KAY EWING'S COOKING SCHOOL COOKBOOK

KAY EWING'S COOKING SCHOOL COOKBOOK

BY

KAY EWING

ILLUSTRATIONS

BY

MARLA REEVES

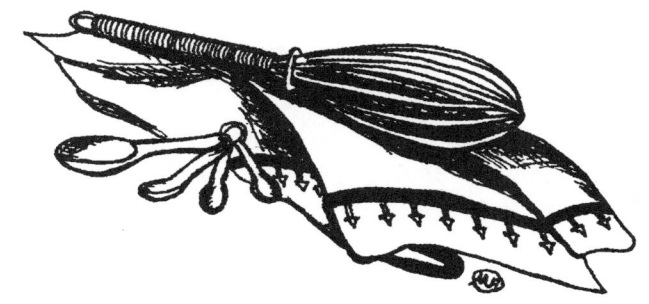

DEDICATION

This book is dedicated to my official taste testers: my husband, Tim Ewing, always supportive & giving; my sister, Marla Reeves, for her enthusiasm, encouragement and creativity; my mother, Bea Miceli, a great cook and my inspiration; and my father, Sam Miceli, who loved and appreciated good food - - - a la famiglia!

Thanks also goes out to all the students who have participated in my cooking classes over the years and who have made teaching such an enjoyable experience for me.

A special thank you to Carol Kaspar, Vickie Smith & Wendy Myers at the Panhandler, for all their help with my classes. Also, to Griff Crutti for his photograph, Marla Reeves for her illustrations and Karen Rosenfeld for her cover design.

Copyright © 1994 by Kay Ewing
Library of Congress Catalog Card Number: 94-90580
Ewing, Kay
  Kay Ewing's Cooking School Cookbook

ISBN 0-9643611-0-8

Published by Kay Ewing's Everyday Gourmet
Baton Rouge, LA
1994

Illustrations by Marla Reeves
Cover design by Karen Rosenfeld
Photograph by Griff Crutti

CONTENTS

APPETIZERS & GARNISHES	1
BACK TO BASICS	11
BRUNCH	23
CAJUN CREOLE	35
CARIBBEAN CUISINE	65
CHINESE	71
DESSERTS	91
ENGLISH TEA	111
FIRESIDE SUPPER	119
FOOD PROCESSOR	127
FRENCH	133
GIFTS OF FOOD	157
ITALIAN	187
PHYLLO PASTRY	215
QUICK & EASY	225
SOUTHWESTERN	237
SUMMER CUISINE	247
TEX-MEX	265
THANKSGIVING	273
YOUNG EVERYDAY GOURMET	279
GENERAL CLASS NOTES	297
INDEX	301

INTRODUCTION

Nine years ago I started Kay Ewing's Everyday Gourmet Cooking School to teach full participation cooking classes to non-professional cooks. My goal was to teach old and new recipes, as well as traditional cooking techniques. The menus featured in this book are a compilation of the most popular classes that I have taught over the years. Most of the menus will offer you a complete meal that you can serve your family and friends. Some, however, feature only one specific item, for example, Desserts. All are taught as full participation classes where the students, after reviewing the recipes, prepare the foods under my supervision. Classes are limited to six students and last approximately three hours. During that time, we share cooking experiences, have lots of laughs and enjoy tasting the various recipes we have cooked.

I hope this book will convey to you some of the joy and pleasure that I have received from both teaching and cooking these menus. Enjoy!

Kay Ewing
September 1994

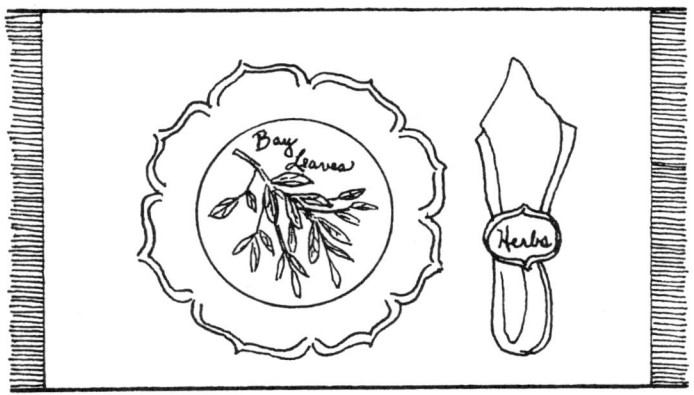

APPETIZERS & GARNISHES

MENUS

TORTILLA BITES
CHEESE STUFFED SHRIMP
AVOCADO CRAB MORNAY

CRAB STUFFED FRENCH BREAD
CREOLE SHRIMP ON PITA ROUNDS
MARINATED SHRIMP KABOBS
BUFFALO CHICKEN WINGS
WITH BLUE CHEESE DIP

HAM & CHEESE PALMIERS
PEPPER JELLY TARTS
CRAB STUFFED MUSHROOMS
OLIVE CHEESE BALLS

GARNISHES

Most cooks are always looking for new appetizers to serve before meals or for parties. The following classes are for recipes that could be made ahead and served or reheated when your guests arrive.

Garnishing suggestions are not that difficult to follow, they just take a little practice, and they always add a special touch to most dishes.

APPETIZERS & GARNISHES

TORTILLA BITES
CHEESE STUFFED SHRIMP
AVOCADO CRAB MORNAY

TORTILLA BITES

1 (8 oz) carton soft cream cheese
1/3 cup sour cream
1 Tablespoon picante sauce
1/2 teaspoon lime juice
1/2 teaspoon finely chopped jalapeno pepper
8 soft flour tortillas
Chilled picante sauce

Mix together cream cheese, sour cream, picante sauce, lime juice and jalapeno pepper until combined. Spread each tortilla with filling and roll up tightly. Cover with plastic wrap and chill. Cut into bite size pieces. Serve with toothpicks and picante sauce. (Serves 8 - 10)

For a decorative presentation, garnish a large plate or platter with leaf lettuce or parsley. Place tortilla bites on lettuce around a hollowed out green pepper filled with picante sauce.

CHEESE STUFFED SHRIMP

1 lb. large shrimp
1 Tablespoon liquid crab boil
2 Tablespoons salt
1 (8 oz) pkg. cream cheese
4 oz. blue cheese
1/4 teaspoon Tabasco
Finely minced parsley
Chilled chili sauce
Mayonnaise

Cook shrimp in a large pot of boiling water seasoned with crab boil and salt until done, about 10 minutes. Drain and cool. Peel shrimp, leaving tail intact. Cut shrimp along back to make a pocket for stuffing, leaving meat at tail and head intact. Spread out to open slightly.
   Blend cheeses and Tabasco in food processor until smooth. Using a pastry bag with a small star tip, pipe mixture into shrimp pocket, then dip in parsley to coat stuffing.
   To serve, place a layer of chili sauce on individual plates. Arrange shrimp in center. Pipe a thin circle of mayonnaise around the outer edge. Run a knife through the mayonnaise to form a decorative border. (Serves 8 - 10)

More enticing than a basic shrimp cocktail!
Never rinse shrimp off after boiling in seasoned water, otherwise you will lose a lot of flavor.

AVOCADO CRAB MORNAY

1/4 cup butter or margarine
1/4 cup flour
1/2 cup chicken broth, heated
1 cup half & half, heated
1/4 cup grated Parmesan cheese
1/2 cup grated Swiss cheese
1/4 cup chopped green onion

1/4 cup chopped parsley
Dash of nutmeg
Dash of cayenne pepper
Salt & pepper to taste
1 large avocado, peeled & diced
1 lb. white crab meat
Prepared puff pastry shells

Melt butter in a medium saucepan over medium heat. Stir in flour with a whisk and cook 2 minutes. Add warm broth and half & half. Stir until smooth. Mix in cheeses, green onion, parsley and seasonings until combined. Gently stir in avocado and crab meat until warmed.

Serve in prepared puff pastry shells or individual ramekins. Garnish with a tomato rose and parsley. Can be made ahead and reheated to serve. (Serves 6 - 8)

**CRAB STUFFED FRENCH BREAD
CREOLE SHRIMP ON PITA ROUNDS
MARINATED SHRIMP KABOBS
BUFFALO CHICKEN WINGS
WITH BLUE CHEESE DIP**

CRAB STUFFED FRENCH BREAD

1 large loaf French bread
8 oz. sharp cheddar cheese
2 Tablespoons butter or margarine
1/4 teaspoon Tabasco

1/2 cup chopped green onion
1/2 lb. fresh white crab meat
Salt & pepper to taste
2 Tablespoons mayonnaise
Paprika for garnish

Preheat oven to 350°. Cut French bread in half lengthwise and hollow out. Grate cheese in food processor. Mix in butter and Tabasco until combined. Fill loaf with cheese mixture. Top with green onion. Mix together crab meat, salt, pepper and mayonnaise and spoon on top of green onion.

Bake for 15 - 20 minutes, until hot and bubbly. Remove, top with paprika, slice and serve. (Serves 12 - 15)

Crawfish or boiled shrimp could be substituted for crab meat. If preparing for tailgating, wrap tightly in foil and place in an ice chest (without ice) to keep warm.

APPETIZERS & GARNISHES

CREOLE SHRIMP ON PITA ROUNDS

1 Tablespoon liquid crab boil
2 Tablespoons salt
1 lemon, halved
1 lb. medium shrimp

2/3 cup vegetable oil
1 Tablespoon white wine vinegar
1/4 teaspoon salt
1 teaspoon sugar
3 Tablespoons Creole mustard
Pita breads and leaf lettuce

Bring a large pot of water, seasoned with crab boil, salt and lemon, to a boil over high heat. Add shrimp and cook until done, about 5 minutes. Drain, cool and peel. Refrigerate.
Mix together all ingredients for Creole sauce with a whisk until blended. Refrigerate.
Cut out several 2" rounds from pita breads which have been split in half.
When ready to serve, top a pita round with a small piece of lettuce. Place a shrimp on top and spoon on a small amount of dressing. (Serves 12)

For an even easier presentation, arrange shrimp on a platter covered with lettuce. Place Creole sauce for dipping in the center and serve pita rounds as an accompaniment.

MARINATED SHRIMP KABOBS

MARINADE:
3/4 cup vegetable oil
1/4 cup red wine vinegar
2 Tablespoons lemon juice
1 clove garlic, minced
1 teaspoon dry mustard

1 teaspoon basil
1 teaspoon salt
1/4 teaspoon pepper
6 whole allspice

Mix all ingredients together with a whisk until blended.

KABOBS:
2 lbs. large shrimp, boiled & peeled
Cherry tomatoes, whole
Artichoke hearts, halved

Cucumber, sliced
Mushrooms, whole
Black olives, whole

On small wooden skewers, alternate a shrimp between each vegetable, starting and ending with shrimp. Place in a glass or plastic dish and pour marinade over kabobs. Cover and refrigerate several hours or overnight, turning occasionally. Remove from marinade to serve. Makes about 15 - 20 kabobs. (Serves 8 - 10)

BUFFALO CHICKEN WINGS
WITH BLUE CHEESE DIP

BLUE CHEESE DIP:
1/2 cup mayonnaise
1/2 cup sour cream
1 clove garlic, minced
1/4 cup chopped green onion
2 oz. (1/4 cup) crumbled blue cheese
Salt & pepper to taste
Celery sticks

Mix all ingredients together for dip, except celery sticks. Chill at least 1 hour.

CHICKEN WINGS:
12 - 14 chicken wings (about 2 lbs.)
2 Tablespoons butter, melted
2 Tablespoons Tabasco
2 teaspoons cider vinegar

Preheat oven to $425°$. Cut and discard tip from each wing. Cut each wing into 2 pieces at joint. Arrange on a rack in a pan covered with foil.
Combine butter, Tabasco and vinegar. Brush half the sauce on the wings. Roast for 20 minutes. Turn wings over, brush with remaining sauce and roast 20 minutes more.
Serve wings on a large platter with celery sticks and blue cheese dip on the side (to cool the mouth!). (Serves 6 - 8)

A very popular and filling appetizer. Great for tailgating!

APPETIZERS & GARNISHES

HAM & CHEESE PALMIERS
PEPPER JELLY TARTS
CRAB STUFFED MUSHROOMS
OLIVE CHEESE BALLS

HAM & CHEESE PALMIERS

1 (9") square frozen puff pastry sheet
1 egg yolk
1 Tablespoon Dijon mustard
1/2 cup finely chopped ham
1/2 cup finely grated Swiss cheese

Let pastry thaw at room temperature for about 15 - 20 minutes on a lightly floured sheet of wax paper.

Preheat oven to 400°. Unfold dough; mix egg yolk and mustard together and brush on pastry (save a little for topping).

Sprinkle ham and cheese over dough. Mark the center and roll up both sides tightly to meet in the middle (chill if too soft to cut). Cut into 1/4" slices and place on a greased foil lined baking sheet. Flatten slightly with the palm of your hand. Brush again lightly with egg wash.

Bake about 20 minutes, until golden brown. Drain on paper towels. (Makes about 2 dozen)

 *Can substitute egg yolk with 1 Tablespoon water and 1/2 cup Parmesan cheese.*

PEPPER JELLY TARTS

1/2 cup butter, softened
1 cup grated cheddar cheese
1 cup flour
Hot pepper jelly

Cream butter and cheese until smooth with an electric mixer or food processor. Add flour and mix thoroughly. Wrap in plastic wrap and chill for at least 30 minutes.

Preheat oven to 400°. Roll dough out on a lightly floured surface and cut out 3 - 4 inch rounds with a cookie cutter. Place 1/2 teaspoon pepper jelly on each round, fold over in a crescent shape and press edges with a fork to seal.

Place on a greased foil lined baking sheet and bake for about 12 - 15 minutes, until lightly browned. (Serves 6)

CRAB STUFFED MUSHROOMS

1 lb. large fresh mushrooms
1/2 cup chopped green onion
8 oz. Monterey Jack cheese, grated
1 cup Italian seasoned bread crumbs
1/2 lb. fresh white crab meat

1 teaspoon salt
1/4 teaspoon cayenne pepper
1/2 teaspoon sugar
2 Tablespoons melted butter
1/4 cup heavy cream

Preheat oven to 375°. Wipe mushrooms clean with a damp paper towel. Remove stems. In a large mixing bowl, combine green onions, cheese, bread crumbs, crab meat, salt, pepper and sugar. Toss to mix. Pour in melted butter and cream and mix well. Fill each mushroom cap with stuffing and pile high. Place on a greased foil lined baking sheet. Bake 10 - 15 minutes, until golden brown and hot. (Serves 6)

Mushrooms tend to absorb water if washed; instead, simply wipe with a damp paper towel to clean.

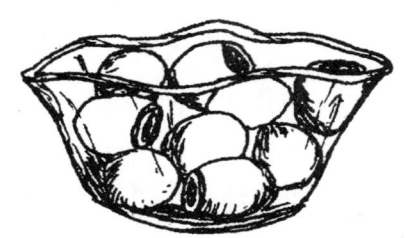

OLIVE CHEESE BALLS

1 cup grated cheddar cheese
3 Tablespoons butter or margarine
1/2 cup flour

1/2 teaspoon salt
1/2 teaspoon paprika
Stuffed green olives

Thoroughly blend cheese, butter, flour, salt and paprika together in a food processor or by hand. Mold small pieces of dough around each olive, making a ball. Refrigerate until ready to bake.
Preheat oven to 400°. Bake olive cheese balls for 15 minutes, until golden brown. (Serves 6 - 8)

Try using black olives for variation.

GARNISHES GARNISHES GARNISHES

Cucumber ***Cartwheels*** - remove alternate strips from top to bottom,
Zucchini then cut into slices.

Tomato ***Rose*** - starting at base of tomato, cut a continuous strip off around entire tomato, including a little meat of the tomato with the peel. Curl entire peel around itself to create a rose.

Lemon ***Basket*** - lay lemon on its side and make a cut a little off
Lime of center to middle of lemon on both sides to create
Orange handle. Then cut from tips of lemon down the middle to center to remove top of basket. Cut away meat of lemon under handle and inside lemon to create a basket. Fill with parsley.

Cup - lay lemon on its side and make zig-zag cuts through the center of lemon, around entire lemon. Pull cups apart and trim off tips. Can be sprinkled with paprika or parsley.

Twists - cut a thin whole slice across lemon. Make a slit to center of slice and twist open.

Wedge Wings - cut lemon in half lengthwise and lay on flat side. Cut a very small angled wedge out of the center. Continue to cut larger wedges each time, cutting all the way through to enable removal of wedges. Line wedges up slightly apart to create wings.

Scored Wedges - remove alternate strips from around lemon, then cut into wedges.

Green Onion ***Brushes*** - cut off root end of green onion. Cut off again slightly
Celery above where white part of onion ends. Make several slits from end of onion toward center, leaving center intact. Repeat on other side. Place brushes in a bowl of iced water until curled.

Mushroom ***Fluted*** - make small wedge cuts, removing wedges as you cut around entire mushroom, leaving center intact.

Flowers - using tip of a paring knife, start at top and make small tip cuts around entire mushroom.

BACK TO BASICS

MENUS

**SENSATION SALAD
CHICKEN & SAUSAGE JAMBALAYA
EASY BOILED RICE
FUDGY BROWNIES**

KITCHEN BASICS

Back to Basics is the one class where the students do all the chopping and preparation for the recipes. They learn the correct way to use a chef's knife, as well as easy ways to cut most vegetables. The recipes are pretty basic and are some true Louisiana favorites. A listing of Kitchen Basics is also given to each student to be used as a handy reference guide.

BACK TO BASICS

SENSATION SALAD
CHICKEN & SAUSAGE JAMBALA
EASY BOILED RICE
FUDGY BROWNIES

SENSATION SALAD

1/2 cup vegetable oil
1/2 cup olive oil
2 Tablespoons lemon juice
1 clove garlic, minced
2 Tablespoons white vinegar

1 cup grated Romano cheese
1/4 cup crumbled blue cheese
2 Tablespoons chopped parsley
Salt & pepper to taste
Iceberg & leaf lettuce combination

Mix all ingredients, except lettuce, together for dressing. Refrigerate in a covered container.

When ready to serve, tear up lettuce and place in a large salad bowl. Stir dressing to recombine. Toss lettuce with a generous amount of dressing (Makes 1 1/2 cups dressing) [Adapted from a recipe in River Road Recipes II]

A wonderful salad served in many local restaurants. Dressing may congeal when chilled. Just set out at room temperature until normal consistency returns.

CHICKEN & SAUSAGE JAMBALAYA

1 whole chicken
1 lb. smoked pork sausage, cut in small slices
1 cup diced ham
1 onion, chopped
2 ribs celery, chopped
1/2 green bell pepper, chopped
1 clove garlic, minced
1 (8 oz) can tomato sauce
1/4 cup chopped green onion
1/4 cup chopped parsley
6 cups cooked rice
Chicken stock
Salt, pepper and cayenne to taste

Remove packing from inside chicken and discard. Rinse chicken under cold water. Place chicken in a large stock pot and add enough water to cover chicken. Bring to a boil over high heat, skimming surface as necessary. Lower heat to low and cook for about 1 hour or until tender. Remove chicken from stock and reserve stock. When chicken is cool enough to handle, remove skin, debone and cut into bite size pieces.

Meanwhile, sauté sausage and ham in a large dutch oven greased with cooking spray, over medium heat, just until lightly browned. Stir frequently. Add onion, celery, green pepper and garlic and sauté until softened. Stir in tomato sauce, green onion and parsley. Lower heat and add chicken. Cook for about 15 minutes, stirring frequently.

Add cooked rice to the meat mixture and enough chicken stock to moisten. Season to taste. Let simmer about 10 minutes to blend flavors. (Serves 6 - 8)

A variation from most jambalayas where everything is cooked together. A great one dish meal that can be made ahead. Add a little broth to moisten before reheating.

EASY BOILED RICE

2 cups long grain white rice
4 cups water
1 teaspoon salt
1 Tablespoon butter or margarine

Measure rice, water, salt and butter into a medium size saucepan greased with cooking spray. Bring to a boil over high heat. Let boil until craterlike holes appear on the surface of the rice and most of the water has evaporated. Cover and turn off the heat. Let steam for about 20 minutes. Fluff with a fork before serving. (Makes 6 cups cooked rice)

A foolproof method of cooking rice. Make ahead, freeze and reheat in microwave when needed. Recipe can also be halved.

FUDGY BROWNIES

1/2 cup butter or margarine
2 oz. unsweetened chocolate
1 cup sugar
2 eggs

1/2 teaspoon vanilla
1/2 cup flour
1/4 teaspoon salt
1 cup chopped pecans

    Preheat oven to $325°$. Place butter and chocolate in a small saucepan over low heat, stirring until melted. Remove from heat and stir in sugar. Mix in eggs and vanilla. Add flour, salt and pecans.
    Pour into a greased 8" square baking pan and bake for 35 - 40 minutes, until tested done.
    Let cool in pan and cut into squares. (Makes 16 squares)

Can be served with ice cream and chocolate sauce for a more substantial dessert. Very fudgy!

THE BASICS

BASIC EQUIPMENT

Knives:

    Cutlery can be made of high-carbon steel or stainless and the end of the blade (tang) should extend all the way to the end of the handle. Knives should be of a weight that is comfortable to handle.

Chef's (French) - 6", 8", 10" or 12" - chopping
Parer - peeling
Slicer - slicing
Serrated - slicing breads, tomatoes, cakes
Sharpening steel - realigns blades of knives, but does not sharpen

When using a chef's knife (or any other knife), <u>always</u> curve fingers back away from the blade, keeping thumb back as well. It takes practice to feel comfortable with this method, but the result will be no more cut fingers.

Measurers:

    Standard measurers have specific purposes and should be used accordingly, especially important in baking.

Dry - set of stacked stainless steel cups used to measure dry ingredients so they can be leveled off.
Liquid - glass measuring cup usually in 1, 2, or 4 cup sizes used for liquids so they won't spill. Should remain on the counter at eye level when measuring.
Spoons - set of graduated sizes, 1/4 teaspoon, 1/2 teaspoon, 1 teaspoon, 1 Tablespoon

Cookware:
Can be made of aluminum, stainless steel (with an aluminum or copper core), cast iron, enamel, copper or non-stick finishes.

Saucepans - 1, 2, 3, 4 qt. sizes
Skillet - 8," 9", 10" or 12" sizes
Dutch oven - round or oval
Stock pot - 6, 8, 10, 12 qt. sizes
Wok - for stir frying

Baking Pans:
Aluminum is best for even baking, some are non-stick or insulated.

Cake Layers - 8" or 9" x 1 1/2" round (usually need 2 or 3)
Square - 8" x 8" x 2" or 9" x 9" x 1 3/4"
Roaster - 13" x 9 1/2" x 2"
Cookie Sheet - small, medium, large
Jelly Roll - 15 1/2" x 10 1/2" x 1"
Loaf Pan - 9" x 5" x 3" or 8" x 4" x 2 1/2"
Muffin Tins - 12 large, 12 miniature
Pie Plate - 9" or 10" round
Tube Pan - 10" x 4"
Bundt Pan
Pizza Pan - 12" or 14"
Baking Dishes & Casseroles - Corning Ware or Pyrex

Utensils:
A sample list of some useful utensils that make cooking easier.

Biscuit/cookie cutter   Bottle opener   Brushes (pastry)   Cake racks   Chopping board   Colander   Corkscrew   Custard cups   Flour sifter   Garlic press   Grater   Jar opener   Kitchen shears   Ladle   Long-handled spoon   Slotted spoon   Fork   Mixing bowls   Pancake turner   Pepper mill   Potato masher   Potato peeler   Rolling pin   Salad spinner   Scale   Scoop   Spatulas   Strainer   Thermometer (candy, meat, oven)   Tongs   Vegetable brush   Wire whisk   Wooden spoons

Servers:
Items that will make serving much easier.

Set of dishes   Set of flatware   Glasses   Wine glasses   Serving spoons & fork   Salt & pepper shakers   Dish towels & cloths   Napkins   Place mats   Tablecloth   Pot holders   Trivets   Butter dish   Bread basket   Glass pitcher

Appliances:
The basic ones that will come in handy many times.

Blender   Can opener   Coffee maker   Food processor   Mixer   Toaster

BASIC MEASUREMENTS

Liquid & Dry:

3 teaspoons = 1 Tablespoon
2 Tablespoons = 1 ounce
4 Tablespoons = 1/4 cup
8 Tablespoons = 1/2 cup = 4 ounces
1 cup = 8 ounces = 1/2 pint
2 cups = 1 pint = 1/2 quart = 1 pound
4 cups = 32 ounces = 2 pints = 1 quart
4 quarts = 1 gallon

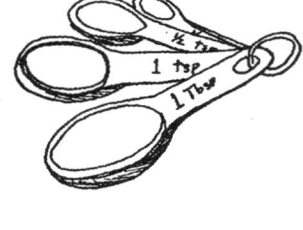

Butter, Shortening, Cheese & other Solid Fats:

1 Tablespoon = 1/8 stick = 1/2 ounce
2 Tablespoons = 1/4 stick = 1 ounce
4 Tablespoons = 1/2 stick = 2 ounces = 1/4 cup
8 Tablespoons = 1 stick = 4 ounces = 1/2 cup
16 Tablespoons = 2 sticks = 8 ounces = 1 cup
32 Tablespoons = 4 sticks = 1 pound = 2 cups

Flour:

1 Tablespoon = 1/4 ounce
4 Tablespoons = 1/4 cup = 1 1/4 ounce
1/2 cup = 2 1/2 ounces
1 cup = 5 ounces
3 1/2 cups = 16 ounces = 1 pound

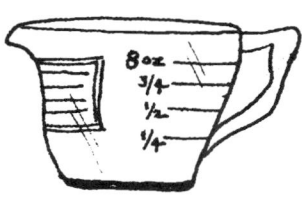

Sugar:

2 cups granulated = 1 pound
2 1/4 cups brown sugar = 1 pound
3 3/4 cups powdered sugar = 1 pound

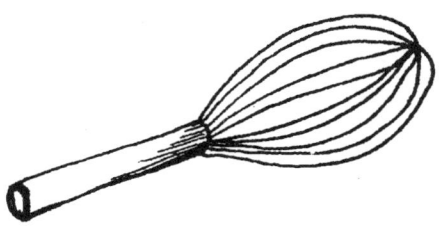

BASIC COOKING METHODS

Bake - to cook in dry heat, in an enclosed oven, usually using a specific temperature.

Boil - to bring liquid to a temperature of $212°F$ at sea level. When boiling, bubbles rise and break on the surface.

Braise - to brown foods slowly in a small amount of fat, then add a small amount of liquid, and slowly cook in a tightly covered utensil.

Broil - to cook under or over direct heat.

Fry - to cook food in hot fat. Pan fry is to cook in a small amount of fat and deep fry is to immerse completely in hot fat.

Grill - to cook by direct heat, over fire or hot coals.

Poach - to simmer food gently in a hot liquid.

Roast - to cook in an enclosed oven by dry heat.

Sauté - to cook in a small amount of fat over direct heat.

Steam - to cook by direct steam on a rack placed in a deep container holding a small amount of boiling water.

BASIC FOODS

Meats:

Beef - round (steak, ground, roast), rump (roast), flank (steak), loin (sirloin, porterhouse, t-bone, club, strip, tenderloin, filet steaks), rib (standing, rolled roasts), chuck (pot roast, steak, ground), plate (short ribs, brisket, corned beef), shank (stew meat), soup bone.

Pork - ham, fat back (salt pork, lard), loin (chops, roast), bacon, spareribs, shoulder, butt, picnic, hock.

Veal - leg (round steak, sirloin, rolled rump, standing rump), loin (chop), rib (chop), shoulder (steak, pot roast), breast (riblets, stew).

Lamb - leg (roast, shank, butt), loin (chop), breast, shank, shoulder (roast, chop), neck, rib (chop, crown roasts), stew.

Poultry: breast, back, wings, leg, thighs, giblet (heart, liver, gizzards), neck.

Game: duck, cornish hens, partridge, pheasant, quail, rabbit, squab, turkey, venison.

Fish: catfish, flounder, red fish, red snapper, trout, etc.

Seafood: Crab, crawfish, lobster, oysters, scallops, shrimp, etc.

Vegetables: artichoke, asparagus, beans (green, lima), beets, broccoli, brussel sprouts, cabbage, carrots, cauliflower, celery, corn, cucumber, eggplant, greens (collards, chard, kale, spinach), garlic, hearts of palm, leek, lettuce (bibb, chicory, endive, escarole, iceberg, leaf, romaine), mushrooms, okra, onions (chives, green, red, scallion, shallot, white, yellow), parsley, parsnip, peas, peppers (chili, green, red, yellow), potatoes (red, sweet, white), pumpkin, radishes, squash (acorn, spaghetti, yellow), tomatoes, turnips, watercress, yams, zucchini.

Fruits: apples, apricot, avocado, banana, berries (blue, cran., rasp., straw.), cherries, coconut, currants, dates, figs, grapefruit, grapes, lemons, limes, mango, melons, nectarines, olives, oranges, papaya, peaches, pineapple, plums, prunes, raisins, tangerines.

Dairy Products: eggs, milk (buttermilk, condensed, dry, evaporated, half & half, heavy cream, ice cream, light cream, sherbert, sour cream, whipping cream, whole milk or yogurt), cheeses.

Fats & Oils: butter, margarine, lard, suet, hydrogenated vegetable shortening, oils, olive oil.

BASIC COOKING TERMINOLOGY

Au Gratin - cooked with crumbs or grated cheese (or both) on top of the dish, the top is then browned in the oven or under the broiler.
Au Jus - served with natural juices or gravy, often beef.
Baste - to moisten food with liquid during cooking to prevent drying out.
Batter - a semi-liquid mixture, usually of eggs, milk and flour that can be poured or dropped from a spoon; to coat with this mixture.
Beat - a process of adding air to a mixture to make it smooth and/or incorporate additional ingredients using a spoon, whisk or electric mixer.
Bind - to unite ingredients with a sauce, such as mayonnaise.
Blanch - to pre-cook foods for a short period of time by plunging them into boiling water, usually to aid in skin removal of fruits and vegetables; parboil.
Blend - to combine ingredients together thoroughly with a spoon or a blender.
Bone - to remove bones from meat or fish.
Bread - to coat food with dried bread crumbs in order to form a crisp crust when baking or frying. The crumbs are usually made to adhere by first dipping food in liquid or beaten egg.

Brown - to cook food until it actually turns brown in color either in the oven, under a broiler, or on top of a stove, usually in a pan with a little fat to seal in flavor.

Butter - to rub the cookware or baking pan to be used with butter or fat to prevent foods from sticking.

Caramelize - to heat sugar until melted and browned.

Chop - to cut food into small pieces (larger than minced).

Clarify - to clarify butter: heat butter until melted, then carefully pour liquid into another container, leaving the creamy milk solid residue behind. To clarify stock: add egg whites or broken egg shells to fat-free stock and simmer uncovered for about 20 minutes.

Coat - to roll or sprinkle food with a layer of another food such as flour, bread crumbs, mayonnaise or a sauce.

Cream - to work butter or shortening alone or with sugar to a creamy, light consistency.

Crisp - to wash lettuce or any other vegetable in cold water in order to firm it or to crisp foods by heating in oven.

Cube - to cut food into uniform cube shapes of small size.

Cut in - to work with a pastry blender or two knives until solid fat and dry ingredients are evenly and finely combined to form small particles, usually the size of peas.

Debone - to remove bones from meat or fish.

Deglaze - to loosen the drippings caked on cookware after browning by adding water, broth, wine or other liquids to make a sauce.

Degrease - to remove fat from surface of liquids.

Dice - to cut food into small cubes or squares.

Dot - to cover surface of food with small amounts of butter before baking or broiling.

Dredge - to coat food with flour, cornmeal, bread crumbs, sugar or some other ingredient.

Drippings - the fat expelled from meat while roasting or frying.

Dust - to sprinkle lightly with flour, sugar or other ingredient.

En Papillote - to place meat or fish in parchment paper or foil with other ingredients and bake in oven.

Fillet - a piece of meat or fish from which all the bones have been removed.

Flake - to break apart a food such as fish, gently with a fork, so that it resembles flakes.

Flour - to coat food or bakeware with flour.

Fold - to blend one mixture with another with a spoon or spatula in a gentle folding motion from the bottom up and over ingredients repeatedly until combined.

Frost - to ice or glaze cakes or other baked goods.

Garnish - a decoration of some colorful food added to a prepared dish to enhance its appearance.

Glaze - to coat or cover food with a glossy coat of icing, aspic, syrup or sauce.

Grate - to rub a food over a grater so that it is reduced to tiny particles or thin shreds.

Grease - to lightly coat a surface with butter, oil or cooking spray.

Grind - to reduce food to a powdery consistency such as that of coffee, pepper or flour.
Ice - to decorate a cake or pastry with icing.
Julienne - to cut food such as carrots, potatoes or cheese into thin, even, matchlike sticks.
Knead - to repeatedly press, pull and fold dough into a smooth mass with hands on a flat, lightly floured surface.
Lard - to insert fat into flesh of meat with a special needle to make meat juicier.
Marinate - to allow food to rest in a mixture to season and sometimes tenderize.
Melt - to heat solid food to a liquid state.
Mince - to cut pieces of food into very small bits.
Mix - to combine, shake or stir ingredients to evenly distribute.
Mold - to prepare food in a specified shape to set or gel.
Pare - to peel the outer skin off with a peeler or sharp knife.
Peel - to remove the outer skin or layer of a food with a sharp knife.
Pinch - approximately 1/8 of a teaspoon or an amount of seasoning that can be held between the forefinger and thumb.
Pit - to remove the seed from food.
Pound - to strike with a heavy blunt instrument to tenderize and/or flatten.
Preheat - to allow oven or pan to reach exact temperature required to cook dish before placing food in.
Proof - to dissolve yeast in a warm liquid until bubbly; to prove that the yeast is alive.
Punch down - to strike risen dough with a fist to allow gas to escape.
Purée - to reduce food to a smooth mixture by use of a sieve, food mill, electric blender or food processor.
Reduce - to evaporate a liquid by boiling uncovered.
Render - to melt solid animal fat by cooking slowly.
Rise - to let yeast dough double in bulk.
Scald - to heat liquid to the point just before it boils or to dip fruits and vegetables in boiling water to skin.
Score - to make shallow slits or gashes with a knife or fork through the outer surface of food.
Sear - to brown meat quickly in a saucepan or skillet over high heat.
Season - to add flavor to a food by the addition of salt, pepper, herb, spice or other seasoning; to coat cast iron or carbon steel cookware with vegetable oil and heat to incorporate a smooth cooking surface and prevent rust from forming.
Separate - to remove egg whites from egg yolks.
Shred - to tear or cut food into thin strips or pieces.
Shuck - to remove covering of a food such as the husks of corn or shells of oysters or clams.
Sift - to put dry ingredients through a fine sieve.
Simmer - to cook food gently in liquid, just below boiling point.
Skewer - a thin metal or wooden pin on which food is secured and cooked.
Skim - to remove fat or particles from surface of a liquid with a spoon, ladle or skimmer.

Sliver - to cut into even, long, thin strips.
Steep - to soak or let stand in a liquid to extract flavor.
Stir - to mix two or more ingredients in a circular motion with a spoon.
Strain - to remove solid foods from liquid by pouring through a sieve, strainer or colander.
Stock - a liquid in which food has cooked.
Tenderize - to soften tough fibers of meat by pounding with a heavy, blunt gavel or tenderize by marination.
Thicken - to make a sauce become thick by the use of thickening agents such as flour, cornstarch or eggs; or by cooking food longer to cause evaporation and, therefore, thicken a sauce or gravy.
Toast - to brown or make crisp with dry heat.
Toss - to combine gently usually with two spoons or forks.
Truss - to secure legs and wings of poultry or game with a string, so the meat will cook more evenly.
Unmold - to loosen and remove the contents of a mold by either immersing in hot water and inverting or running the blade of a thin knife around the edge of mold and inverting.
Whip - to beat rapidly to induce expansion and fluffiness by beating in air, usually with a whisk or electric mixer.

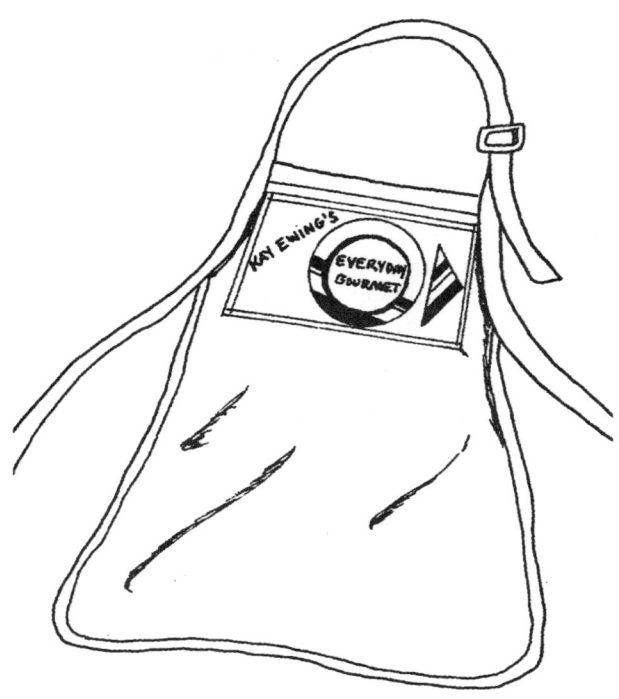

BRUNCH

MENUS

COFFEE MOCHA PUNCH
CHEESE GRITS
SAUCED FRUIT
SHIRRED EGGS WITH CREOLE SAUCE
BRIOCHE TWISTS

SPICY TOMATO JUICE
CARAMEL FRUIT
BREADED PARSLEY POTATOES
CAJUN EGG BAKE
MARDI GRAS KING CAKE

HOT CHOCOLATE EGGNOG
CINNAMON PINWHEELS
CHEESY CHILIE EGGS
JALAPEÑO CHEESE GRITS
SESAME CORNMEAL BISCUITS
MILK CHOCOLATE DIPPED FRUIT

Brunch is a great way to entertain with some very enjoyable foods. It's an often overlooked meal that is usually very easy to prepare, with many recipes that can be made ahead.

BRUNCH

```
COFFEE MOCHA PUNCH
CHEESE GRITS
SAUCED FRUIT
SHIRRED EGGS WITH CREOLE SAUCE
BRIOCHE TWISTS
```

A brunch menu with a southern twist. Great to serve during the holiday season.

COFFEE MOCHA PUNCH

2 quarts brewed coffee, chilled
1 quart chocolate milk
1/2 gallon vanilla ice cream
1 cup heavy cream, whipped
1 oz. semisweet chocolate, grated

Stir coffee and chocolate milk together in a punch bowl. Spoon in vanilla ice cream. Stir slightly to combine. Place dollops of whipped cream on top and sprinkle with grated chocolate for garnish. (Serves 16 - 20)

Recipe can be halved. Can also be served hot or spiked with Kahlúa.
A truly delicious punch that will get rave reviews, especially from coffee lovers.

CHEESE GRITS

4 cups water
1 teaspoon salt
1 cup Quick Grits
1/4 cup butter or margarine
1 cup grated cheddar cheese
1/2 roll garlic cheese
1/2 roll jalapeño cheese
1 teaspoon Worcestershire sauce
Paprika for garnish

Bring 4 cups of water to a boil in a large saucepan, greased with cooking spray, over high heat. Add salt and grits, stirring to combine. Lower heat to low, cover and cook, stirring frequently, until water is absorbed, about 5 minutes. Add butter, cheeses and Worcestershire, stirring until melted. Place in a greased casserole dish and sprinkle with paprika for garnish. (Serves 8)

A real basic as far as southerners are concerned. Most people who say they don't like grits, are surprised when they taste cheese grits.

SAUCED FRUIT

1 (8 oz) pkg. cream cheese, cut up
1/4 cup sugar
1/2 cup sour cream
2 Tablespoons fresh orange juice

Fresh pineapple, apples,
  grapes, mandarin oranges,
  bananas, strawberries, etc.
Chopped pecans

Place cream cheese, sugar, sour cream and orange juice in food processor and blend until combined. Chill.

Prepare fruit and cut into bite size pieces. If using a fresh pineapple, cut in half lengthwise, including leaves. Cut pineapple out of each half, leaving the shell intact. Mix all fruit together and place in pineapple halves to serve. Spoon sauce over fruit and sprinkle with chopped pecans. (Serves 6 - 8)

SHIRRED EGGS WITH CREOLE SAUCE

CREOLE SAUCE:
3 Tablespoons vegetable oil
1 onion, chopped
1/2 green pepper, chopped
1/2 cup chopped celery
1 clove garlic, minced
4 large fresh tomatoes, peeled
  & chopped or 2 cans diced
  tomatoes, drained

1/2 cup chopped green onion
2 Tablespoons chopped
  parsley
1 cup chicken broth
1 cup Burgundy or
  Pinot Noir wine
Salt & pepper to taste
1/2 teaspoon thyme
1 teaspoon sugar

Heat oil in a large skillet or saucepan over medium high heat. Add onion, green pepper, celery and garlic. Sauté until tender. Add tomatoes, green onion and parsley, stirring to combine. Mix in chicken broth, wine and seasonings. Bring mixture to a boil, lower heat to medium and cook until sauce is reduced and thickened, about 30 minutes.

SHIRRED EGGS:
1 cup heavy cream
1 teaspoon dry mustard
2 teaspoon Worcestershire sauce

8 - 16 eggs
Salt & pepper to taste
1/2 cup finely chopped ham
Parsley sprigs for garnish

Preheat oven to 375°. Whisk together cream, mustard and Worcestershire sauce in a small bowl. Place 2 Tablespoons of cream mixture in the bottom of 8 greased individual au gratin dishes. Break 1 or 2 eggs carefully into each dish. Season with salt and pepper and sprinkle with a little ham. Bake for 8 - 12 minutes or until eggs are cooked to desired degree of firmness.

Serve shirred eggs with Creole sauce spooned over each and topped with a sprig of parsley. (Serves 8) [Adapted from a recipe by Terry Thompson]

BRIOCHE TWISTS

2 pkgs. dry yeast (4 1/2 teaspoons)
1/2 teaspoon sugar
1/3 cup warm water (105-115°)
3/4 cup butter or margarine
1/3 cup milk
1/2 cup sugar
1 teaspoon salt
1/4 teaspoon ground nutmeg
5 eggs
5 1/2 - 6 cups unbleached flour
1 egg beaten with 1 Tablespoon water

Dissolve yeast and sugar in warm water. Let proof for 10 minutes. Meanwhile, heat butter and milk in microwave, just until butter is melted. Place in a large mixing bowl. Stir in sugar, salt and nutmeg. Whisk in eggs, add yeast mixture and mix well. Mix in 2 cups of flour with whisk to combine. Switch to a spatula or spoon to stir in 3 more cups of flour. Turn out on a floured surface and knead to form a smooth dough, adding more flour if necessary. Knead for about 5 minutes. Place in a greased bowl, cover and let rise in a warm spot for about 1 1/2 hours, until doubled.

Punch dough down and cut in half. Keep dividing each piece in half until you have 32 pieces. Roll out each piece with hands into an 8" long rope. Twist together 2 ropes, pinching together at ends. Place on 2 greased foil lined baking sheets, forming 16 twists in all. Place in a warm spot and let rise about 30 minutes.

Preheat oven to 350°. Brush twists lightly with egg and water mixture and bake for about 20 minutes, until golden brown. If baking on 2 shelves, switch position of baking sheets after 10 minutes. (Makes 16 twists)

If yeast doesn't bubble up while proofing, discard and try again with fresher yeast. Keep dough a little on the sticky side while kneading. If too much flour is added, dough will become dry.

BRUNCH

**SPICY TOMATO JUICE
CARAMEL FRUIT
BREADED PARSLEY POTATOES
CAJUN EGG BAKE
MARDI GRAS KING CAKE**

A perfect menu for Mardi Gras season. Learn to make your own King Cake and you may never buy another one.

SPICY TOMATO JUICE

**1 (46 oz) can V-8 juice
1/4 cup chopped green onion
1 small cucumber, peeled & chopped
1 Tablespoon horseradish
1 teaspoon Worcestershire sauce
Juice of 1 lemon or lime
1 clove garlic, mashed
8 drops Tabasco
Salt & pepper to taste
Lemon or lime slices**

Mix together all ingredients in a large pitcher or bowl. Cover and refrigerate several hours or overnight.

Strain and taste for seasonings. Refrigerate until ready to serve. Serve garnished with lemon or lime slices. Can be spiked with Vodka, if desired. (Serves 6 - 8)

CARAMEL FRUIT

**8 oz. cream cheese, cut up
1 cup dark brown sugar
1 teaspoon vanilla
1 Tablespoon milk
Fruit: apples, bananas, pineapple, mandarin oranges, grapes, cherries, strawberries, pears, etc.
Chopped pecans**

In a food processor, combine cream cheese, brown sugar, vanilla and milk. Process until smooth. Place in a covered container and chill until ready to use.

Prepare fruit shortly before serving and place in a large bowl, tossing to combine. To serve, spoon caramel sauce over individual servings of fruit and top with chopped pecans. (Serves 8)

BREADED PARSLEY POTATOES

4 - 6 medium red potatoes, peeled
1/4 cup butter or margarine
1/2 cup chopped green onion
1 clove garlic, minced

1/2 cup chopped parsley
1/2 cup Italian seasoned
   bread crumbs
1/4 cup butter or margarine
Salt & pepper to taste

 Cut potatoes into quarters, then into chunks. Place in a large saucepan and cover with water. Bring to a boil over high heat. Lower heat to medium and cook until tender, about 10 minutes.
 Meanwhile, in a skillet over medium heat, melt butter and sauté green onions, garlic and parsley until softened. Add bread crumbs and cook, stirring for a few minutes, until combined.
 Drain potatoes well and toss with 1/4 cup butter. Season with salt and pepper and place in a greased casserole. Sprinkle bread crumb mixture over potatoes. Serve immediately or keep warm in a low oven until ready to serve. (Serves 8)

CAJUN EGG BAKE

1 dozen eggs
1 cup milk
Salt & pepper to taste
1 Tablespoon Creole mustard
1/2 teaspoon Tabasco

2 Tablespoons butter
1/2 cup chopped green
   onion
1/4 cup chopped green
   pepper
1 cup sliced mushrooms
1/2 cup chopped ham
1 cup grated cheddar cheese
Tomato rose & green pepper
   slice for garnish

 Preheat oven to 375°. Beat eggs with a wire whisk in a large bowl. Mix in milk and seasonings.
 Melt butter in a large skillet over medium heat. Sauté green onions, green pepper, mushrooms, and ham until softened. Remove from heat. Combine with egg mixture and pour into a large greased casserole. Top with grated cheese. Bake for about 15 - 20 minutes, until tested done. Garnish with a green pepper slice and a tomato rose in the center. (Serves 8)

MARDI GRAS KING CAKE

1/2 cup milk
1/2 cup sugar
1/2 cup butter or margarine
1 1/2 teaspoons salt
2 pkgs. dry yeast (4 1/2 teaspoons)
1/3 cup warm water (105-115°)
1/2 teaspoon sugar

3 eggs
1 teaspoon lemon zest
1/2 teaspoon nutmeg
4 1/2 - 5 cups flour
1 plastic baby doll or
    a dried kidney bean

Heat milk, sugar, butter and salt in a small saucepan over medium heat, stirring frequently, just until butter is melted. Pour into a large bowl to cool.

Mix yeast with warm water and sugar. Let stand about 10 minutes until bubbly.

Add yeast mixture to cooled milk. Use a whisk to beat in eggs, lemon rind, nutmeg and 2 cups flour until combined. Stir in remaining 2 1/2 cups flour with a spoon. Turn out on a floured surface and knead until smooth and elastic, adding more flour, if necessary, to keep from sticking. Place dough in a greased bowl, cover with a towel or plastic wrap and let rise in a warm place for 1 1/2 hours or until doubled.

Punch dough down and knead for a few minutes. Divide dough into thirds. Roll each portion out by hand into 26" long strips. Braid the strips and shape into a circle on a greased baking sheet with a small greased bowl in the center, to hold the shape of the bread as it bakes. Overlap the ends of the braid and pinch the ends together to form the circle. Carefully insert the baby doll or bean into the dough from the bottom. Place in a warm spot and let rise about 1/2 hour.

Preheat oven to 375°. Bake king cake for about 20 minutes until nicely browned. Let cool in the pan, then place on a wire rack with wax paper underneath.

GLAZE:
1 1/2 cups powdered sugar
1 teaspoon lemon juice

3 Tablespoons water
1 drop yellow food coloring

Combine all ingredients, mixing well, and frost cooled cake. While icing is still moist, sprinkle alternating stripes of purple, gold and green sugars all around cake. Let dry before covering.

COLORED SUGARS:
Purple = 1/4 cup sugar + 3 drops red food coloring + 1 drop blue
Gold = 1/4 cup sugar + 2 drops yellow + 1 drop red
Green = 1/4 cup sugar + 2 drops green

Place sugar and food coloring in 3 small Ziploc bags. Shake and knead until color is evenly distributed in sugar.
   (continued on next page)

FILLED KING CAKE:
1/2 cup butter or margarine, softened
1 cup light brown sugar
2 teaspoons cinnamon
1/2 cup chopped pecans

Mix together butter, brown sugar and cinnamon until combined. To shape dough, divide in half. Roll out each half into a 26" x 8" rectangle. Spread filling down the center of each half. Fold dough over filling and roll up. Place seam side down on a greased foil lined baking sheet with a greased bowl in the center to hold the shape. Pinch ends together to form a circle and place the baby doll into the dough. Let rise in a warm spot for 30 minutes. Follow previous directions for baking, etc.

According to tradition, whoever gets the baby in their piece of King Cake has the honor of supplying the next King Cake during Mardi Gras season---so pass the recipe on!

HOT CHOCOLATE EGGNOG
CINNAMON PINWHEELS
CHEESY CHILIE EGGS
JALAPEÑO CHEESE GRITS
SESAME CORNMEAL BISCUITS
MILK CHOCOLATE DIPPED FRUIT

HOT CHOCOLATE EGGNOG

3 cups dairy eggnog
1 cup chocolate milk
1 cup whipped cream
Chocolate shavings

Heat eggnog and chocolate milk in a large pot over medium heat or in the microwave until warmed. Serve with a dollop of whipped cream and chocolate shavings on top. (Serves 4)

Make chocolate shavings by running a vegetable peeler over a square of semisweet chocolate.

CINNAMON PINWHEELS

4 slices soft white bread
1/4 cup soft cream cheese
1/4 cup chopped pecans

1/4 cup sugar
1 teaspoon cinnamon
1/4 cup butter, melted

Preheat oven to 350°. Trim the crusts from the bread. Flatten slices with a rolling pin. Spread a thin layer of cream cheese on each slice and sprinkle with pecans. Roll up bread slices and cut each roll into thirds.

Mix sugar and cinnamon together in a small bowl. Dip each roll into the melted butter, then in the cinnamon sugar. (Don't dip the open ends of the rolls!) Place rolls seam side down on a foil lined baking sheet. Bake for about 15 minutes or until crisp and golden. Serve warm or cool. (Makes 12)

Kids will also enjoy making and eating this easy breakfast treat.

CHEESY CHILIE EGGS

1 lb. ground pork sausage
2 (4 oz) cans diced green chilies, drained
2 cups grated cheddar cheese
2 cup grated Monterey Jack cheese

1 dozen eggs
1 cup milk
Salt and pepper to taste
Dash of Tabasco
Green pepper slices & cherry tomato halves

Preheat oven to 375°. Brown sausage in a large skillet over medium high heat and drain well. Place in a greased 9 x 13 inch baking dish. Top with chopped chilies and sprinkle with cheeses. Beat eggs with milk in a large bowl and season with salt, pepper and Tabasco. Pour over cheeses.

Bake for 25 - 30 minutes, until firm. Garnish with green pepper slices and cherry tomato halves. (Serves 12 - 14)

A touch of the southwest flavors this delicious and very easy egg dish. Can be made partially the night before; add eggs and bake the next day.

JALAPEÑO CHEESE GRITS

4 cups water
1 teaspoon salt
1 cup Quick Grits

1/4 cup butter or margarine
1/2 roll jalapeño cheese
1 cup grated cheddar cheese

Bring 4 cups of water to a boil in a large saucepan, greased with cooking spray, over high heat. Stir in salt and grits; lower heat to low. Cook, stirring occasionally, until water is absorbed. Add butter and cheeses and heat until melted. (Serves 8)

Serve immediately or place in a greased baking dish, cover and reheat later.

SESAME CORNMEAL BISCUITS

1/2 cup yellow cornmeal
1 1/2 cups flour
1/2 teaspoon salt
4 teaspoons baking powder
1/2 teaspoon cream of tartar

2 Tablespoons sugar
1/2 cup butter
2/3 cup milk
Milk & sesame seeds

Preheat oven to $425°$. In a large mixing bowl, stir together cornmeal, flour, salt, baking powder, cream of tartar and sugar. With a pastry blender or fingers, cut in butter until mixture resembles fine crumbs. Add milk and stir to hold dough together.
Turn out on a lightly floured surface and knead a few times until smooth. Pat into an 8" square, about 1/2" thick. Cut dough into 16 squares with a knife.
Place on a foil lined baking sheet. Brush biscuits with milk, then sprinkle with sesame seeds. Bake for 15 minutes, until nicely browned. Serve hot with butter. (Makes 16)

MILK CHOCOLATE DIPPED FRUIT

1 (12 oz) pkg. semisweet chocolate chips
1 (14 oz) can sweetened condensed milk
2 Tablespoons butter or margarine

1 Tablespoon vanilla
Fruit: strawberries, grapes,
  orange slices, cherries, etc.

In a small saucepan over low heat, combine chocolate chips and condensed milk. Cook and stir until mixture thickens, about 10 minutes. Remove from heat, stir in butter and vanilla. Dip fruit, one at a time, into warm chocolate mixture and place on wax paper. Chill until firm. Best served the same day as prepared.

CAJUN CREOLE

MENUS

LOUISIANA SPICY SHRIMP RÉMOULADE
EASY BOILED SHRIMP
SESAME CATFISH WITH
NEW ORLEANS TARTAR SAUCE
PECAN ICE CREAM ROLL WITH
CHOCOLATE FUDGE SAUCE

RED BELL PEPPER SOUP
HONEY NUT SALAD
CAJUN PEPPERED SHRIMP & GRITS
LEMON CELEBRATION CAKE

CREOLE SQUASH SOUP
SAUCED SWEET POTATOES
SOUTHERN PECAN CHICKEN
CHOCOLATE PECAN TART

OYSTERS BIENVILLE
TROUT WITH SEAFOOD SAUCE
PECAN RICE
SWEET POTATO SOUFFLÉ

SHRIMP CORN SOUP
SAUTÉED CATFISH WITH
CREOLE MUSTARD SAUCE
BRABANT POTATOES
PRALINE ICE CREAM MERINGUES
& PRALINE SAUCE

CRAB CORN BISQUE
SALADE OF HEARTS
LOUISIANA MEAT PIES
SAUCE PIQUANT
PECAN TORTE

CREAM OF ARTICHOKE SOUP
& CHEESE TOASTS
WARM SPINACH SALAD
LOUISIANA CRAB CAKES
& COCKTAIL SAUCE
MILE HIGH PIE & CHOCOLATE SAUCE

CREOLE CHEESE SOUP
WITH GARLIC CROUTONS
SAUTÉED CATFISH
WITH SEAFOOD DRESSING
PRALINES & CREAM DREAM

CREAMY ONION SOUP
FRESH GREEN BEAN CAESAR SALAD
SQUASH & SHRIMP WITH PASTA
PEACHES & CREAM TORTE

Cajun Creole cuisine is one of the most popular regional cuisines in the country. With the abundance of seafood in south Louisiana, most of these menus take advantage of the fresh foods that are available to us. Some recipes will remind you of the wonderful meals served in great New Orleans restaurants, while others are reminiscent of the more simple foods of Cajun country.

LOUISIANA SPICY SHRIMP RÉMOULADE
SESAME CATFISH WITH NEW ORLEANS TARTAR SAUCE
PECAN ICE CREAM ROLL & CHOCOLATE FUDGE SAUCE

LOUISIANA SPICY SHRIMP RÉMOULADE

3 Tablespoons vegetable oil
3 Tablespoons olive oil
2 Tablespoons vinegar
1 Tablespoon paprika
1/2 teaspoon white pepper
1 Tablespoon chopped parsley

1/2 teaspoon salt
1/4 cup Creole mustard
1/2 rib celery, chopped
1 green onion, chopped

1 lb. shrimp, boiled & peeled
Shredded lettuce

Mix all sauce ingredients in a food processor or blender until combined. Chill.

To serve, place boiled shrimp on individual beds of shredded lettuce and top with sauce. (Recipe can be doubled) (Serves 6)

EASY BOILED SHRIMP:
1 - 2 lbs. medium or large shrimp
2 Tablespoons liquid crab boil

2 lemons, cut in half
3 Tablespoons salt

Fill a large stock pot with water and place over high heat. Bring to a boil and add shrimp, crab boil, lemons and salt. Return to a boil and lower heat to medium. Cook until shrimp are tender but not overdone, about 7 - 10 minutes. Taste test is best.

When cooked, pour shrimp into a colander to cool. Do not rinse. Peel when cool enough to handle.

A real favorite in many New Orleans restaurants.
Can be served as an appetizer or a salad.

SESAME CATFISH WITH NEW ORLEANS TARTAR SAUCE

1 lb. catfish fillets, cut into nuggets
Salt & pepper
1 egg, beaten
1/2 cup flour
1/2 cup water
Dash of Tabasco
2 cups Italian seasoned bread crumbs
3 Tablespoons sesame seeds
Vegetable oil

Season catfish nuggets with salt & pepper. Mix egg, flour, water and Tabasco together in a small bowl. In another bowl, combine bread crumbs and sesame seeds for coating.

Cover the bottom of a large skillet with a layer of oil and heat on medium high.

Dip each catfish nugget into batter, then roll in coating. Place several pieces in oil and fry until golden on both sides. Drain on paper towels and keep warm in the oven. Repeat with remaining fish.

Serve with New Orleans Tartar Sauce. (Serves 6)

NEW ORLEANS TARTAR SAUCE

1 cup mayonnaise
1 Tablespoon Creole mustard
1/4 teaspoon Tabasco
2 Tablespoons sweet pickle relish
2 Tablespoons chopped green onion
1 Tablespoon chopped parsley

Mix all ingredients until combined. Cover and chill.

Creole mustard gives this tartar sauce extra flavor!

PECAN ICE CREAM ROLL

1 1/2 cups pecan halves
3 Tablespoons cocoa
6 eggs, separated
1/2 teaspoon cream of tartar

1 cup sugar, divided
1/2 teaspoon vanilla
Powdered sugar
1 quart vanilla ice cream

Grease a 15 1/2 x 10 1/2 x 1 inch jelly roll pan and line with wax paper and grease again. Preheat oven to 350°.

Place pecans in a food processor and chop until finely ground. Add cocoa and combine. Set aside.

In a large bowl, beat egg whites with an electric mixer until foamy. Add cream of tartar and beat until soft peaks form. Gradually add 1/4 cup sugar and beat until stiff but not dry.

In another bowl, combine egg yolks, 3/4 cup sugar and vanilla. Beat until pale and thick, about 3 minutes. Gradually fold in nut mixture alternately with egg whites.

Pour into prepared pan and bake for about 20 minutes or until top springs back when touched and edges shrink slightly. Cool in pan for 15 minutes.

Sprinkle powdered sugar on a cotton towel and invert cake on towel. Gently peel off wax paper.

Soften ice cream slightly. Spread on cake and roll cake up, using towel, from the long side. Sprinkle with more powdered sugar, wrap in foil and freeze. Serve slices with Chocolate Fudge Sauce. (Serve 10 - 12)

You will be surprised at how easy this cake is to handle---it's a grande finale for any meal!

CHOCOLATE FUDGE SAUCE

4 oz. unsweetened chocolate
3 Tablespoons butter
2/3 cup water

1 2/3 cups sugar
6 Tablespoons corn syrup
1 teaspoon vanilla

Melt chocolate and butter in a small saucepan over low heat. Separately, heat water to boiling, then stir into chocolate. Add sugar and corn syrup, stirring until smooth. Turn heat up to medium and bring to a boil, stirring constantly. Lower heat to maintain boiling point and let simmer for about 9 minutes, without stirring.

Remove from heat and cool 10 minutes. Stir in vanilla and serve warm. Can be stored, covered, in refrigerator and reheated as needed. (Makes 2 1/2 cups)

CREOLE SQUASH SOUP
SAUCED SWEET POTATOES
SOUTHERN PECAN CHICKEN
CHOCOLATE PECAN TART

CREOLE SQUASH SOUP

2 Tablespoons butter or margarine
1 onion, chopped
1 clove garlic, minced
4 or 5 yellow squash, quartered & sliced
3 cups chicken broth
1 (8 oz) can tomato sauce

1/2 teaspoon sugar
1/4 teaspoon thyme
1/4 teaspoon oregano
2 Tablespoons chopped parsley
Salt & pepper to taste
Dash of cayenne
Grated Romano cheese

Melt butter in a large saucepan over medium heat. Add onion and garlic and sauté until tender. Add all remaining ingredients and bring to a boil. Cover, lower heat and simmer about 30 minutes until tender. Can serve garnished with Romano cheese, if desired. (Serves 6 - 8)

A very easy, yet tasty, low fat soup!

SAUCED SWEET POTATOES

3 lbs. sweet potatoes
1/4 cup butter or margarine
1/4 cup heavy cream
1/4 cup sugar
1 teaspoon vanilla

1/2 cup butter or margarine
1/4 cup flour
3/4 cup light brown sugar
1/2 cup water
1/2 cup miniature marshmellows

Place sweet potatoes in a large pot, cover with water and bring to a boil over high heat. Cook until tender, drain and rinse with cold water. Peel and place potatoes in a large mixing bowl. Add butter, cream, sugar and vanilla. Mash together until smooth and spoon into a medium size greased baking dish.
Preheat oven to 350°. In a small saucepan over medium heat, melt butter. Stir in flour and cook for 2 minutes. Add brown sugar and combine. Stir in water and marshmellows and cook, stirring constantly, until marshmellows melt and sauce thickens.
Pour sauce over sweet potatoes, cover with foil and bake for 15 - 20 minutes until hot. (Serves 8 - 10)

SOUTHERN PECAN CHICKEN

6 - 8 boneless chicken breasts
Salt & pepper
2 eggs
2 teaspoons Creole mustard
1/2 cup finely chopped pecans
1 cup plain bread crumbs

1/4 cup butter or margarine
1/4 cup vegetable oil

<u>Sauce:</u>
1/4 cup butter
1/2 cup coarsely chopped pecans
1 teaspoon lemon juice

Lay chicken breasts out on wax paper. Season with salt and pepper. In a small bowl, beat eggs with mustard. In another bowl, combine pecans and bread crumbs. Dip chicken in egg mixture then coat with bread crumb mixture.

Preheat oven to 350^0. In a large skillet over medium high heat, melt 2 Tablespoons butter and 2 Tablespoons oil. Sauté half the chicken until golden brown on each side. Place in an ovenproof dish. Wipe out skillet, pouring off any drippings. Sauté the rest of the chicken in the remaining 2 Tablespoons of butter and oil.

Place in oven and bake for 15 minutes.

Make sauce by melting butter in a small saucepan over low heat. Stir in pecans and lemon juice. Serve over chicken. (Serves 6 - 8)

 *Can substitute fish for the chicken for an equally good variation. Wipe out skillet between batches so second batch will have a clean, fresh look after browning.*

CHOCOLATE PECAN TART

CRUST:
1 1/2 cups flour
2 Tablespoons sugar
3/4 cup butter, cut up
2 - 3 Tablespoons ice water

Preheat oven to 400°. Place flour, sugar and butter in a food processor fitted with the metal blade. With machine running, add water just until dough forms a ball. Remove dough and pat with fingers into a greased 9" - 10" fluted tart pan. Press dough out to cover bottom and up sides at least 1". Cover with a piece of foil, greased on the bottom, directly on top of dough and fill with dried beans or pie weights. Also, place a piece of foil under the tart pan to catch any drippings. Bake at 400° for 10 minutes. Reduce heat to 375° and bake 10 minutes more. Remove foil and weights carefully and return crust to oven to bake 5 minutes. Remove from oven and turn temperature to 425°.

FILLING:
1 1/2 cups coarsely chopped pecans (preferably by hand)
1 cup heavy cream
3/4 cup sugar

Place all ingredients in a small saucepan, stirring to blend, and bring to a boil over medium heat. Cook for 6 minutes, without stirring. Pour into crust and bake at 425° for 15 minutes. Remove and make chocolate glaze while tart cools.

GLAZE:
5 oz. semisweet chocolate
2 Tablespoons butter or margarine
1 Tablespoon water
Fresh strawberries

In a double boiler, melt chocolate, butter and water until smooth and shiny, over hot but not boiling water. Spread glaze over filling to cover. Cool and refrigerate until glaze hardens.

To serve, decorate plates using four 1" strips of wax paper to create a crisscross pattern on plate. Sift cocoa over plate and carefully remove strips of wax paper. Place a thin slice of tart in center of plate and dust tart with sifted powdered sugar. Garnish with a fan cut strawberry, if desired. Store in refrigerator.

Use real butter in the crust, you will taste the difference.
Serve small pieces---it's like eating candy!

SHRIMP CORN GUMBO
SAUTÉED CATFISH WITH
CREOLE MUSTARD SAUCE
BRABANT POTATOES
PRALINE ICE CREAM MERINGUES

SHRIMP CORN GUMBO

1/4 cup vegetable oil
1/4 cup flour
1 onion, chopped
1 clove garlic, minced
1/2 green pepper, chopped
1/2 cup chopped celery
1 lb. medium shrimp, peeled

1 (1 lb) can tomatoes
1 (1 lb) can whole kernel corn
1/2 lb. okra, sliced
1 cup chicken broth
Salt, pepper, cayenne to taste
1/4 cup chopped green onion
2 Tablespoons chopped parsley

Heat oil in a large saucepan over medium heat. Add flour and stir constantly until roux becomes a deep golden brown. Add onion, garlic, green pepper and celery. Lower heat to low and cook, stirring constantly until softened. Stir in shrimp and cook until pink. Add tomatoes, corn, okra, chicken broth, salt, pepper and cayenne. Cover and simmer for 30 minutes, stirring occasionally. Add green onions and parsley. Cook 5 minutes more. Taste for seasonings and add more broth to thin, if necessary. (Serves 8)

The addition of okra makes this dish more like a gumbo than a soup. Its a terrific combination of flavors!

SAUTÉED CATFISH WITH CREOLE MUSTARD SAUCE

**6 catfish fillets
Salt, pepper, flour
6 Tablespoons butter or margarine
4 Tablespoons vegetable oil
1/3 cup chopped green onion**

**1 large tomato, peeled,
seeded & chopped
Salt & pepper to taste
1/4 cup dry white wine
1/4 cup heavy cream
2 teaspoons Creole mustard**

Season catfish fillets with salt and pepper. Heat 2 Tablespoons butter and 2 Tablespoons oil in a large skillet over medium heat. Dredge 3 fillets with flour and sauté until golden brown on each side. Place in a ovenproof dish in a warm oven. Pour off oil and add 2 Tablespoons butter and 2 Tablespoons vegetable oil to skillet. Flour remaining fish and sauté. Discard any leftover oil in skillet.

In same skillet, melt the remaining 2 Tablespoons butter and sauté green onions for about 1 minute. Add tomato and cook 2 minutes. Season with salt and pepper. Add wine and reduce slightly. Lower heat and stir in cream and mustard. Heat thoroughly and serve immediately over catfish fillets. (Serves 6)

A wonderful sauce that would work equally well with chicken or shrimp.

BRABANT POTATOES

**2 large white baking potatoes,
unpeeled and scrubbed
Large pot of boiling salted water**

**Salt, pepper or Cajun
seasoning to taste
Vegetable oil**

Quarter the potatoes lengthwise, then cut into 1" cubes. Add to boiling water; cover and cook over high heat just until tender, about 7 minutes. Drain immediately and rinse with cold water to cool. Sprinkle with seasonings, tossing gently.

Heat about a 1 inch layer of oil in a large skillet over medium high heat. Add potatoes and fry until golden brown on all sides, about 12 - 15 minutes, stirring occasionally. Drain on paper towels and serve immediately or keep warm in oven. (Serves 6)

A very versatile potato dish; try it with other entrées!

PRALINE ICE CREAM MERINGUES

MERINGUES:
3 egg whites
1/4 teaspoon cream of tartar
Pinch of salt
1/2 cup sugar
1/4 cup chopped pecans
1 teaspoon vanilla

Preheat oven to 275°. Beat egg whites, cream of tartar and salt with an electric mixer until foamy. Gradually add sugar and beat until stiff peaks form. Fold in nuts and vanilla.

Cover a baking sheet with aluminum foil and grease. Pipe or shape into 6 individual meringue shells with bottom of a spoon. Bake for 1 hour, until light brown and crisp. (Can leave in oven to cool)

PRALINE SAUCE:
1/2 teaspoon baking soda
1/2 cup buttermilk
1 cup sugar
2 Tablespoons light corn syrup
1 teaspoon vanilla
1/2 cup chopped pecans

Vanilla ice cream

Stir soda into buttermilk. Combine with remaining ingredients in a large saucepan and place over medium high heat. Bring to a boil, lower heat to low and simmer for 10 minutes, until slightly thickened. Let cool slightly before serving.

To serve, place a scoop of vanilla ice cream in a meringue shell and top with praline sauce. (Serves 6)

Praline sauce can be made ahead, refrigerated and reheated gently when ready to serve.

CREAM OF ARTICHOKE SOUP
WARM SPINACH SALAD
LOUISIANA CRAB CAKES
& COCKTAIL SAUCE
MILE HIGH PIE
& CHOCOLATE SAUCE

CREAM OF ARTICHOKE SOUP

1/4 cup butter or margarine
1/2 onion, chopped
1/2 cup chopped celery
1/4 cup flour
4 cups chicken broth, warmed
2 (14 oz) cans artichoke hearts, drained & chopped

1 teaspoon lemon juice
1/4 teaspoon thyme
1/8 teaspoon cayenne pepper
Salt & pepper to taste
1 cup heavy cream
Grated Parmesan cheese & chopped parsley

Melt butter in a large saucepan over medium heat. Add onion and celery and sauté until softened. Stir in flour and cook, stirring constantly, for about 3 minutes. Add broth, artichokes, lemon juice, thyme, red pepper, salt & pepper. Bring mixture to a boil. Lower heat, cover and cook for about 15 minutes.

Purée soup in food processor or blender for a smooth consistency. Return to heat and stir in cream. Serve when warmed, garnished with Parmesan cheese and parsley and with cheese toasts on the side. (Serves 8)

CHEESE TOASTS:
Slices of French bread
Butter

Grated Parmesan cheese
Paprika

Preheat oven to 375°. Spread a little butter on each slice of French bread and top with cheese and paprika. Toast until golden, about 10 minutes. Serve with soup.

WARM SPINACH SALAD

1 pkg. fresh spinach, washed
1 cup sliced fresh mushrooms
1 hard boiled egg, chopped
1/4 cup grated Parmesan cheese
Salt & pepper to taste
4 slices bacon
1 teaspoon Dijon mustard
1 teaspoon sugar
1/4 cup red wine vinegar
1/4 cup chopped green
  onion
1/3 cup olive oil

In a large heatproof bowl, place spinach, mushrooms, egg, cheese, salt and pepper.
Cook bacon in a large skillet over medium heat until crisp. Remove, drain and crumble into salad bowl. In bacon drippings, stir in Dijon mustard, sugar, vinegar and green onion. Bring to a boil and slowly add olive oil, whisking constantly.
Remove from heat and invert skillet over salad bowl. Hold over bowl for about 1 minute. Toss salad and serve immediately. (Serves 6 - 8)
[Adapted from a recipe by Terry Thompson]

LOUISIANA CRAB CAKES

1 lb. fresh white or backfin,
  crab meat, drained
3/4 cup cracker crumbs
  (about 20 saltines)
1 egg, slightly beaten
1/2 cup chopped green onion
2 Tablespoons mayonnaise
1 Tablespoon Worcestershire
1 Tablespoon Creole mustard
1/4 teaspoon Tabasco
1/2 teaspoon salt
1/4 teaspoon pepper
Additional cracker crumbs
  (about 10 saltines)
Vegetable oil

In a large bowl, gently mix all ingredients except additional cracker crumbs and oil. Shape into 3" patties. Coat with additional cracker crumbs and chill until ready to cook.
Cover bottom of a large skillet with a layer of oil. Place on medium high heat. Fry crab cakes until golden brown on each side. Drain on paper towels. Can keep warm in a low heated oven. Serve hot with Cocktail Sauce and lemon cups or wedges. Recipe can be doubled. (Makes about 8 cakes)

COCKTAIL SAUCE

1 cup ketchup
3 teaspoons prepared horseradish
1 teaspoon lemon juice
1/2 teaspoon Worcestershire

Mix all ingredients, cover and refrigerate until ready to serve.

MILE HIGH PIE

CRUST:
1 1/2 cups flour
1/4 teaspoon salt
1/2 cup shortening (Crisco)
4 - 5 Tablespoons ice cold water

Preheat oven to $450°$. Mix flour and salt together in a large bowl. Cut in shortening with a pastry cutter to the size of small peas. Add one Tablespoon of ice water at a time and mix in with a spatula until moistened. Form into a ball with your fingers. Roll out on a lightly floured surface and place into a greased 9" pie pan. Trim any excess, turn edge under and flute. Prick all over with a fork. Bake for about 15 minutes, until nicely browned. Cool completely.

FILLING:
1 pint vanilla ice cream
1 pint strawberry ice cream
1 pint chocolate ice cream

Layer ice creams in cooled pie shell and freeze until firm.

MERINGUE:
8 egg whites
1/2 teaspoon vanilla
1/4 teaspoon cream of tartar
3/4 cup sugar

Preheat broiler. With an electric mixer, beat egg whites with vanilla and cream of tartar until soft peaks form. Gradually add sugar, beating until stiff and glossy. Spoon over ice cream to edge of pie shell. Broil for about 30 seconds to brown top. Freeze until ready to serve. (Serves 8)

CHOCOLATE SAUCE

1/2 cup butter or margarine
12 oz. semisweet chocolate chips
  (2 cups)
1 cup sugar
1 teaspoon vanilla
1 cup heavy cream

In a medium saucepan over low heat, melt butter and stir in chocolate chips until melted. Add sugar, vanilla and heavy cream. Simmer for about 10 minutes until smooth, stirring frequently. Cool slightly before serving. (Makes 2 cups) [Based on a recipe from the Caribbean Room at the Ponchartrain Hotel, New Orleans]

A very impressive dessert. Be prepared for raves!

CAJUN CREOLE

**RED BELL PEPPER SOUP
HONEY NUT SALAD
CAJUN PEPPERED SHRIMP & GRITS
LEMON CELEBRATION CAKE**

RED BELL PEPPER SOUP

3 Tablespoons olive oil
1 onion, chopped
3 red bell peppers, chopped
1 large carrot, peeled & chopped

1 clove garlic, minced
6 cups chicken broth
Salt, pepper, cayenne to taste
Chopped parsley for garnish

Heat oil in a large saucepan over medium heat. Sauté vegetables, stirring frequently, until softened, about 15 minutes. Add broth and seasonings. Bring to a boil, lower heat, cover and simmer about 20 minutes. Purée in a food processor or blender and pour through a strainer back into the saucepan. Reheat and serve garnished with chopped parsley. (Serves 6)

Straining the soup will remove bits of skin from the peppers and produce a smooth consistency. A very beautiful soup!

HONEY NUT SALAD

1/2 cup vegetable oil
1/4 cup cider vinegar
3 Tablespoons honey
2 Tablespoons Dijon mustard

Leaf or iceberg lettuce
1 (11 oz) can mandarin
  oranges, drained
1/2 cup toasted pecan halves
Salt & pepper to taste

Mix dressing ingredients together in a small bowl with a wire whisk until blended. Tear lettuce into a large salad bowl. Add oranges, pecans, salt and pepper. Toss with enough dressing to coat. (Makes 1 cup dressing)

*A simple honey mustard dressing!
Also good on spinach salads.*

CAJUN PEPPERED SHRIMP & GRITS

GRITS:
6 cups water
2 teaspoons salt
1 1/2 cups Quick Grits
2 Tablespoons butter
1 roll garlic cheese
1 cup grated cheddar cheese
1 teaspoon Worcestershire

Preheat oven to 350°. Grease a large saucepan with cooking spray, add water and bring to a boil over high heat. Stir in salt and grits. Lower heat and cook, stirring occasionally, until water is absorbed and grits thicken. Add butter, cheeses and Worcestershire. Cook until cheese melts. Pour in a greased casserole dish and bake for about 20 minutes to set.

SHRIMP:
1/2 cup butter or margarine
1/4 cup olive oil
3 lbs. medium shrimp, peeled
1 clove garlic, minced
1 cup chopped green onion
1 cup sliced mushrooms
1/2 cup chopped parsley
1/2 teaspoon salt
1 teaspoon pepper
1/4 teaspoon cayenne pepper
1/2 teaspoon paprika
1/4 teaspoon basil, thyme & oregano
1 Tablespoon lemon juice
Fresh hot French bread

In a large saucepan, melt butter and oil over medium heat. Add shrimp and sauté just until pink. Stir in all other ingredients and seasonings. Simmer about 10 minutes. Mixture will be very saucy.

Serve a scoop of grits surrounded with shrimp and sauce. Serve with hot French bread for dipping. (Serves 8)

A delightful combination of flavors straight from the South! Try serving this impressive dish for Brunch.

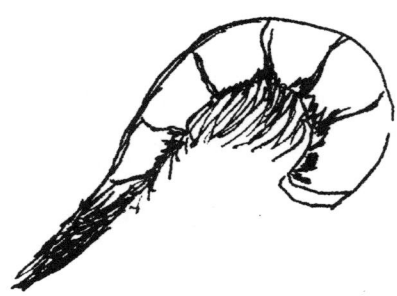

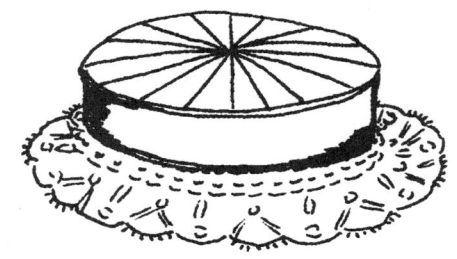

LEMON CELEBRATION CAKE

1 cup butter or margarine
2 cups sugar
3 eggs
Zest of 1 lemon

2 teaspoons baking powder
1/2 teaspoon salt
2 cups flour
1 cup sour cream

Preheat oven to 325°. Grease a celebration cake pan or bundt pan.
In the large bowl of an electric mixer, cream butter and sugar until fluffy, about 4 minutes. Add eggs, one at a time, until mixed. Add zest, baking powder and salt. Mix in flour alternately with sour cream until blended.
Pour into prepared pan and bake about 40 - 45 minutes, until tested done. Let cool in pan 10 minutes. Remove and place on rack to cool completely before glazing.

GLAZE:
2 cups sifted powdered sugar
3 Tablespoons lemon juice

1 drop yellow food coloring
About 1 Tablespoon water
Decorative sprinkles

Mix powdered sugar, lemon juice, food coloring and enough water together in a small bowl to obtain a smooth consistency. Spread glaze over cake and top with decorative sprinkles for a festive appearance.

A celebration cake pan is an 11" nonstick pan with 16 decorative divisions marked in the pan. It makes a very beautiful presentation.

OYSTERS BIENVILLE
TROUT WITH SEAFOOD SAUCE
PECAN RICE
SWEET POTATO SOUFFLÉ

OYSTERS BIENVILLE

- 1/2 cup butter or margarine
- 1/2 cup flour
- 1 cup chopped green onion
- 2 cups chicken broth, warmed
- 2 cups boiled shrimp, peeled & finely chopped
- 2 cups fresh mushrooms, finely chopped
- 3 egg yolks
- 1/2 cup half & half cream
- Salt & pepper to taste
- 1/2 teaspoon cayenne pepper
- 2 - 3 dozen oysters, drained
- 1/4 cup Italian seasoned bread crumbs
- 1/2 cup grated Parmesan cheese

Melt butter in a large saucepan over medium high heat. Stir in flour and cook, stirring constantly, until lightly browned. Add green onions and sauté lightly. Gradually add warm broth, stirring constantly. Lower heat and simmer until thick. Add chopped shrimp and mushrooms and cook 5 minutes. Whisk together egg yolks and half & half. Very slowly add some of the warm sauce to the egg mixture, stirring constantly. Gradually add egg mixture to sauce and stir over low heat until thickened. Season to taste.

Preheat oven to 400°. Place drained oysters in oyster shells or ovenproof ramekins. If using shells, arrange on a layer of rock salt in a large baking pan. Bake for 7 minutes. Remove from oven and drain any excess liquid from oysters.

Spoon sauce over each oyster to cover. Combine bread crumbs and Parmesan cheese and sprinkle on top of each sauced oyster. Return to oven and bake for 10 minutes until bubbly hot. (Serves 6 - 8)

A great old New Orleans recipe!
The sauce is what makes this dish special.

TROUT WITH SEAFOOD SAUCE

1/2 cup butter
1/2 lb. fresh white crab meat
1/2 lb. shrimp, boiled & peeled
Juice of 1 lemon
Salt & pepper to taste
2 Tablespoons chopped parsley

6 trout fillets
Salt, pepper & flour
3 Tablespoons vegetable oil
3 Tablespoons butter

To make sauce, melt butter in a small saucepan over low heat. Add crab, shrimp, lemon juice, salt, pepper and parsley. Heat and keep warm.

Season trout fillets with salt and pepper. Heat oil and butter in a large skillet over medium high heat. Coat half the fillets with flour and sauté until golden brown on each side. Place in a warm oven. Flour remaining fillets and sauté until golden.

To serve, top each piece of sautéed trout with seafood sauce. (Serves 6)

Crawfish may be substituted for crab and shrimp. Always coat fillets just before browning so flour isn't absorbed.

PECAN RICE

1/2 cup butter or margarine
1/2 cup chopped green onion
1/2 cup chopped bell pepper
1/2 cup chopped celery
1/4 cup chopped parsley

1 cup chopped pecans
Salt & pepper to taste
Dash of Tabasco
3 cups cooked Pecan Rice
  or plain rice

Melt butter in a medium saucepan over medium heat and sauté green onions, bell pepper, celery and parsley until tender. Stir in pecans and cook until lightly browned. Add seasonings and stir in cooked rice. Serve immediately or place in a casserole and reheat later. (Serves 6)

SWEET POTATO SOUFFLÉ

6 large sweet potatoes
6 Tablespoons butter
1 cup heavy cream
1/2 cup sugar

1/3 cup dark brown sugar
3 eggs, lightly beaten
1 teaspoon vanilla
Powdered sugar

Boil potatoes in a large pot of water over high heat until tender. Drain and allow to cool slightly. Peel and place in a large mixing bowl.

Preheat oven to $350°$. Beat potatoes with an electric mixer, adding butter, cream, sugar, dark brown sugar, eggs and vanilla. Beat until very smooth. Pour into a greased soufflé dish or 2 qt. casserole and bake for about 1 hour or until firm.

Sprinkle generously with powdered sugar and serve immediately. (Serves 6 - 8)

A very different, not too sweet dessert!
Sweet potatoes are easier to peel after they have been boiled.

CRAB CORN BISQUE
SALADE OF HEARTS
LOUISIANA MEAT PIES
SAUCE PIQUANT
PECAN TORTE

CRAB CORN BISQUE

- 3 ears fresh corn or 1 (12 oz) can of corn, drained
- 2 slices of bacon
- 1 Tablespoon butter or margarine
- 2 Tablespoons flour
- 1 onion, chopped
- 1 cup chopped celery
- 1 medium red potato, peeled & cubed
- 2 cups chicken broth
- 1 cup milk
- Salt & pepper to taste
- Dash of cayenne pepper
- 1 cup heavy cream
- 1/2 lb. fresh white crab meat
- 1/4 cup chopped green onion
- 1/4 cup chopped parsley

Cut corn off cob and reserve. In a large saucepan over medium heat, cook bacon until crisp. Remove, drain and crumble. Add butter to saucepan and stir in flour until smooth. Cook about 3 minutes. Add onion, celery and potato and sauté until softened, about 5 minutes, stirring frequently. Stir in broth, milk, reserved corn and seasonings. Bring to a boil, reduce heat to low and simmer, covered, for about 20 minutes. Stir in cream, crab meat, green onion, parsley and bacon. Taste for seasonings. (Serves 6)

 *1/2 lb. shrimp can be substituted for crab meat; cook with onion, celery and potato.*

SALADE OF HEARTS

DRESSING:
1/2 teaspoon sugar
1/4 teaspoon dry mustard
1 Tablespoon white wine vinegar
1/2 cup olive oil
Salt & pepper to taste

Whisk all ingredients together in a small bowl. Chill.

SALADE:
Boston or red leaf lettuce
1 can hearts of palm, drained
1 can artichoke hearts, drained
1 jar (2 oz) whole pimientos
1 hard boiled egg, grated

On individual salad plates, place a large leaf of lettuce. Slice hearts of palm in thirds, vertically, and cut artichoke hearts in half. Arrange palm in middle, artichoke on sides, sprinkle with egg and cross pimiento pieces on top. Spoon on dressing. (Serves 6)

Hearts of palm are a nice change of pace in this delicate salade!

LOUISIANA MEAT PIES
SAUCE PIQUANT

PASTRY:
- 2 1/2 cups flour
- 1 teaspoon sugar
- 1 teaspoon salt
- 1 egg
- 1/2 cup very cold butter, cut into 8 pieces
- 1/2 cup cold milk

Measure flour, sugar and salt into a food processor. Pulse to combine. Add egg and butter. Process just until crumbly. With machine running, add milk through feed tube and process just until dough comes together and forms a ball. Remove, cover with plastic wrap and chill. Triple recipe, separately, to use all of filling.

MEAT FILLING:
- 1 lb. loose pork sausage
- 1 lb. lean ground meat
- 1/2 cup vegetable oil
- 1/2 cup flour
- 1 onion, chopped
- 1/2 cup chopped celery
- 1/2 green pepper, chopped
- 1/2 cup chopped green onion
- 1 1/2 cups beef broth
- 1/4 teaspoon sage
- 1/4 teaspoon thyme
- 1/4 cup chopped parsley
- Salt & pepper to taste
- Dash of cayenne pepper

In a large skillet or saucepan over medium high heat, brown sausage. Remove and drain on paper towels. Add ground meat to skillet and brown. Remove and drain on paper towels also. Lower heat to medium and add oil. When oil is hot, stir in flour and cook, stirring constantly, to a medium brown roux. Lower heat as necessary. Add chopped vegetables and sauté until softened. Stir in beef broth and seasonings. Add sausage and ground meat. Cook for about 10 minutes, stirring occasionally and skim off any excess grease. Remove from heat and cool.

SAUCE PIQUANT

- 2 Tablespoons vegetable oil
- 1/2 onion, chopped
- 1 clove garlic, minced
- 1/4 green pepper, chopped
- 1 (10 oz) can diced Ro-Tel tomatoes & chilies
- 1 (16 oz) can tomato sauce
- 1/2 teaspoon sugar
- Salt & pepper to taste

Heat oil in a large skillet over medium heat. Sauté chopped vegetables until softened. Add tomatoes and tomato sauce. Stir in sugar, salt and pepper. Bring to a boil, lower heat and simmer for about 20 minutes.
(continued on next page)

TO ASSEMBLE:
1 egg
2 Tablespoons milk

Preheat oven to 375°. Roll out one recipe of dough on a lightly floured surface to about 1/4" thick. Cut out 4" rounds and roll each circle out again to thin out. Place about 2 Tablespoons cooled meat mixture down center of circle. Fold over to enclose meat in a crescent shape. Crimp edges on both sides with tines of a fork. Place on a greased foil lined baking sheet.

Make an egg wash by beating 1 egg with 2 Tablespoons milk. Brush each meat pie with egg wash. Repeat assembly of meat pies using the remaining 2 recipes of dough.

Bake for about 30 minutes, until golden brown. Serve with Sauce Piquant. (Makes about 2 dozen meat pies)

Meat pies can be frozen before or after baking.
A great crowd pleasing recipe!

PECAN TORTE

3 eggs, separated
3/4 cup sugar
1/2 teaspoon vanilla
1 teaspoon baking powder
Pinch of salt

1 1/2 cups finely chopped pecans
1 Tablespoon flour
Powdered sugar for garnish
1 pint vanilla ice cream

Preheat oven to 350°. Beat egg yolks in a mixing bowl with an electric mixer until thick and lemon colored, about 5 minutes. Gradually beat in about half of 3/4 cup sugar until blended.

In another bowl, beat egg whites until frothy. Gradually beat in remaining half of sugar and beat until stiff. Mix in vanilla.

Stir baking powder, salt, pecans and flour together in a small bowl. Gently fold into egg whites; then fold egg yolks into egg white mixture.

Pour into a greased 9" tart pan. Bake about 25 minutes. Cool in pan.

Before serving, place 4, 1" strips of wax paper over torte and sprinkle with powdered sugar. Remove strips and repeat in opposite direction, forming a crisscross design.

Remove ice cream from freezer and allow to melt at room temperature, stirring frequently, until a liquid consistency. Keep in refrigerator until ready to serve.

To serve, spoon some ice cream sauce in the bottom of a plate or bowl. Place a slice of pecan torte on top. (Serves 8)

A delicious nutty dessert that's easy, yet impressive!
Melted ice cream makes a great dessert sauce.

CREOLE CHEESE SOUP
WITH GARLIC CROUTONS
SAUTEED CATFISH
WITH SEAFOOD DRESSING
PRALINES & CREAM DREAM

CREOLE CHEESE SOUP

1/4 cup butter or margarine
1 onion, chopped
1/4 green pepper, chopped
1/2 cup chopped celery
1/3 cup flour
2 cups milk, heated
2 cups chicken broth, heated

2 cups grated sharp cheddar cheese
2 Tablespoons tomato paste
1 Tablespoon Worcestershire
Salt & pepper to taste
1/4 teaspoon Tabasco
Chopped parsley for garnish

In a large saucepan over medium heat, melt butter and sauté onion, green pepper and celery until softened. Add flour and cook, stirring constantly, for about 3 minutes. Slowly add milk and chicken broth. Mix in cheese, tomato paste and seasonings. Cover, lower heat and simmer for about 15 - 20 minutes, stirring occasionally. Serve garnished with garlic croutons and chopped parsley. (Serves 6)

 *A wonderful soup with the colors of fall!*

GARLIC CROUTONS

4 slices white or wheat bread
1/4 cup butter, melted

1 clove garlic, minced

Preheat oven broiler. Trim crusts from bread and cut bread slices into cubes. Place bread cubes on a foil lined baking sheet. Mix butter and garlic together and brush over cubes. Toast under broiler, watching carefully, until browned. Toss to ensure even browning.

SAUTÉED CATFISH WITH SEAFOOD DRESSING

1 lb. medium shrimp
1 1/2 cups water
1 medium eggplant
2 cups water
1/2 cup butter or margarine
1 onion, chopped
1/4 green pepper, chopped
1/2 cup chopped celery
1 clove garlic, minced
Salt & pepper to taste
1/4 teaspoon thyme, basil, oregano & cayenne pepper

1 lb. fresh white crab meat
1/4 cup chopped green onion
1/4 cup chopped parsley
1/2 cup Italian seasoned bread crumbs
8 catfish fillets, slit down the center
Salt, pepper and flour
Vegetable oil
8 lemon slices

Place shrimp in a medium saucepan with 1 1/2 cups water. Bring to a boil over high heat and cook about 3 minutes. Strain and reserve stock. Peel shrimp and chop coarsely.

Peel eggplant and cut into small cubes. Place in a medium saucepan with 2 cups water. Bring to a boil over high heat, lower heat to medium and cook about 5 minutes. Drain thoroughly and mash with a fork against strainer to remove water.

Melt butter in a large skillet over medium heat. Sauté onion, green pepper, celery and garlic until tender, about 5 minutes. Season shrimp and eggplant with salt and pepper and add to skillet along with 1/2 cup reserved shrimp stock. Mix in thyme, basil, oregano and cayenne pepper. Lower heat and simmer for 10 minutes. Gently stir in crab meat, green onion, parsley and bread crumbs. Cook 5 minutes. Taste for seasonings.

Preheat oven to 350°. Season catfish fillets with salt and pepper. In a large skillet over medium heat, place a thin layer of oil. While oil is heating, coat 4 fillets with flour. Sauté fish until golden brown on both sides. Remove and place in a large baking dish. Repeat with remaining fish fillets.

Place a generous portion of dressing on top of each fillet. Top with a lemon slice and spoon on a little reserved stock over each piece. Bake for 15 - 20 minutes. (Serves 8)

Seafood dressing would also make a great filling for stuffed eggplant.

PRALINES & CREAM DREAM

1 cup light brown sugar
1/4 cup light corn syrup
1/2 cup half and half cream
2 Tablespoons butter

1 cup coarsely chopped
  pecans
1/2 teaspoon vanilla
Vanilla ice cream

In a small saucepan, combine brown sugar, corn syrup and cream. Place over medium heat and cook for 7 - 8 minutes. Stir in butter, pecans and vanilla. Remove and cool completely.

To serve, spoon alternate layers of ice cream and praline sauce in a wine glass or parfait glass. (Serves 6)

**CREAMY ONION SOUP
FRESH GREEN BEAN CAESAR SALAD
SQUASH & SHRIMP WITH PASTA
PEACHES & CREAM TORTE**

CREAMY ONION SOUP

4 or 5 yellow onions, chopped
4 cups chicken broth
1/4 cup butter or margarine
1/4 cup flour
1 teaspoon sugar

Salt & pepper to taste
1/4 teaspoon Tabasco
1/2 teaspoon Anisette or
  Pernod
Grated cheddar cheese &
  chopped parsley

Place half the chopped onions and 4 cups broth in a large saucepan over high heat and bring to a boil. Lower heat to medium, cover and cook about 25 minutes.

In another saucepan, melt butter over medium heat. Add the rest of the onions and sauté until transparent, about 15 minutes. Stir in flour and cook 3 minutes. Add sugar, salt, pepper, Tabasco, Anisette and the chicken broth and onion mixture. Cook about 10 minutes over low heat.

Serve garnished with cheese and parsley. (Serves 6)

Anisette gives a subtle yet unique flavor to this soup.

GREEN BEAN CAESAR SALAD

                               1 cup sliced fresh
                                  mushrooms
       ...ice   1/4 cup toasted walnuts
       ...shire sauce   1/2 cup grated Parmesan or
                                  Romano cheese

...green beans in a large pot of boiling water over high heat for about 15 minutes, until tender. Drain and cool.

Whisk olive oil, lemon juice, Worcestershire, salt and pepper together until combined.

Place green beans in a serving bowl. Add mushrooms and toss with dressing. Sprinkle with walnuts and top with cheese. (Serves 6)

SQUASH & SHRIMP WITH PASTA

1/2 cup butter or margarine	1/4 teaspoon oregano
1 onion, halved & sliced	1/4 teaspoon basil
1/2 green pepper, chopped	Salt, pepper & cayenne
1/2 red bell pepper, chopped	pepper to taste
2 cloves garlic, minced	1 cup chicken broth
4 yellow squash, halved & sliced	2 lbs. medium shrimp, peeled
2 zucchini, halved & sliced	1/2 cup chopped green onion
2 tomatoes, peeled & chopped	1/4 cup chopped parsley
2 teaspoons sugar	1 lb. vermicelli pasta
	1 cup grated Romano or Parmesan cheese

Melt butter in a large saucepan over medium heat and sauté onion, peppers and garlic until tender, about 10 minutes. Add squash, zucchini, tomatoes, seasonings and broth. Cover and cook 10 minutes. Stir in shrimp, green onion and parsley. Simmer about 10 more minutes until shrimp are pink. Taste for seasonings.

Meanwhile, cook pasta in a large pot of boiling salted water until done (al dente). Drain and stir into sauce. Turn off heat. Add cheese and stir gently to combine. Let stand for a few minutes for pasta to absorb sauce. Serve with additional cheese. (Serves 8)

A superb summertime dish when vegetables are at their peak. Other pastas may be substituted.

PEACHES & CREAM TORTE

3 - 4 fresh peaches (or I lb. frozen peach slices)
1/4 cup butter or margarine
1/2 cup sugar
2 eggs

1 teaspoon baking powder
1/4 teaspoon salt
1 cup flour
1/2 cup milk
1/2 teaspoon almond extract
1/4 cup sugar

SAUCE:
1/2 cup heavy cream
1/4 cup sifted powdered sugar
1/2 teaspoon vanilla

Preheat oven to 350°. Peel peaches and slice thin.

Cream butter and sugar with an electric mixer until smooth and creamy, about 5 minutes. Add eggs, one at a time, beating well. Add baking powder and salt. Mix in flour alternately with milk, beating until smooth. Add almond extract.

Pour batter in a greased 9" tart or cake pan. Arrange peach slices on top of batter, in a decorative circle. Sprinkle peaches with 1/4 cup sugar. Place tart pan on a piece of foil to catch any spillovers. Bake for 30 - 35 minutes until tested done. Remove from oven and place on a rack to cool slightly.

Make sauce by mixing together cream, sugar and vanilla until blended. Do not beat. Pour sauce over torte and let stand to absorb. Serve warm or cool. Store in refrigerator. (Serves 8)

If using frozen peaches, defrost, slice in half for thinner slices and blot off any excess water. Especially good with Louisiana peaches!

CARIBBEAN CUISINE

MENU

CRAB TARTLETS
PARADISE SALAD
PINEAPPLE SHRIMP CARIBE
LEMON MERINGUE CAKE

A taste of the islands can be sampled in this menu of tropical recipes--- a nice departure from the ordinary!

CRAB TARTLETS
PARADISE SALAD
PINEAPPLE SHRIMP CARIBE
LEMON MERINGUE CAKE

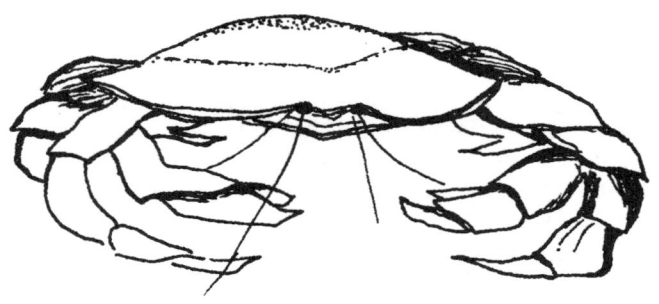

CRAB TARTLETS

18 slices of sandwich bread
1 (4 1/4 oz) can crab meat
1/4 cup mayonnaise
1/2 cup grated Swiss cheese
1 teaspoon lemon juice

1 teaspoon Dijon mustard
1/8 teaspoon cayenne pepper
1/2 teaspoon Worcestershire
Salt & pepper
Parsley for garnish

Preheat oven to 375°. Roll each slice of bread out with a rolling pin and cut out center with a 2 1/2 inch daisy cookie cutter. Gently press each piece into a greased mini-muffin pan. Bake about 5 - 8 minutes until lightly browned.

Meanwhile, drain crab meat well. Mix with remaining ingredients in a small bowl. Spoon filling into tartlet shells and top with a tiny piece of parsley. Bake about 8 minutes or until hot. (Makes about 18)

 *Shells & filling can be made ahead and assembled later.*

PARADISE SALAD

VINAIGRETTE:
3/4 cup olive oil
1/4 cup balsamic vinegar
1/4 teaspoon salt
1/8 teaspoon pepper

GLAZED PECANS:
1 Tablespoon butter
1 Tablespoon sugar
1 teaspoon water
1 cup pecan halves

1 red onion, sliced thin
1 red pepper, sliced thin
Red leaf lettuce
1 avocado, sliced
1/2 cup Gorgonzola cheese, crumbled

Make vinaigrette by whisking oil, vinegar, salt and pepper together. Chill. Make glazed pecans by melting butter in a small skillet over medium heat. Mix in sugar and water and cook until bubbling. Add pecans and stir constantly until sugar begins to caramelize, about 5 minutes. Pour out onto a foil lined baking sheet, separate and cool.

Grill onion and pepper slices until softened. (Stove top grill works great!)

To assemble, make individual salads of lettuce, avocado, grilled onions, peppers, gorgonzola cheese, vinaigrette and glazed pecans. (Serves 6 - 8)

One of the best salads you will ever make---a super combination of ingredients!

PINEAPPLE SHRIMP CARIBE

2 lbs. medium shrimp, peeled
Salt & pepper
2 Tablespoons vegetable oil
1 onion, chopped
1 clove garlic, minced
1/2 green pepper, chopped
4 tomatoes, peeled & chopped
1 Tablespoon lime juice

1/2 teaspoon coriander
1/2 teaspoon turmeric
1/2 teaspoon cumin
1/4 teaspoon ginger
1/8 teaspoon cayenne pepper
Salt & pepper to taste
1 (20 oz) can pineapple chunks, in its own juice
1 Tablespoon cornstarch

Season shrimp with salt & pepper. Heat oil in a large saucepan over medium high heat. Sauté onion, garlic and green pepper until tender. Add shrimp and cook about 2 minutes, until pink. Stir in tomatoes and all seasonings. Lower heat and cook, stirring occasionally, for about 10 minutes. Add pineapple chunks and juice. Dissolve cornstarch in 2 Tablespoons cold water and mix into sauce. Cook until thickened. Serve over rice. (Serves 6 - 8)

LEMON MERINGUE CAKE

CAKE:
1/2 cup butter or margarine
1/2 cup sugar
4 egg yolks
2 teaspoons baking powder
1/8 teaspoon salt
1 cup flour
1/2 teaspoon almond extract
1/4 cup milk

Preheat oven to 350°. Grease two 8" round cake pans. Cream butter and sugar with an electric mixer until smooth, about 3 minutes. Add egg yolks, one at a time, and mix well. Mix in baking powder, salt and flour alternately with almond and milk. Divide evenly between the two cake pans.

MERINGUE:
4 egg whites
1 cup sugar
1/2 teaspoon almond extract
1/2 cup chopped almonds

Beat egg whites with an electric mixer until soft peaks form. Gradually beat in sugar until stiff and meringue holds its shape. Fold in almond extract and chopped almonds. Spread meringue over cake batter in both pans. Bake about 20 - 25 minutes. Cool in pans.

FILLING:
3/4 cup sugar
3 Tablespoons cornstarch
2 teaspoons flour
1 1/4 cups water
2 egg yolks
Zest of 1 lemon
1/4 cup lemon juice
1 Tablespoon butter

Cool Whip, powdered sugar & toasted sliced almonds

Place sugar, cornstarch & flour in a small non-aluminum saucepan. Slowly whisk in water to combine. Place over medium high heat and bring to a boil, stirring constantly. Boil for 1 minute until sauce thickens. Remove and turn heat to low.

In a small bowl, whisk egg yolks, zest and lemon juice together. Quickly whisk in about 1/2 cup hot mixture to gently warm egg yolks. Then stir yolk mixture into saucepan to combine. Cook about 3 minutes, stirring constantly. Remove from heat and stir in butter until melted. Place in a another bowl to cool. Cover with plastic wrap directly on the surface and chill.

To assemble, place a cake layer, meringue side down, on a plate and top with half of the lemon filling. Place other cake layer, meringue side up, on top and spread with remaining filling. Trim off any excess meringue.

Spread Cool Whip around sides of cake and garnish top with toasted sliced almonds. Sprinkle top with powdered sugar. Chill.

 Best made on the same day as served.

CHINESE

MENUS

FRIED WON TONS
SWEET & SOUR PORK
HOT MUSTARD SAUCE
MOO GOO GAI PAN
SHRIMP CANTONESE
PINEAPPLE IMPERIAL

SHRIMP & PORK EGG ROLLS
SWEET & SOUR SAUCE
HOT MUSTARD SAUCE
LEMON CHICKEN WITH PEA PODS
SHRIMP WITH LOBSTER SAUCE
FORTUNE COOKIES

VELVET CORN SOUP
WALNUT CHICKEN
TOMATO PEPPER BEEF
SHRIMP & VEGETABLE STIR-FRY
STIR-FRIED SPICED APPLES

SHRIMP TOAST
SPINACH MUSHROOM SOUP
SHRIMP FRIED RICE
ALMOND CHICKEN
SWEET & SOUR PORK

STEAMED SHRIMP DUMPLINGS &
PLUM SAUCE
CASHEW CHICKEN
MU SHU PORK &
MANDARIN PANCAKES

Chinese menus usually require advance preparation, since the cooking goes so fast. Simply allow time to chop the vegetables and meats, and assemble all of your ingredients before stir-frying. You will find that most Chinese recipes taste best when they are cooked and served immediately.

```
FRIED WON TONS
SWEET & SOUR SAUCE
HOT MUSTARD SAUCE
MOO GOO GAI PAN
SHRIMP CANTONESE
PINEAPPLE IMPERIAL
```

FRIED WON TONS

2 Tablespoons peanut or vegetable oil
1/2 lb. pork, chopped
1/2 lb. shrimp, peeled & chopped
2 Tablespoons soy sauce
1 Tablespoon rice wine or pale dry sherry
1/2 teaspoon salt
1/4 cup chopped water chestnuts
1/2 cup chopped green onion

1 teaspoon cornstarch, dissolved in 1 Tablespoon water

1 pkg. won ton wrappers

Peanut oil for frying

Heat oil in a wok or large skillet over high heat. Add the pork and stir-fry for about 1 minute or until meat loses its reddish color. Add the shrimp and stir-fry for another minute, until pink. Add soy sauce, rice wine, salt, water chestnuts and green onions. Stir-fry for 1 minute. Stir cornstarch and water to recombine and add to wok. Stir until mixture thickens. Remove and transfer to a bowl to cool to room temperature.

To assemble, place about 1 teaspoon of filling in the center of a won ton wrapper. Moisten edges of wrapper with a little water (use fingers) and bring one corner over the filling to the opposite corner of the wrapper, to form a triangle. Pull the two bottom corners of the folded triangle to meet in the center and moisten to hold together. Place each filled won ton on a wax paper lined baking sheet. Cover with plastic wrap and refrigerate if holding longer than 30 minutes.

Heat enough oil in a wok or skillet to deep fry won tons ($375°$). Fry a few at a time until crisp and golden on each side. Drain on paper towels and keep warm in a $250°$ oven. Serve with Sweet & Sour Sauce and Hot Mustard Sauce. (Serves 6 - 8)

Pork & shrimp add a lot of flavor to this great appetizer!

SWEET & SOUR SAUCE

1/2 cup white vinegar
1/2 cup water
1/4 cup light brown sugar

1/4 cup sugar
1/4 cup cornstarch
1/2 cup pineapple juice

In a small saucepan over medium high heat, bring vinegar, water and sugars to a boil. Combine cornstarch and pineapple juice together. Add to hot mixture and cook until thickened. (Makes 2 1/4 cups)

 *Any leftover sauce can be stored in the refrigerator. It will congeal but will return to a sauce consistency when reheated.*

HOT MUSTARD SAUCE

2 - 3 Tablespoons dry mustard   **Water**

Place dry mustard in a small bowl and stir in enough water to make a thin paste.

 *Hot mustard is exactly that-----hot! Use sparingly.*

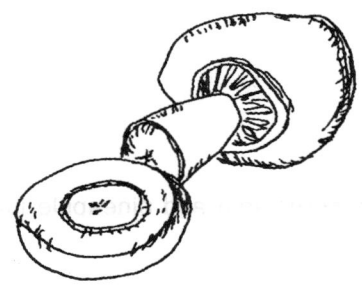

MOO GOO GAI PAN

MARINADE:
1 egg white, lightly beaten
1 Tablespoon vegetable oil
1 Tablespoon rice wine
1/4 teaspoon salt
Pepper to taste
1 Tablespoon cornstarch

1 lb. boneless chicken breast, cut into bite size strips

SAUCE:
1 Tablespoon soy sauce
1 Tablespoon oyster sauce
1 Tablespoon rice wine
1/2 teaspoon sugar
1 teaspoon sesame oil

3 Tablespoons vegetable oil
1 clove garlic, mashed
1 cup sliced mushrooms
1 (8 oz) can sliced water chestnuts
1/2 cup snow peas
1 Tablespoon cornstarch
2 Tablespoons water
1 cup chicken broth
Soy sauce to taste

Mix together marinade ingredients in a medium size bowl and stir in chicken to coat completely. Marinate for 30 minutes.

Combine sauce ingredients in a small bowl and set aside.

Heat 3 Tablespoons oil in a wok or large skillet over medium high heat. Stir-fry garlic just until browned; remove and discard. Add marinated chicken and stir-fry until lightly browned. Add sauce, then stir in mushrooms, water chestnuts and snow peas. Cook 1 minute.

Dissolve cornstarch in water. Add chicken broth to wok. Heat until bubbly. Stir in cornstarch mixture and heat thoroughly until sauce thickens. Taste for soy sauce and serve immediately with rice. (Serves 4 - 6)

SHRIMP CANTONESE

1 lb. medium shrimp, peeled
Salt & pepper to taste
2 Tablespoons vegetable oil
1 Tablespoon oyster sauce
1 onion, halved & sliced
1 cup sliced celery
1/2 pkg. (5 oz) fresh spinach,
   washed, drained & torn
1 cup sliced mushrooms
1 (8 oz) can bamboo shoots
Salt, pepper and soy sauce
   to taste
1 cup chicken broth
1 Tablespoon cornstarch
1/4 cup water

Season shrimp with salt & pepper. In a wok or large skillet, heat oil over medium high heat. Stir-fry shrimp until pink, about 2 minutes. Add oyster sauce, onion and celery. Stir-fry for 2 minutes. Add spinach, mushrooms, drained bamboo shoots, salt, pepper and soy sauce. Stir-fry another minute. Add broth and cook until bubbly. Mix cornstarch with water to dissolve. Add to sauce, stirring until thickened and heated through. Serve immediately with rice. (Serves 4 - 6)

PINEAPPLE IMPERIAL

6 slices (1/2" thick) fresh or
   canned pineapple
2 egg whites
1/2 cup light brown sugar
1/4 cup chopped almonds

Preheat broiler. Drain pineapple and pat dry with paper towels. Place on a greased foil lined baking sheet.
   Place egg whites in a small bowl and beat with an electric mixer until soft peaks form. Gradually beat in sugar until stiff and glossy.
   Spoon meringue on top of pineapple slices to form a mound. Sprinkle with chopped almonds and broil until lightly browned. Refrigerate until ready to serve. (Serves 6)

VELVET CORN SOUP
WALNUT CHICKEN
TOMATO PEPPER BEEF
SHRIMP & VEGETABLE STIR-FRY
STIR-FRIED SPICED APPLES

VELVET CORN SOUP

2 egg whites
2 Tablespoons milk
3 cups chicken broth
1 (17 oz) can cream style corn
Salt & pepper to taste

1 Tablespoon cornstarch
2 Tablespoons water
1/4 cup finely chopped ham
2 Tablespoons chopped green onion

In a small bowl, beat egg whites, with a whisk, until frothy. Add milk.

In a medium saucepan, bring chicken broth to a boil over high heat. Add corn, salt and pepper and return to a boil. Dissolve cornstarch in water and stir into soup. Cook, stirring constantly, until soup thickens and becomes clear. Turn off heat and immediately pour in egg white mixture, stirring only once.

Quickly ladle into soup bowls and sprinkle with chopped ham and green onion. (Serves 4 - 6)

WALNUT CHICKEN

3 boneless chicken breasts, cut into 1/4" x 2" strips
Salt & pepper
2 Tablespoons vegetable oil
1/2 cup walnut halves or pieces
1/2 onion, sliced
1/2 cup sliced celery

1 cup chicken broth
2 Tablespoons soy sauce
2 Tablespoons cornstarch
1/2 cup chicken broth
1/2 cup snow peas
1 (8 oz) can sliced water chestnuts, drained

Season chicken with salt and pepper. Heat oil in a wok over medium high heat. Stir-fry walnuts quickly until lightly colored, being careful not to burn. Remove and drain on paper towels. Add chicken to wok and stir-fry until no longer pink. Add onion and celery and stir-fry for about 2 minutes. Stir in broth and soy sauce; cook about 3 minutes. Mix cornstarch and broth and stir into chicken mixture until thickened. Add snow peas, water chestnuts and walnuts. Cook only until heated through. Taste for seasonings and serve immediately with rice. (Serves 4 - 6)

TOMATO PEPPER BEEF

1 lb. beef flank steak or other
   tender beef cut
Salt & pepper
1 Tablespoon cornstarch
2 Tablespoons rice wine or pale
   dry sherry
1 Tablespoon soy sauce
2 Tablespoons vegetable oil

1/2 onion, sliced
1/2 green pepper, chopped
3 small tomatoes, peeled,
   halved & cut into wedges
1 cup sliced mushrooms
2 teaspoons cornstarch
1/2 cup chicken broth
1 teaspoon sugar
1 Tablespoon soy sauce

    Cut beef against the grain into 1/4" x 2" strips. Season with salt and pepper. Mix cornstarch, wine and soy sauce together. Add beef and marinate about 20 minutes. Heat oil in a wok over medium high heat. Add beef and stir-fry for 2 minutes. Add onion and green pepper and stir-fry for 2 minutes. Stir in tomatoes and mushrooms and cook for about 2 minutes. Mix cornstarch with broth and add to wok with sugar and soy sauce. Cook about 2 minutes more. Taste for seasonings and serve immediately with rice. (Serves 4 - 6)

SHRIMP & VEGETABLE STIR-FRY

1 lb. medium shrimp, peeled
Salt & pepper
2 Tablespoons vegetable oil
1/2 onion, sliced
1/4 green bell pepper, slivered
1/4 red bell pepper, slivered
1 zucchini, halved & sliced

1 yellow squash, halved &
   sliced
1/2 cup chicken broth
2 Tablespoons oyster sauce
2 Tablespoons soy sauce
1 Tablespoon cornstarch
1/2 cup chicken broth

    Season shrimp with salt and pepper. Heat oil in wok over medium high heat. Add shrimp and stir-fry just until pink. Add onion, green pepper, red pepper, zucchini and yellow squash and stir-fry about 3 minutes. Add broth, oyster sauce and soy sauce. Cook 3 minutes more. Mix cornstarch with broth and add to wok. Cook until thickened. Taste for seasonings and serve immediately with rice. (Serves 4 - 6)

STIR-FRIED SPICED APPLES

2 Tablespoons butter or margarine
3 red delicious apples, peeled, cored & sliced thin
1/4 cup light brown sugar
1 teaspoon cinnamon
1/8 teaspoon nutmeg
Chopped pecans or almonds
Vanilla ice cream

Heat butter in a wok over medium heat. Add apple slices and stir-fry for about 3 minutes. Add brown sugar, cinnamon and nutmeg. Stir-fry until combined. Sprinkle some nuts on top and serve over vanilla ice cream. (Serves 4 - 6)

 *Not your typical Chinese dessert, but a stir-fry recipe none the less!*

SHRIMP & PORK EGG ROLLS
SWEET & SOUR SAUCE
HOT MUSTARD SAUCE
LEMON CHICKEN WITH PEA PODS
SHRIMP WITH LOBSTER SAUCE
HOMEMADE FORTUNE COOKIES

SHRIMP & PORK EGG ROLLS

3 Tablespoons peanut oil
1/2 lb. lean boneless pork, finely chopped
1/2 lb. raw shrimp, peeled & chopped
2 cups finely chopped celery
1 Tablespoon soy sauce
1 Tablespoon Chinese rice wine or pale dry sherry
1/2 teaspoon salt
1/2 teaspoon sugar
1/2 cup sliced mushrooms
1/2 lb. fresh bean sprouts
1 Tablespoon cornstarch dissolved in 2 Tablespoons cold water
1 pkg. egg roll wrappers
3 cups peanut oil

    Place oil in a wok or large skillet over high heat. Add pork and stir-fry for 2 minutes, or until it loses its reddish color. Add shrimp and stir-fry for another minute. Add celery, soy sauce, wine, salt and sugar. Stir-fry for 3 minutes more. Add mushrooms and bean sprouts; stir-fry 1 minute. Stir cornstarch and water to recombine and add to wok, stirring until liquid has thickened slightly. Transfer to a large bowl and cool to room temperature before using.
    To assemble egg rolls, place a large spoonful of filling diagonally across the center of an egg roll wrapper. Lift the lower triangular flap over the filling and tuck the point under it, leaving the upper point of the wrapper exposed. Bring each of the two small end flaps in on top of the enclosed filling and press down firmly. Brush the upper exposed triangle with water and roll wrapper into a neat sealed package. Cover with a dry towel or plastic wrap and refrigerate if holding longer than 30 minutes before frying.
    To cook, set a wok or deep fryer over medium high heat. Add 3 cups of oil and heat until a haze forms ($375°$). Place 4 - 6 egg rolls in hot oil and deep fry for 3 to 4 minutes, or until golden brown and crisp. Drain on paper towels. Keep warm in a low oven.
    Serve with Sweet & Sour Sauce and Hot Mustard Sauce.

Lots of filling make these exceptionally good.

SWEET & SOUR SAUCE
(see index)

HOT MUSTARD
(see index)

LEMON CHICKEN WITH PEA PODS

6 boneless chicken breasts
Juice of 2 lemons
1/4 teaspoon grated fresh ginger
1 clove garlic, minced
2 Tablespoons cornstarch
1 Tablespoon vegetable oil
1 Tablespoon cold water
2 Tablespoons vegetable oil
1 cup chicken broth
Salt, pepper & soy sauce
  to taste
1 cup fresh pea pods
  (snow peas)

Cut chicken into thin strips. Place in a bowl and add lemon juice, ginger, garlic, cornstarch, oil and water. Stir to combine and marinate for about 10 minutes.

Heat 2 Tablespoons oil in a wok or large skillet over medium high heat. Add chicken mixture and stir-fry for 3 - 4 minutes, until chicken is no longer pink. Add broth and bring to a boil. Season with salt, pepper and soy sauce to taste. Add pea pods and cook until heated. Serve immediately with rice. (Makes 4 servings)

Pea Pods become very soft if cooked too long, so add at the last minute. Remove strings, as from a green bean, before using. A delightful lemon flavor makes this a very light tasting dish.

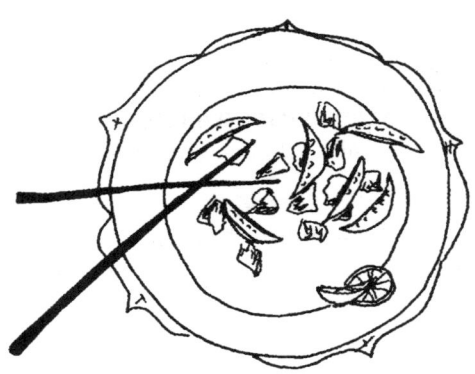

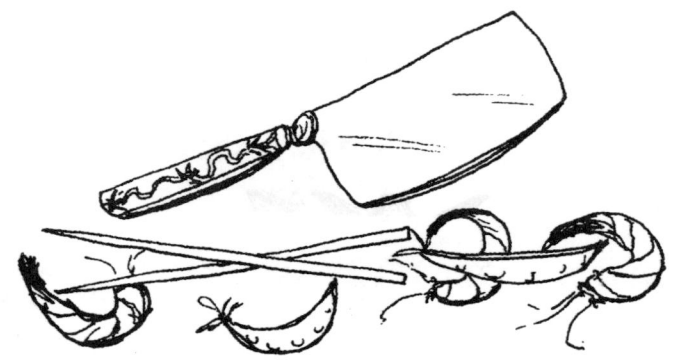

SHRIMP WITH LOBSTER SAUCE

MARINADE:
2 teaspoons Chinese rice wine
  or pale dry sherry
1 teaspoon cornstarch
1/4 teaspoon grated fresh ginger
Salt & pepper to taste

1 lb. fresh medium shrimp, peeled

SAUCE:
1 cup chicken broth
1 teaspoon cornstarch
4 teaspoons oyster sauce

2 Tablespoons vegetable oil
1/2 cup chopped onion
1/2 cup chopped green
  pepper
1 clove garlic, minced
2 Tablespoons fermented
  black beans, rinsed &
  chopped
2 egg whites, lightly beaten

Combine marinade ingredients; add shrimp and mix well. Let marinate for 20 minutes.
Mix ingredients for sauce and set aside.
Heat oil in a wok or large skillet over medium high heat. Stir-fry shrimp for about 2 minutes, until pink. Add onion, green pepper, garlic and black beans. Stir-fry 2 minutes. Stir sauce to recombine and add to wok. Bring to a boil. Pour in egg whites in a slow stream, stirring constantly and serve immediately with rice. (Serves 4)

*A real favorite among Chinese food lovers!
This dish is named after the sauce served with
Lobster Cantonese.*

HOMEMADE FORTUNE COOKIES

Flour
3 Tablespoons butter or
  margarine, softened
3 Tablespoons sugar

1 egg white
1/2 teaspoon vanilla
1/3 cup flour

    Make up fortunes; type, cut out, and fold. Grease a large baking sheet and dip the rim of a 3 inch cookie cutter or glass in flour. Use cookie cutter to mark baking sheet with 6 circles, 1 inch apart.
    Preheat oven to 400°. In a small bowl, beat butter, sugar, egg white and vanilla with an electric mixer until blended. Stir in 1/3 cup flour and combine. With a small spatula, spread about a teaspoonful of batter in each outlined circle.
    Bake for 4 - 5 minutes or until edges are lightly browned. Remove from oven and quickly loosen cookie with spatula and turn bottom side up. Place folded fortune in center. Gently fold cookie in half, working very quickly, and hold edges together for a few seconds. Place center of fold over the rim of a bowl and gently press down to bend cookie in the middle. Repeat with remaining cookies. If cookies cool too quickly, return to oven briefly to soften, for easy folding. (Makes 6)

It's so much fun to serve homemade fortune cookies with your own fortunes inside. Be creative with your fortunes; your guests will love them!

SHRIMP TOAST
SPINACH MUSHROOM SOUP
SHRIMP FRIED RICE
ALMOND CHICKEN
SWEET & SOUR PORK

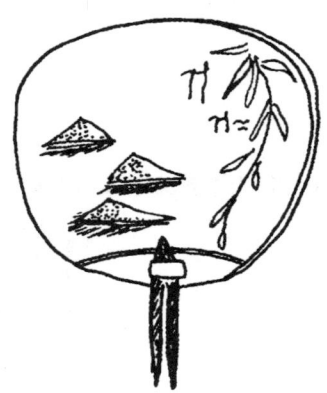

SHRIMP TOAST

1/2 lb. medium shrimp, peeled
2 Tablespoons fresh pork fat
1/4 cup water chestnuts
1 Tablespoon rice wine
1 teaspoon salt

1 egg, lightly beaten
2 Tablespoons cornstarch
4 slices white sandwich bread
Fresh parsley leaves
3 cups peanut oil

Chop shrimp, pork fat and water chestnuts together as fine as possible (can use a food processor). Add rice wine, salt, egg and cornstarch and mix thoroughly to form a paste.

Trim the crusts from bread slices and discard. Cut bread into quarters or triangles. Spread an equal amount of paste on bread pieces, mounding slightly in the center. Gently press a fresh parsley leaf into the center of each mound.

Heat oil in a wok or deep fryer until 375°. Place about 6 bread pieces, shrimp side down, into hot oil and fry for 1 minute. Gently turn them over and cook 1 minute longer, until golden brown. Then, turn them over again and cook for 1 minute more. Drain on paper towels and keep warm in a low oven until ready to serve. (Makes 16)

SPINACH MUSHROOM SOUP

4 cups chicken broth
1 cup sliced fresh mushrooms
1 clove garlic, minced
1/2 pkg. (5 oz) fresh spinach,
  washed, drained & torn
1/2 teaspoon sugar
1 Tablespoon soy sauce
Salt & pepper to taste

1 teaspoon cornstarch
2 Tablespoons water

1 egg, lightly beaten
1/4 teaspoon sesame oil

1/4 cup chopped green
  onion

Bring chicken broth to a boil in a large saucepan over high heat. Reduce heat to low and add mushrooms, garlic, spinach, sugar, soy sauce, salt and pepper. Let simmer for 10 minutes.

Stir cornstarch in water to dissolve. Add to soup in a slow, steady stream. Cook and stir until slightly thickened. Remove from heat.

Pour in egg slowly, stirring with a fork so it cooks in strands. Stir in sesame oil.

Ladle soup in individual bowls and garnish with chopped green onions. Serve immediately. (Serves 6)

SHRIMP FRIED RICE

1 teaspoon cornstarch dissolved
  in 2 teaspoons water
1/4 lb. shrimp, peeled & chopped
Salt & pepper to taste
2 Tablespoons vegetable oil

3 eggs, beaten
Salt & pepper to taste
1 Tablespoon oil

3 Tablespoons oil
1 cup chopped green onion
3 cups cooked white rice
Salt & pepper to taste
Soy sauce to taste

Mix dissolved cornstarch with shrimp, salt and pepper. Heat 2 Tablespoons oil in a wok over medium high heat and stir-fry shrimp until pink and firm. Remove.

Season beaten eggs with salt and pepper. Add 1 Tablespoon oil to the wok and cook eggs until soft and fluffy. Remove.

Add 3 Tablespoons oil to wok and stir-fry green onions for about 30 seconds. Add rice, stirring until heated through. Mix in shrimp and eggs and stir-fry about 1 minute, to heat and combine. Add salt, pepper and soy sauce to taste. (Serves 4 - 6)

Other meats or seafood can be substituted for shrimp.

ALMOND CHICKEN

1/4 teaspoon salt
1/4 teaspoon pepper
1 teaspoon cornstarch
1 Tablespoon soy sauce
1 egg white
1 lb. boneless chicken breast, cut into bite size pieces

SAUCE:
1 Tablespoon rice vinegar
2 Tablespoons soy sauce
1/4 teaspoon salt
1 teaspoon sugar
1/2 teaspoon cornstarch
1/2 cup water

2 Tablespoons vegetable oil
1/2 cup slivered almonds

1 Tablespoon oil
3 small slices ginger root
1/2 cup chopped green pepper
1/2 cup chopped green onion
1 (8 oz) can bamboo shoots, drained

Mix together salt, pepper, cornstarch, soy sauce and egg white until combined. Add chicken, stirring to coat, and marinate for 20 minutes.
Mix together all ingredients for sauce.
Heat 2 Tablespoons oil in a wok over medium high heat. Add almonds and stir-fry until golden brown. Remove with a slotted spoon and drain on paper towels.
Immediately add chicken mixture to wok and stir-fry until browned, about 4 minutes. Remove and keep warm.
Add 1 Tablespoon oil to wok. Stir-fry ginger for about 30 seconds, remove and discard. Add green pepper, green onions and bamboo shoots. Stir-fry for 3 minutes. Add chicken, prepared sauce, and heat thoroughly before serving with rice. (Serves 4 - 6)

SWEET & SOUR PORK

1 egg, lightly beaten
1 teaspoon salt
1/4 cup cornstarch
1/4 cup flour
1/4 cup chicken broth

1 lb. pork, cut into
  bite size pieces

Peanut oil for frying

1 Tablespoon vegetable oil
1 clove garlic, minced
1 green pepper, chopped
1 large carrot, slivered
1/2 cup chicken broth
1/4 cup sugar
1/4 cup red wine vinegar
1 teaspoon soy sauce
1 Tablespoon cornstarch
  dissolved in 2 Tablespoons
  water

In a large bowl, mix egg, salt, cornstarch, flour and chicken broth until combined. Add pork and stir to coat.

Heat enough peanut oil in a wok to deep fry the pork (375°). Drop in half the pork cubes, one by one. Fry until crisp and golden brown. Remove with a slotted spoon and repeat with the rest of the pork. Drain on paper towels and keep warm in a low oven.

To make the sauce, heat 1 Tablespoon oil in a wok over medium high heat. Add garlic, green pepper and carrot. Stir-fry about 3 minutes. Add broth, sugar, vinegar and soy sauce and bring to a boil. Cook about 1 minute. Stir cornstarch mixture to recombine and add to sauce. Cook until thickened. Add fried pork to sauce. Heat thoroughly and serve with rice. (Serves 4 - 6)

A little trouble to prepare, but definitely worth it!
Chicken or shrimp can be substituted for pork.

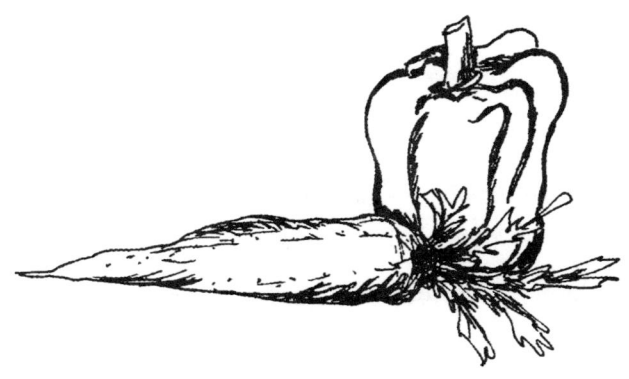

STEAMED SHRIMP DUMPLINGS & PLUM SAUCE
CASHEW CHICKEN
MU SHU PORK & MANDARIN PANCAKES

STEAMED SHRIMP DUMPLINGS

1/2 lb. shrimp, boiled, peeled & chopped
Salt & pepper
1/4 cup chopped green onion
1/4 cup chopped water chestnuts
1 Tablespoon soy sauce
1 Tablespoon honey
24 dumpling wrappers or won ton skins cut into 3" circles

Combine shrimp, salt, pepper, green onions, water chestnuts, soy sauce and honey together in a small bowl.

Place about 1 teaspoon filling in center of wrapper. Moisten edges with a little water. Bring sides up to meet and pleat edges, pressing together to hold. Cover with plastic wrap and refrigerate if not using immediately.

Place about 1" of water in a wok and bring to a boil over high heat. Arrange dumplings apart from each other on a greased steamer rack and place in wok. Cover and let steam about 15 minutes. Serve with Plum Sauce. (Makes about 24)

A simply wonderful appetizer with no added fat!

PLUM SAUCE

1/2 cup plum jam
2 Tablespoons apricot preserves
1 Tablespoon vinegar

Mix together all ingredients until combined. Serve with dumplings.

You'll never need to buy store bought again!

CASHEW CHICKEN

1 lb. boneless chicken breast
1 teaspoon cornstarch
1 Tablespoon soy sauce
1 Tablespoon rice wine
1/2 teaspoon sesame oil

2 Tablespoons vegetable oil
1/2 cup sliced carrots

1/2 cup sliced celery
1/2 cup chopped green onion
1 1/2 cups chicken broth
2 Tablespoons hoisin sauce
1/2 cup cashews
2 Tablespoons cornstarch
   dissolved in 2 Tablespoons
   water

Cut chicken into bite size pieces. Mix together cornstarch, soy sauce, rice wine and sesame oil in a small bowl. Stir in chicken to coat and marinate for 15 minutes.

Heat vegetable oil in a wok over medium high heat. Add marinated chicken and stir-fry until no longer pink. Add carrots, celery and green onion and stir-fry for 1 minute. Mix in chicken broth and hoisin sauce. Cook 3 minutes. Add cashews and dissolved cornstarch and cook until thickened. Serve with rice. (Serves 4 - 6)

Hoisin sauce adds lots of flavor to this delicious recipe.

MU SHU PORK & MANDARIN PANCAKES

PANCAKES:
2 cups flour
1 cup boiling water

1 Tablespoon sesame oil

Measure flour into a mixing bowl. Make a well in the center and add boiling water. With a spoon, mix flour and water together. Using hands, start kneading mixture together, then transfer to a lightly floured surface. Knead for about 5 minutes, until smooth. Cover with plastic wrap and let rest for 15 minutes.

Divide dough in half. Roll each half into a 6" log shape and divide into 6 pieces. On a lightly floured surface, flatten each piece with the palm of your hand into a circle. Roll out into a 6" circle, turning and flouring to keep from sticking as necessary. Brush 6 circles lightly with sesame oil and top with an unoiled circle. Roll on both sides to hold together. Brush off any excess flour.

Place a small heavy skillet over medium heat until hot. Cook pancakes, one at a time, until puffed and lightly browned, turning over to cook both sides. Gently separate the halves and stack in an ovenproof dish, covering with foil to keep warm. Place in a low oven to keep warm or make ahead and reheat in steamer or oven. (Makes 12)

(continued on next page)

MU SHU PORK:
1/2 cup dried mushrooms
1 lb. boneless pork
Salt & pepper
1 teaspoon sugar
1 teaspoon cornstarch
1 Tablespoon vegetable oil
1 Tablespoon rice wine
1 Tablespoon soy sauce
1/2 teaspoon sesame oil

1 Tablespoon vegetable oil
4 eggs, lightly beaten
Salt & pepper
1 Tablespoon vegetable oil
1/2 cup chopped green onion
1 can bamboo shoots
2 cups shredded cabbage
1 Tablespoon soy sauce
Hoisin sauce

Soak mushrooms in 1 cup boiling water for 30 minutes to rehydrate. Drain, blot dry and cut into shreds. Meanwhile, cut pork into thin slices. Season with salt and pepper. Mix sugar, cornstarch, vegetable oil, rice wine, soy sauce and sesame oil together in a small bowl. Add pork, stirring to coat, and marinate for 10 - 15 minutes.

Heat vegetable oil in a wok over medium high heat. Season eggs with salt and pepper and add to wok. Stir-fry until set. Remove and chop coarsely.

Heat vegetable oil in the wok and add pork. Stir-fry about 3 minutes, until no longer pink. Add green onions, drained bamboo shoots, cabbage and prepared mushrooms. Stir-fry 1 minute. Add soy sauce and cooked eggs. Stir to combine. Serve immediately by spreading a small amount of hoisin sauce on a pancake, top with pork mixture and roll up to enclose filling. Eat with hands, like a sandwich. (Serves 4 - 6)

A nice variation from the typical stir-fry with rice!
Beef or chicken can be used for variation.

DESSERTS

MENUS

FROZEN STRAWBERRY CREAM
IN CHOCOLATE LACE CUPS
SWEETHEART ALMOND CAKES
CHOCOLATE MOUSSE CAKE
IN MERINGUE CRUST

BÛCHE DE NOËL
MERINGUE MUSHROOMS
CHOCOLATE ÉCLAIRS
ALMOND TARTLETS

GERMAN CHOCOLATE TORTE
CHOCOLATE CHIP CHOCOLATE
CREAM PUFFS
SWEETHEART BROWNIE WAFFLES
WITH WARM BANANA SAUCE

MOCHA HOT CHOCOLATE
CHOCOLATE MINT DEMITASSE
CREAM
WHITE CHOCOLATE MOUSSE CUPS
IN STRAWBERRY SAUCE
POACHED PEARS
WITH FUDGE SAUCE

CHAMPAGNE PUNCH
WITH FROZEN FRUIT MOLD
PETIT FOUR HEARTS
RED VELVET CAKE
MICROWAVE PRALINES

Desserts are some of the most impressive and enjoyable recipes you can prepare. These classes will give you a wonderful selection to choose from when looking for that special recipe to indulge your guests.

DESSERTS

**FROZEN STRAWBERRY CREAM
IN CHOCOLATE LACE CUPS
SWEETHEART ALMOND CAKES
CHOCOLATE MOUSSE CAKE
IN PECAN MERINGUE CRUST**

FROZEN STRAWBERRY CREAM IN CHOCOLATE LACE CUPS

CHOCOLATE LACE CUPS:
1/4 cup light corn syrup
1/4 cup butter or margarine
1/2 cup flour
1/4 cup light brown sugar
1/4 cup chopped slivered almonds

ICING:
1/2 cup powdered sugar
1 Tablespoon cocoa
1 Tablespoon hot water

Preheat oven to 300°. In a small saucepan over medium heat, bring corn syrup to a boil. Add butter, reduce heat to low and cook until butter melts, about 2 minutes. Remove from heat. Stir in flour, brown sugar and almonds.

Drop Tablespoons of dough, 4 inches apart, on a greased foil lined baking sheet. Shape each mound of dough into a circle.

Bake about 12 - 15 minutes, until cookies bubble and turn golden brown. Cool for 1 minute on baking sheet. Remove with a spatula and immediately shape inside small custard cups to form and cool.

After cookies have cooled, make icing by sifting powdered sugar and cocoa in a small bowl. Stir in 1 Tablespoon hot water to form icing. Drizzle icing in a crisscross pattern over outside of cookie cups. Let cool to harden icing.

FROZEN STRAWBERRY CREAM:
1 (16 oz) bag frozen strawberries
1 Tablespoon lemon juice
1 (14 oz) can sweetened condensed milk
1 cup heavy cream
Fresh strawberry fans for garnish

Place frozen strawberries in a food processor with the metal blade in place. Add lemon juice. Pulse 5 times. Add condensed milk. Process just until mixed. Add cream and process until smooth. Place in a covered bowl and freeze until ready to serve.

Serve frozen strawberry cream in chocolate lace cups and garnish with strawberry fans made by cutting slits through a berry towards the stem, while leaving the stem in tact. Press lightly with fingers to fan out.

SWEETHEART ALMOND CAKES

1/2 cup butter or margarine
1 (8 oz) can almond paste
3/4 cup sugar
3 eggs

1/2 teaspoon baking powder
1/2 cup flour
Zest of 1 orange
1/2 cup sliced almonds

Preheat oven to $350°$. Place foil liner papers in mini muffin tins or grease mini muffin tins.
Beat butter and almond paste with an electric mixer until creamy. Add sugar and beat until light and fluffy. Add eggs, one at a time, until combined. Mix in baking powder and flour until smooth. Stir in orange zest.
Spoon about 1 teaspoon of batter in each mini cup. Sprinkle each cake with a few almond slices. Bake about 15 minutes until golden. Cool in pans 5 minutes. Remove to a rack to cool completely, then remove foil cups, if used. (Makes about 4 dozen)

ICING:
1/2 cup powdered sugar
1 drop red food coloring
About 1 Tablespoon hot water

Mix together all ingredients until smooth. Drizzle over each almond cake.

A great treat for almond lovers, for a special dessert on Valentine's Day or for a wedding shower!

CHOCOLATE MOUSSE CAKE IN PECAN MERINGUE CRUST

MERINGUE CRUST:
3 egg whites
1/4 teaspoon cream of tartar
1 cup sugar
30 (2") saltine crackers, ground to fine crumbs
1 cup chopped pecans

Preheat oven to 350°. Grease a 9" or 10" pie pan. Beat egg whites and cream of tartar with an electric mixer on high speed until soft peaks form. Lower speed and gradually add sugar. Turn mixer to high and beat until stiff. Fold in ground cracker crumbs and chopped pecans. Spoon into pan, spreading over bottom and up sides.

Bake for about 15 minutes, just until lightly golden. Remove from oven to cool. Press down gently in center to create a well.

CHOCOLATE MOUSSE CAKE:
1/2 cup butter or margarine
2 oz. unsweetened chocolate
2 eggs
1 cup sugar
1/4 cup flour
2 teaspoons vanilla
Powdered sugar
Vanilla ice cream

Melt butter and chocolate in a small saucepan over low heat until smooth (or use microwave). Cool slightly. Beat eggs and sugar with an electric mixer for about 4 minutes. Add flour, vanilla and chocolate mixture and mix to combine. Pour into meringue crust and bake at 350° for 35 minutes, until set. Let cool.

Garnish with sifted powdered sugar and serve with vanilla ice cream.

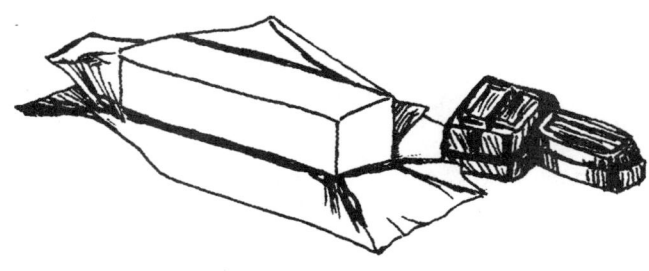

DESSERTS

**GERMAN CHOCOLATE TORTE
CHOCOLATE CHIP CHOCOLATE
CREAM PUFFS
SWEETHEART BROWNIE WAFFLES
WITH WARM BANANA SAUCE**

You can never have too much chocolate, or can you? This class is a chocoholics dream!

GERMAN CHOCOLATE TORTE

4 oz. German's sweet chocolate
1/2 cup butter or margarine
1 1/2 cups sugar
6 eggs
1 teaspoon vanilla

1 1/4 cups flour
1 cup finely ground pecans
1 teaspoon salt
1/4 teaspoon baking soda
3/4 cup buttermilk

Preheat oven to $350°$. Grease a 15" x 10" jelly roll pan. Melt chocolate and butter in a small saucepan over low heat. Let cool. Beat sugar, eggs and vanilla with an electric mixer for about 8 minutes, until very pale. Mix in melted chocolate and butter. Mix together dry ingredients and add alternately to batter, with buttermilk, until combined. Pour into pan and bake for 20 - 25 minutes, until tested done. Cool in pan. When cooled completely, cut cake, starting at the short side, into thirds.

TOPPING:
2 cups heavy cream, very cold
1 cup powdered sugar, sifted
1/4 cup cocoa, sifted

1 cup shredded coconut
1 cup chopped pecans
16 pecan halves

Stir heavy cream, powdered sugar and cocoa together with a whisk to combine. Beat with an electric mixer until stiff.
To assemble, place one layer of cake on a large platter, putting strips of wax paper around edges to catch drippings. Spread cake with about 1/4 of whipped cream mixture, some coconut and chopped pecans. Top with second layer and repeat. Top with third layer and spread with cream mixture over top and sides of cake. Make a 1" border on top with coconut and place pecan halves in a row around the inside of the coconut. Press remaining coconut and chopped pecans into sides of cake. Chill. (Serves 8 - 10)

CHOCOLATE CHIP CHOCOLATE CREAM PUFFS

PASTRY:
2 eggs
1/4 cup butter or margarine
1/2 cup water
1/2 cup flour
1 oz. semisweet chocolate

Beat eggs with a whisk until combined. Place butter and water in a small saucepan over medium heat, and bring to a boil. Add flour and beat with a wooden spoon until it forms a ball. Remove from heat and whisk in eggs. Beat until smooth, thick and sticky. Place in a bowl, cover with plastic wrap and chill for 15 minutes.

Preheat oven to 400°. Use a paring knife to shave off 1 Tablespoon semisweet chocolate and fold into pastry dough. Reserve remaining chocolate. Use a teaspoon to measure out 1" balls of dough onto a greased foil lined baking sheet. Keep as smooth as possible. Bake for about 25 minutes until golden brown. Remove and make a small slit in side of each puff to release steam. Let cool in pan. (Makes 16)

CHOCOLATE FILLING:
1 cup milk
3 egg yolks
1/2 cup sugar
3 Tablespoons cornstarch
2 teaspoons cocoa
1 teaspoon vanilla

In a small saucepan over medium heat, bring milk to a boil. Meanwhile, whisk egg yolks and sugar together in a small bowl. Add cornstarch and cocoa to yolks and mix until smooth. When milk boils, add to yolk mixture very slowly, stirring constantly until combined. Return to saucepan and whisk until mixture boils and thickens. Cook 1 minute. Remove from heat and add vanilla. Place in another bowl, cover with plastic wrap directly on surface and chill.

CHANTILLY CREAM:
1 cup heavy cream
1/2 cup powdered sugar
1 teaspoon vanilla

Beat all ingredients together in a small bowl just until slightly thickened. Chill.

To assemble, fill cream puffs with chocolate filling. Chill.

To serve, sprinkle cream puffs with sifted powdered sugar. Melt leftover semisweet chocolate with 1 Tablespoon water until smooth. Let cool. Cover bottom of dessert plate with chantilly cream. Place 2 cream puffs in center. Make small dots of chocolate around edge and draw a toothpick through chocolate to decorate.

SWEETHEART BROWNIE WAFFLES WITH WARM BANANA SAUCE

1 1/2 cups cake flour
3/4 cup sugar
1/4 cup cocoa
1 teaspoon baking powder
1/2 teaspoon baking soda
1/4 teaspoon salt

2 eggs
1 1/2 cups buttermilk
1 teaspoon vanilla
1/2 cup butter or margarine,
   melted & cooled
1/2 cup chopped pecans

Sift together dry ingredients into a large bowl. Whisk eggs into buttermilk and add vanilla. Stir into dry ingredients. Add melted butter and pecans.

Heat waffle iron. Pour in a generous 1/2 cup batter and cook about 3 minutes, until done. Remove to a baking sheet and repeat. Waffles can be reheated in a warm oven. (Makes about 8 - 10)

WARM BANANA SAUCE:
1/4 cup butter or margarine
1/2 cup light brown sugar
4 - 6 bananas, sliced

1 teaspoon vanilla
Vanilla ice cream
Strawberries for garnish

Melt butter in a large skillet over low heat. Add sugar and mix well. Add bananas and saute just until heated but still firm. Stir in vanilla.

Serve waffles warm with a scoop of vanilla ice cream and top with warm banana sauce. Garnish with strawberry fans.

What a way to greet the morning or end a special meal!

DESSERTS

BÛCHE DE NOËL
MERINGUE MUSHROOMS
CHOCOLATE ÉCLAIRS
ALMOND TARTLETS

BÛCHE DE NOËL

CAKE:
1/2 cup flour
1/4 cup cocoa
3/4 teaspoon baking powder
1/8 teaspoon salt
4 egg whites
1 Tablespoon cold water
1/2 cup sugar

4 egg yolks
1/3 cup sugar
1/2 teaspoon vanilla

Powdered sugar

Preheat oven to 350°. Grease a jelly roll pan (15 x 10 x 1 inch). Line with wax paper, grease again and sprinkle with flour, shaking off any excess. Sift together flour, cocoa, baking powder and salt.

In a mixing bowl, combine egg whites and 1 Tablespoon water. Beat with an electric mixer on high until soft peaks form. Gradually beat in 1/2 cup sugar and beat until stiff and glossy.

In another bowl, beat egg yolks on medium speed until thickened, about 3 minutes. Gradually beat in 1/3 cup sugar. Add vanilla and beat until smooth, about 1 minute more. Fold egg yolk mixture into egg whites. Then fold in dry ingredients just until blended. Spread batter evenly into prepared pan.

Bake for 12 - 15 minutes, until center springs back when lightly touched.

Meanwhile, sprinkle a large cotton dish towel with powdered sugar. Turn hot cake out onto towel and roll cake up, starting at the long end, in the towel. Place on a wire rack to cool.

FILLING:
1 cup heavy cream, very cold
1 Tablespoon sugar

1 teaspoon vanilla

Combine ingredients in a mixing bowl and beat until stiff. Chill.
(continued on next page)

ICING:
3 oz. unsweetened chocolate
3 cups sifted powdered sugar
6 Tablespoons butter, softened
1 teaspoon vanilla
5 - 6 Tablespoons milk

Melt chocolate in microwave over very low heat and cool. Beat powdered sugar and butter until combined. Add vanilla, milk and melted chocolate, beating until smooth and spreadable.

To assemble, fill cake with whipped cream filling. Roll cake and place seam side down on a platter. Slice off one end of cake and place on top of cake to resemble a branch stub. Ice entire cake. Mark icing with tines of a fork and sprinkle with powdered sugar (to look like snow). Decorate with meringue mushrooms. Can also be served without icing; just sprinkle with powdered sugar.

 *Bûche de Noël is also known as a Yule Log and traditionally prepared at Christmas.*

MERINGUE MUSHROOMS

3 egg whites
1/8 teaspoon cream of tartar
3/4 cup sugar
1/2 teaspoon vanilla
1/4 teaspoon almond extract

Preheat oven to $300°$. Place egg whites in a mixing bowl and beat with an electric mixer until foamy. Add cream of tartar and beat until soft peaks form. Add sugar gradually and beat on high until stiff and glossy and sugar is dissolved. Add extracts.

Using a pastry bag fitted with a medium round tube, pipe mushroom caps and stems out onto a greased foil lined baking sheet, keeping tops smooth. Bake for 10 minutes. Turn oven off and leave mushrooms in oven to cool and dry thoroughly.

Assemble by cutting a small slit in the bottom of the mushroom caps, cutting stems at an angle and inserting into caps. Or, melt 1 oz. semisweet chocolate, dip tops of stems in chocolate and "glue" to caps. Let stand upside down until dry.

Dust caps lightly with sifted cocoa. Store in a loosely covered container. Decorate yule log with mushrooms and serve a mushroom with each piece of cake. (Makes about 2 1/2 dozen)

CHOCOLATE ÉCLAIRS

CREAM PUFF PASTRY:
3/4 cup water
1/3 cup butter or margarine
1/8 teaspoon salt
3/4 cup flour
3 eggs

Preheat oven to $400°$. Place water, butter and salt in a medium saucepan and bring to a boil over medium high heat. Remove from heat. Add flour all at once and stir with a wooden spoon. Return to low heat and beat with spoon until it forms a ball. Remove again and beat in eggs, one at a time, until shiny and satiny and dough breaks away in strands. Drop on a greased foil lined baking sheet in 4 x 1 1/2 inch strips, smoothing out ends and tops and slightly indenting sides with moistened fingers; or pipe from a pastry bag.

Bake for 20 - 25 minutes until golden brown. Remove and place on a rack to cool. Cut a slit in the side of each pastry to let steam escape. Cool completely before filling and glazing. (Makes about 8)

PASTRY CREAM FILLING:
1 cup milk
1/4 cup sugar
3 Tablespoons flour
1/4 teaspoon salt
4 egg yolks, slightly beaten
2 teaspoons vanilla
2 Tablespoons butter or
   margarine

Heat milk in a non-aluminum saucepan over medium heat until hot but not boiling. Combine sugar, flour and salt in a mixing bowl, stirring to mix. Slowly whisk in hot milk, stirring steadily to combine. Pour mixture back into saucepan and cook over low heat, whisking constantly until mixture boils and becomes very thick and smooth.

Remove from heat and beat in egg yolks. Return to heat and boil for about 1 minute, beating constantly. Remove from heat and beat for another minute to cool slightly. Stir in vanilla and butter. Place in a bowl, cover with plastic wrap directly on the surface and chill.

CHOCOLATE GLAZE:
1 cup sifted powdered sugar
2 Tablespoons cocoa, sifted
1/2 teaspoon vanilla
2 Tablespoons hot water

Combine ingredients in a small bowl until smooth.

To assemble, remove any uncooked dough from inside pastries. Fill each éclair with pastry cream filling. Place wax paper under a rack to catch any drippings and top with chocolate glaze. Chill.

Store uncovered in the refrigerator so éclairs don't get too moist. A classic all-time favorite!

ALMOND TARTLETS

PASTRY:
2 cups flour
1/4 teaspoon salt
1 cup cold butter
2 Tablespoons cold water

Place flour and salt in a large mixing bowl. Cut butter into small pieces and work into the flour with fingertips until crumbly. Sprinkle cold water over dough and work it in until dough holds together, adding more water only if necessary. Wrap pastry in plastic wrap and chill for about 30 minutes.

FILLING:
3/4 cup heavy cream
3/4 cup sugar
1 cup sliced almonds
1/4 teaspoon almond extract
1 Tablespoon Grand Marnier liqueur

In a small saucepan over medium heat, warm cream and sugar, stirring until sugar is dissolved and mixture is translucent, about 10 minutes. Remove from heat and stir in sliced almonds, almond extract and Grand Marnier. Let cool.

Remove half of dough and roll out on a lightly floured surface. Cut into tartlet shapes, using molds as a guide, and press dough into greased tartlet molds. Place on a foil lined baking sheet. Prick dough with a fork all over and chill for 10 minutes.

Preheat oven to 425°. Repeat with remaining dough.

Bake for 10 minutes. Remove from oven and spoon filling into partially baked shells, being careful not to overfill. Return to oven and bake about 12 minutes until golden brown. Remove and place on a rack to cool. When cool enough to handle, remove from pans to cool completely, being careful not to break. (Makes about 2 1/2 dozen)

Use the tip of a knife to help remove tartlets from molds. These are especially good and loaded with almond flavor!

```
MOCHA HOT CHOCOLATE
CHOCOLATE MINT DEMITASSE CREAM
WHITE CHOCOLATE MOUSSE CUPS
IN STRAWBERRY SAUCE
POACHED PEARS WITH FUDGE SAUCE
```

Another chocolate desserts class---I haven't heard any complaints yet!

MOCHA HOT CHOCOLATE

4 oz. German's sweet chocolate **Fresh hot coffee**
1 (14 oz) can sweetened condensed milk **Whipped cream**

Melt chocolate and condensed milk in top of a double boiler over low heat, stirring occasionally, until smooth.

To serve, place about 2 Tablespoons chocolate mixture in a cup or mug and fill with hot coffee. Whisk until combined and top with whipped cream. Chocolate mixture can be stored in a covered jar in the refrigerator and heated before using.

Milk can be substituted for coffee, if desired.

CHOCOLATE MINT DEMITASSE CREAM

6 oz. semisweet or bittersweet **3 Tablespoons Peppermint**
  chocolate, melted **Schnapps**
1 egg **3/4 cup milk**
2 Tablespoons sugar **Whipped cream for garnish**
1 teaspoon vanilla

Mix all ingredients in a food processor until smooth. Pour into 6 demitasse cups and chill until firm. Serve with whipped cream on top. (Serves 6)

WHITE CHOCOLATE MOUSSE CUPS IN STRAWBERRY SAUCE

MOUSSE:
8 oz. white chocolate
2 Tablespoons butter
3 eggs, separated
2 Tablespoons white Crème de Cacao
1 cup whipping cream
1/4 cup powdered sugar

Melt chocolate and butter in top of a double boiler over simmering water until smooth. Remove to a large bowl to cool slightly. Beat in egg yolks until blended. Stir in Crème de Cacao.
In a small bowl, beat whipping cream to soft peaks with an electric mixer. Add powdered sugar and beat until stiff. Fold into chocolate mixture.
In another bowl, beat egg whites until stiff but not dry. Fold into chocolate mixture. Cover with plastic wrap and chill several hours.

CHOCOLATE CUPS:
8 oz. semisweet chocolate
2 Tablespoons butter

Line a regular size muffin tin with 8 foil liner papers. In top of a double boiler over simmering water, melt chocolate and butter until smooth. Using a teaspoon, place a spoonful of chocolate into each foil liner and spread entire cup with a thin layer of chocolate. Freeze 5 - 10 minutes. Apply a second layer with a pastry brush. Freeze until firm. Remove by tearing foil liner away from chocolate very carefully. Store in freezer. Reserve any remaining melted chocolate in a small bowl for garnishes.

STRAWBERRY SAUCE:
1 qt. fresh strawberries
1/4 cup powdered sugar

Wash and hull strawberries, reserving 8 for garnish. Purée in food processor until smooth. Strain to remove seeds and mix in sugar thoroughly. Cover with plastic wrap and chill.

GARNISHES:
Dip or brush reserved strawberries, with hulls on, with remaining chocolate. Place on a rack in refrigerator to set. Use a toothpick to hold strawberries while dipping.
Make chocolate lace by placing remaining melted chocolate in a small parchment pastry bag and piping lace designs onto wax paper. Freeze to set. Remove carefully.
To serve, spoon strawberry sauce into a dessert plate. Place a chocolate cup in the center and fill with mousse. Place a chocolate covered strawberry next to cup and a lace garnish on top of mousse. (Serves 8)

DESSERTS

POACHED PEARS WITH FUDGE SAUCE

6 Bosc pears, ripe yet firm
2 Tablespoons lemon juice
3 cups water
1/2 cup sugar
1/2 cup white Crème de Cacao

Peel pears, leaving stems intact, and remove core from the bottom with a small melon scoop, being careful not to break through the pear. Place in a large bowl of water and add lemon juice.

In a large saucepan, combine 3 cups water, sugar and Crème de Cacao. Bring to a boil over high heat, stirring until sugar is dissolved. Place pears upright in saucepan, reduce heat to medium, cover and simmer about 10 minutes, until tender yet firm. Let cool in syrup and refrigerate in syrup.

FUDGE SAUCE:
4 oz. semisweet or bittersweet chocolate
3/4 cup sugar
3 Tablespoons butter
1 cup heavy cream
1 teaspoon vanilla

In a small saucepan over low heat, combine chocolate, sugar, butter and cream. Slowly bring to a boil and cook 5 minutes. Remove from heat and add vanilla. Cool slightly before serving.

FILLING:
8 oz. soft cream cheese
1/4 cup chopped pecans
1/3 cup powdered sugar
2 teaspoons Crème de Cacao
Chopped pecans for garnish

Mix together cream cheese, pecans, powdered sugar and Crème de Cacao until blended in a small bowl. Chill.

To serve, remove poached pears from syrup and blot dry with paper towels. With a small spoon, stuff each cored pear with cream cheese filling. Place pear upright on a serving plate and cover with warm Fudge Sauce. Sprinkle with chopped pecans. (Serves 6)

The cream cheese filling really makes these pears special! Be sure to use Bosc pears; they stay firm after poaching.

CHAMPAGNE PUNCH WITH FROZEN FRUIT MOLD
PETIT FOUR HEARTS
RED VELVET CAKE
MICROWAVE PRALINES

This dessert menu would be perfect for a bridal shower or small reception.

CHAMPAGNE PUNCH WITH FROZEN FRUIT MOLD

1 1/2 cups water
3/4 cup sugar
1 (6 oz) can frozen orange juice
3 Tablespoons lemon juice

12 oz. pineapple juice
1 banana, mashed

1 bottle chilled champagne

Bring water to a boil, stir in sugar to dissolve. Add remaining ingredients, except champagne, and mix thoroughly. Pour into a 4 cup ring mold and freeze until solid.

To serve, unmold frozen fruit mold into a punch bowl. Pour chilled champagne over mold. Flavors will blend as mold starts to melt. (Serves 8-10)

For more servings, make another fruit mold and chill another bottle of champagne.

PETIT FOUR HEARTS

CAKE:
1 1/4 cup butter, softened
1 cup sugar
1 (8 oz) can almond paste
5 eggs
1 teaspoon vanilla
3/4 cup flour
2 Tablespoons cornstarch

Preheat oven to 375°. Grease and flour a 15 1/2" x 10 1/2" x 1" jelly roll pan. In a large mixing bowl, beat butter, sugar and almond paste until light and fluffy, about 5 minutes. Add eggs, one at a time, until combined. Add vanilla. In a small bowl, combine flour and cornstarch, then fold into the creamed mixture until blended. Pour into prepared pan, spreading evenly. Bake for 15 minutes or until top is golden. Cool in pan on a wire rack. When completely cool, cut into heart shapes with a cookie cutter.

Cake can be made ahead and refrigerated before cutting.

FONDANT GLAZE:
3 3/4 cups powdered sugar
1/4 cup light corn syrup
1/4 cup water
2 Tablespoons vegetable oil
1 teaspoon vanilla
2 drops red food coloring

In a mixing bowl, combine all ingredients, except food coloring. Beat with an electric mixer on low speed to blend. Increase speed and beat until smooth. Add food coloring and mix in completely. Spoon over cakes placed on a wire rack, set over a baking pan, to catch drippings. Cover cakes completely, tops and sides, with glaze. Let stand at room temperature until fondant dries, about 2 hours, or refrigerate to set quickly.

DECORATIVE FROSTING:
1 (8 oz) pkg. cream cheese, softened   1 cup powdered sugar

In a small mixing bowl or food processor, beat cream cheese and sugar until smooth. Put in a pastry bag and pipe out decorative designs on petit fours.

Petit Fours can be stored in refrigerator for several days.
A bit time consuming, but worth every minute!

DESSERTS

RED VELVET CAKE

1/2 cup butter or margarine
1 1/2 cups sugar
2 eggs
2 Tablespoons cocoa
2 (1/2 oz) bottles red food coloring

1 teaspoon salt
2 1/4 cups flour
1 cup buttermilk
2 teaspoons vanilla
1 Tablespoon white vinegar
1 teaspoon baking soda

Preheat oven to 350°. Cream butter and sugar with an electric mixer until light and fluffy, about 4 minutes. Add eggs and beat 2 minutes. In a small bowl, mix cocoa into red food coloring to form a paste. Add slowly to batter. Mix in salt. Starting and ending with flour, add to batter alternately with buttermilk, mixing well after each addition. Add vanilla, vinegar and soda, blending well.

Pour batter into three 8" cake pans (or two 9" pans) greased and lined with wax paper and greased again. Bake for 20 - 25 minutes or until tested done. Cool on wire racks for 15 minutes, remove from pans, and cool completely. Ice with frosting.

FROSTING:
1 cup butter or margarine
3 Tablespoons flour
3 3/4 cups powdered sugar

1 teaspoon vanilla
1/4 teaspoon almond extract
3 - 4 Tablespoons milk

Cream butter with electric mixer until smooth. Blend in flour, 1 Tablespoon at a time, beating thoroughly after each addition. Add powdered sugar, a small amount at a time, beating constantly. Add extracts and enough milk to obtain a good spreading consistency. Spread frosting between cake layers and on top and sides of cake.

Place small pieces of wax paper just under the edges of a cake when frosting, to catch any excess. Remove when finished and the cake plate will be clean.

MICROWAVE PRALINES

1 (1 lb) box light brown sugar
  (2 1/4 cups)
1 cup whipping cream

2 Tablespoons butter
2 cups pecan halves
1 teaspoon vanilla

In a large microwave proof bowl, stir together brown sugar and whipping cream until combined. Micro on high for 11 minutes or until it reaches a soft ball stage ($235°$). Stir in butter, pecans and vanilla. Allow to cool, stirring occasionally, about 5 minutes. Then stir vigorously until mixture starts to thicken and looses its gloss. Drop by the spoonful onto a greased foil lined baking sheet and let cool completely before removing. (Makes about 2 dozen)

A very quick & easy way to prepare pralines.

ENGLISH TEA

MENU

**PARTY PINWHEELS
RIBBON SANDWICHES
TOMATO EGG ROUNDS
SWEET SCONES
LEMON CURD
SHORTBREAD HEARTS
ORANGE TEA CAKES
CHERRY TARTLETS**

English tea has become a very popular and enjoyable way of entertaining. Tea should be served in courses, starting with a variety of sandwiches. Shortbread, lemon curd and scones are served next. Tea cakes and tartlets are the last course. Fresh pots of hot tea should accompany the courses. Try serving a different tea with each course such as Darjeeling with sandwiches, Apricot with scones and English Breakfast with tea cakes.

**PARTY PINWHEELS
RIBBON SANDWICHES
TOMATO EGG ROUNDS
SWEET SCONES
LEMON CURD
SHORTBREAD HEARTS
ORANGE TEA CAKES
CHERRY TARTLETS**

BREWED TEA

Warm a teapot (china or earthenware) with hot water. Drain. Bring water to a boil in a tea kettle using 3/4 cup (6 oz) for each cup of tea. Pour hot water into the china teapot. Add approximately 1 teaspoon tea leaves per cup of tea to the teapot. Let brew 3 - 5 minutes and strain into individual tea cups to serve.

Serve with cold milk, sugar or lemon.

PARTY PINWHEELS

5 slices thin white bread
5 thin slices ham

8 oz. soft pineapple cream cheese
25 pimiento stuffed olives

Remove crusts from bread with a serrated knife and roll out each slice with a rolling pin to flatten. Place 1 slice of ham on each slice of bread. Spread each with some cream cheese. Place 5 olives across the bottom in a single row. Roll up jelly roll style and cut into 5 pinwheels. (Makes 20)

Store sandwiches covered with damp paper towels, in a covered container, to maintain freshness. Refrigerate.

RIBBON SANDWICHES

12 slices thin white bread
8 slices whole wheat bread
8 oz. soft cream cheese
1 - 2 Tablespoons heavy cream

1/4 cup chopped pecans
8 oz. Cheez Whiz spread, softened
1 - 2 Tablespoons heavy cream

Remove crusts from bread with a serrated knife. Mix cream cheese with heavy cream and pecans until spreadable. Mix Cheez Whiz with heavy cream.

Spread cream cheese mixture on 2 slices of white bread and spread Cheez Whiz on 2 slices of whole wheat. Stack alternately, cheese side up, beginning with white bread and ending with a plain slice of white bread.

Use a serrated knife to cut in half lengthwise and into 4 slices crosswise, yielding 8 sandwiches. Repeat 4 times. (Makes 32 sandwiches)

TOMATO EGG ROUNDS

12 slices wheat bread
Durkee sauce
5 hard boiled eggs, sliced

8 cherry tomatoes, sliced
Parsley for garnish

Cut bread into 24 rounds using a 2" biscuit cutter. Spread each round with a small amount of Durkee sauce. Top with a slice of egg and a tomato slice. Place a dab of Durkee sauce on top and garnish with a tiny piece of parsley. (Makes 2 dozen)

SWEET SCONES

2 cups flour
3 Tablespoons sugar
1/2 teaspoon salt
2 1/2 teaspoons baking powder

1/2 cup butter or margarine
1/2 cup milk
1/4 cup currants
Milk & sugar

Preheat oven to 425°. In a large bowl, mix flour, sugar, salt and baking powder. Cut in butter with a pastry cutter until the size of small peas. Add milk and currants and mix to form a firm dough.

Roll out on a lightly floured surface. Cut into 3" rounds or small wedges. Place on a greased foil lined baking sheet and brush tops with milk. Sprinkle with sugar. Bake for 12 - 15 minutes.

Try these scones for breakfast!
If currants aren't available, substitute raisins or other dried fruits.

LEMON CURD

3 eggs, beaten
2/3 cup sugar

1/3 cup fresh lemon juice
2 Tablespoons butter

Combine all ingredients in a small non-aluminum saucepan. Place over medium heat and cook, stirring or whisking constantly, until thick and bubbly. Cool. Store covered in refrigerator. (Makes 1 cup)

 *Always use fresh lemon juice, it makes a difference!*

SHORTBREAD HEARTS

1/2 cup butter
1/2 cup powdered sugar
1 teaspoon vanilla
1/2 teaspoon almond extract

2 Tablespoons cornstarch
1/8 teaspoon salt
1 cup flour
2 oz. semisweet chocolate
Powdered sugar

Preheat oven to 350°. Beat butter with an electric mixer until smooth and creamy. Add sugar and beat until light and fluffy. Add vanilla and almond. Mix in cornstarch, salt and flour.

Roll dough out on a lightly floured surface to 1/8". Cut with a 2" heart cookie cutter and place on a greased foil lined baking sheet. Bake 15 - 20 minutes until golden. Cool on sheet.

Melt chocolate in top of a double boiler or carefully in microwave. Brush chocolate on half of each cookie. Let dry a little and sprinkle with some sifted powdered sugar. Store in a single layer. (Makes 2 dozen)

ORANGE TEA CAKES

1/4 cup butter or margarine
3/4 cup sugar
1 teaspoon baking powder
1/8 teaspoon salt

1 teaspoon almond extract
1 cup cake flour
1/2 cup milk
2 egg whites

Preheat oven to 350°. Grease an 8" square baking pan. Using an electric mixer, cream butter and sugar, beating until smooth and light. Mix in baking powder, salt and almond. Add cake flour alternately with milk.

In another bowl, beat egg whites until stiff but moist. Gently fold into batter. Pour into prepared pan and bake about 25 minutes, until tested done. Let cool in pan 5 minutes, turn out and cool on a rack.

FROSTING:
2 Tablespoons butter or margarine
1 cup sifted powdered sugar

2 teaspoons orange extract
1 - 2 Tablespoons milk
Orange zest for garnish

Cream butter with electric mixer in a small bowl. Beat in sugar. Add extract and milk and beat until smooth. Frost cake on top only and let stand to dry before cutting into 5 rows, each way. Top each cake with a piece of orange zest. (Makes 25 tea cakes)

A wonderful little cake that you will want to serve on many occasions. Lemon extract can be substituted for orange, if desired.

CHERRY TARTLETS

PASTRY:
1 cup flour
1/4 teaspoon salt
1/4 cup butter, cut up
1/3 cup sour cream

Preheat oven to $425°$. Place flour, salt and butter in a food processor with the metal blade in place. Process for 10 seconds. Add sour cream and process just until dough begins to form a ball.

Press about 1 Tablespoon dough into individual greased tartlet pans and prick with a fork. Place on a baking sheet and bake for about 15 minutes, until golden. Cool in pans for 5 minutes. Remove to a rack to cool completely.

FILLING:
1 (1 lb) can dark sweet cherries
1/4 cup sugar
2 1/2 Tablespoons cornstarch
1/2 teaspoon lemon juice
1 oz. semisweet chocolate, melted
1/2 cup whipping cream
2 Tablespoons powdered sugar

Make filling by placing 1/2 cup cherry juice into a small saucepan. Combine sugar and cornstarch and add to juice. Stir in lemon juice until smooth. Place over medium heat, stirring until thickened, about 10 minutes. Remove and stir in drained cherries. Cool.

Brush melted chocolate on bottom of tartlet shells. Fill shells with about 2 teaspoons filling. Beat whipping cream with powdered sugar until stiff. Top each tartlet with a dollop of whipped cream or pipe out with a star tip. Chill. (Makes about 18)

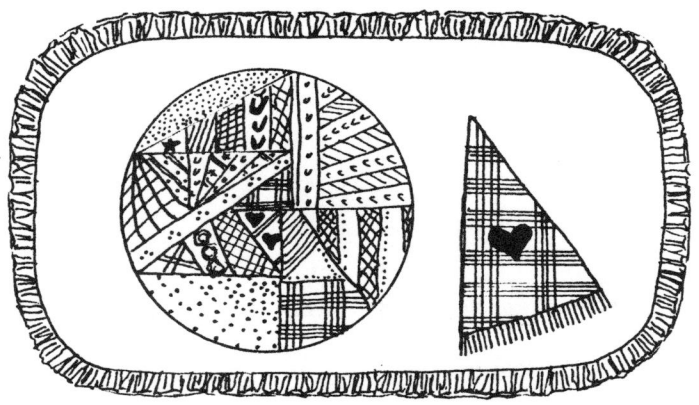

FIRESIDE SUPPER

MENUS

CREAMY BROCCOLI SALAD
ONION HERB BREAD
CHICKEN ANDOUILLE GUMBO
CARAMEL CUSTARD

HOT SPICED CIDER
BAKED ARTICHOKE DIP
BEAN & BACON SOUP
LENTIL SOUP
OATMEAL BREAD
FRENCH APPLE TORTE

Imagine a cold winter night, with a warm fire burning, and enjoy these menus of hearty, comfort foods.

FIRESIDE SUPPER

**CREAMY BROCCOLI SALAD
ONION HERB BREAD
CHICKEN ANDOUILLE GUMBO
CARAMEL CUSTARD**

CREAMY BROCCOLI SALAD

1 bunch fresh broccoli, rinsed
1/2 cup sliced fresh mushrooms
1/3 cup vegetable oil
2 Tablespoons lemon juice
1/2 teaspoon salt
1/4 teaspoon pepper

3 strips bacon, cooked & crumbled
8 cherry tomatoes, quartered
1/3 cup sour cream
1 Tablespoon Dijon mustard

Cut broccoli florets from stems. Discard stems and coarsely chop florets. Place in a salad bowl with mushrooms, oil, lemon juice, salt and pepper. Mix and chill 30 minutes.
Just before serving, add bacon, tomatoes, sour cream and Dijon mustard to broccoli mixture. (Serves 6)

ONION HERB BREAD

1/2 cup milk
1 Tablespoon sugar
1 teaspoon salt
2 Tablespoons butter or margarine
1/2 cup warm water (110°)
1 pkg. active dry yeast

1 teaspoon sugar
2 1/4 cups flour
1 Tablespoon instant minced
  onion
1/4 teaspoon dried dill weed
1/4 teaspoon dried rosemary

In a small saucepan over medium heat, warm milk, sugar, salt and butter just until butter melts. Remove to cool. Dissolve yeast and sugar in a small bowl with warm water. Let stand 10 minutes.

In a large mixing bowl, measure flour, onion, dill and rosemary. Mix milk and yeast together and stir into flour to form a sticky dough. Place in a greased bowl, cover and let rise in a warm spot for about 1 hour.

Preheat oven to 350°. Stir dough down and turn into a greased 8" round cake pan. Bake about 45 - 50 minutes until nicely browned. Cut into wedges.

A very dense, hearty bread---great with soups and gumbos.

CHICKEN ANDOUILLE GUMBO

1 lb. andouille sausage, cut in
  1/4" slices
1 chicken, cut up & skinned or
  8 - 12 chicken pieces
Salt, pepper, flour
1/2 cup vegetable oil
1/2 cup flour
1 onion, chopped
1/2 bell pepper, chopped
2 cloves garlic, minced

1 cup chopped celery
1 (1 lb) can tomatoes, mashed
1 (6 oz) can tomato paste
4 cups chicken broth, heated
1 lb. fresh or frozen okra,
  sliced
Salt, pepper, cayenne to taste
1/2 cup chopped green onion
1/4 cup chopped parsley
Boiled rice

In a large pot over medium heat, lightly brown sausage and remove. Salt, pepper and flour chicken pieces. Heat oil and brown chicken in batches. Add flour to oil and stir constantly until roux is golden brown. Add onion, bell pepper, garlic and celery. Stir constantly until softened. Add tomatoes, tomato paste, chicken broth, okra, salt, pepper, cayenne, chicken and sausage. Bring to a boil, lower heat and simmer for about 1 1/2 hours, stirring occasionally. Skim off any grease. Add green onion and parsley. Cook for 5 minutes more. Taste for seasonings. Serve over rice. (Serves 8 - 10)

Be patient when making a roux, it takes 20 - 30 minutes to brown. Stir constantly and lower the heat, as necessary, to keep from burning. If andouille sausage is not available, use a spicy smoked pork sausage instead.

CARAMEL CUSTARD

1 cup sugar
3 eggs
1 (12 oz) can evaporated milk

1/4 cup water
1 teaspoon vanilla
Dash of nutmeg

Preheat oven to 350°. Grease six (6 oz) individual ovenproof baking bowls. Measure 1 teaspoon sugar from the 1 cup sugar and place in the bottom of each bowl. Place bowls in a large deep baking pan and bake until sugar becomes light brown. Cool slightly.

Beat eggs with a whisk and add sugar, evaporated milk, water, vanilla and nutmeg. Pour evenly into bowls. Add hot water to the baking pan to come half way up sides of bowls. Bake for about 40 minutes or until tested done with a knife. Remove bowls from pan and cool on a wire rack. Cover each bowl with plastic wrap and refrigerate.

To serve, run a knife around bowls to loosen custard. Turn out on plates and let sauce drip over custard. (Serves 6)

A smooth, comforting dessert with a simple yet elegant flavor.

**HOT SPICED CIDER
BAKED ARTICHOKE DIP
BEAN & BACON SOUP
LENTIL SOUP
OATMEAL BREAD
FRENCH APPLE TORTE**

Either of these soups will help to take the chill off those cold winter nights, especially during football season. Be sure to include the Oatmeal Bread as an accompaniment.

HOT SPICED CIDER

1/2 gallon apple cider
2 (6 oz) cans pineapple juice
1 cup orange juice
1/4 cup lemon juice

4 cinnamon sticks
20 whole cloves
20 whole allspice
1/2 cup sugar

Mix all ingredients in a large saucepan over low heat until piping hot. Serve in mugs. Can be spiked with rum, if desired. (Serves 8)

BAKED ARTICHOKE DIP

1 (14 oz) can artichoke hearts, drained
1 cup grated Parmesan cheese
1/2 cup mayonnaise
1/2 cup sour cream
1/2 teaspoon Tabasco
Melba or sesame rounds

Preheat oven to 350°. Chop artichoke hearts very finely. Combine artichokes with remaining ingredients. Pour into a greased baking dish or casserole.
Bake 30 minutes, until lightly browned. Serve warm with melba or sesame rounds. (Serves 6 - 8)

BEAN & BACON SOUP

1 lb. dry navy beans
8 slices bacon
1 onion, chopped
2 cloves garlic, minced
1/2 green pepper, chopped
2 carrots, peeled & chopped
2 qts. water
1 (8 oz) can tomato sauce
1 teaspoon Worcestershire
Salt & pepper to taste
1 bay leaf
1/4 cup chopped parsley

Bring about 1 qt. of water to a boil in a large stock pot. Add beans and cook 5 minutes. Drain.
Return pot to stove and cook bacon over medium heat until crisp. Remove bacon, drain and crumble. Pour off all but 2 Tablespoons of drippings. Sauté onion, garlic and green pepper until tender. Stir in carrots, water, tomato sauce, Worcestershire sauce, salt, pepper, bay leaf and crumbled bacon (reserve about 2 Tablespoons for garnish). Bring to a boil, cover and let simmer for about 3 hours, stirring occasionally, and adding more water if necessary. Add parsley about 5 minutes before serving. Sprinkle reserved bacon on top of each bowl of soup. (Serves 6 - 8)

LENTIL SOUP

1 lb. dry lentil beans
2 qts. water
1 lb. smoked pork sausage, sliced
Ham hock and 1 cup diced ham
2 onions, chopped

2 cloves garlic, minced
1 cup chopped celery
1 cup sliced carrots
2 (1 lb) cans tomatoes
Salt & pepper to taste

Add lentil beans to 2 quarts of boiling water. Remove from heat and let stand.
In a large stock pot, sauté sausage, ham hock and ham over medium high heat, until lightly browned. Add onions and garlic and sauté until tender. Add celery, carrots, tomatoes, lentils and water and bring to a boil. Season with salt and pepper and let simmer about 3 hours, stirring occasionally. (Makes 3 qts.)

OATMEAL BREAD

2 Tablespoons butter, melted
1 teaspoon salt
1/2 cup light brown sugar
1 cup Quick Oatmeal, uncooked

2 1/2 cups warm water (110°)
1 pkg. active dry yeast
5 cups unbleached flour

In a large bowl, place melted butter, salt, brown sugar and oatmeal. Pour warm water over ingredients and stir until dissolved. Sprinkle on yeast and mix in. Stir in 2 cups flour until combined. Add the other 3 cups of flour and mix well. Turn out on a lightly floured surface and knead about 5 minutes, adding a little more flour if too sticky. When smooth, place in a greased bowl, cover with plastic wrap or a towel, place in a warm spot and let rise until doubled, about 1 1/2 hours.
Punch dough down and divide in half. Shape into 2 loaves and place in greased 9 x 5 inch loaf pans. Turn over once. Let rise again, about 30 minutes.
Preheat oven to 350°. Bake bread for 35 - 40 minutes. Remove from pans and cool completely on racks before storing. (Makes 2 loaves)
[Adapted from a recipe by Mary Frances Ewing]

 *Slice any leftover bread. Wrap well and freeze. Makes great toast!*

FRENCH APPLE TORTE

1/2 cup butter
1/3 cup sugar
1 teaspoon vanilla
1 cup flour
1 (8 oz) pkg. cream cheese, softened
1/4 cup sugar
1 egg
1/2 teaspoon vanilla

4 red delicious apples
1/2 teaspoon cinnamon
1/3 cup sugar
1/2 cup sliced or slivered almonds
1 cup heavy cream, whipped with 1 Tablespoon Amaretto

Cream butter, sugar and vanilla with an electric mixer until smooth. Blend in flour. Spread crust mixture over bottom and 1 1/2 inches up sides of a 9 inch springform pan. Chill.

Beat cream cheese with sugar. Add egg and vanilla, beating until smooth. Spread cheese mixture evenly over crust.

Preheat oven to $450°$. Peel, core and cut apples in half. Slice thin and toss with cinnamon and sugar. Spread over cheese layer. Sprinkle with almonds. Place a piece of foil under pan to catch any drippings.

Bake for 10 minutes. Reduce heat to $400°$ and bake 25 minutes more. Cool in pan and loosen rim. Serve topped with whipped cream.

Can be prepared in advance, refrigerated and served later.

FOOD PROCESSOR

MENU

MAYONNAISE
WHITE SHRIMP RÉMOULADE
FIVE CHEESE PIZZA
MEDITERRANEAN PIZZA
APPLE KUCHEN

The food processor is one of the most versatile tools in your kitchen. It enables oil to form an emulsion when making mayonnaise. It kneads bread dough easily when making pizza dough. It takes the guess work out of making pastry dough. It also slices and grates foods quicker than any other method. It chops beautifully, and when using the pulse button, you can control the texture. Always be careful when handling the metal blade, as it is very sharp. Try to keep your machine out and you will use it more often.

FOOD PROCESSOR

MAYONNAISE
WHITE SHRIMP RÉMOULADE
FIVE CHEESE PIZZA
MEDITERRANEAN PIZZA
APPLE KUCHEN

MAYONNAISE

2 egg yolks
1 egg
1 teaspoon white wine vinegar
1 teaspoon Dijon mustard

1/4 teaspoon salt
1/8 teaspoon white pepper
3/4 cup vegetable oil

Use metal blade of processor to combine egg yolks, egg, vinegar, mustard, salt and pepper for about 30 seconds.

With machine running, pour about 1/4 cup oil slowly through the feed tube pusher or by drops. Gradually dribble in the remaining oil very slowly until all is incorporated and an emulsion is formed. Taste for seasonings. Store in refrigerator in a tightly covered container for about 10 days. (Makes 1 cup)

Most feed tube pushers have a small hole in the bottom that's perfect for adding the oil slowly. If your machine doesn't have one, simply add oil by drops through the feed tube. Homemade mayonnaise is nothing like store bought ---it's much better!

WHITE SHRIMP RÉMOULADE

1 cup mayonnaise
1/4 cup Creole mustard
1 teaspoon lemon juice
1/2 teaspoon Worcestershire sauce
Dash of Tabasco

1 teaspoon sweet pickle relish
Salt & pepper to taste
1 lb. boiled shrimp, peeled
Shredded iceberg lettuce

Mix all ingredients for rémoulade together in the food processor until combined. To serve, place boiled shrimp on a bed of lettuce for each serving and top with rémoulade sauce. (Serves 6)

A nice variation from traditional rémoulade sauce! When pouring a sauce from the workbowl, be sure to hold blade in place either with a finger on top or from underneath the bowl, so the blade doesn't fall out.

PIZZA

1 (1/4 oz) pkg. active dry
   yeast (2 1/4 teaspoons)
1 cup warm water (105 - 115°)
1 teaspoon sugar

2 2/3 cups unbleached flour
1 teaspoon salt
1 teaspoon vegetable oil

Mix yeast with warm water and sugar and let stand for about 10 minutes, until bubbly.

With metal blade in place, add flour, salt and oil to work bowl of food processor. With machine running, pour yeast through feed tube until absorbed. Let machine run for about 45 seconds to knead dough.

Place dough in a greased bowl, cover and let rise in a warm spot for about 1 1/2 hours, or until doubled.

Preheat oven to 400°. Punch dough down and divide in half. Roll out each piece on a lightly floured surface to fit two 12" pizza pans. Grease pans and place dough in each pan, stretching to fit. Top with desired ingredients and bake for about 30 - 35 minutes until bottom of crust is browned. Switch shelves after 15 minutes to ensure even browning of both pans.

The processor does all the kneading for you---it takes all the work out of making bread dough, all you need is the time to let it rise.

FIVE CHEESE PIZZA

1 Tablespoon olive oil
1 tomato, sliced
1 clove garlic, minced
1 teaspoon basil
Pepper to taste
1/4 cup grated Parmesan cheese

1/4 cup grated Swiss cheese
1/4 cup grated Romano
   cheese
2 Tablespoons crumbled feta
   cheese
1/2 cup grated mozzarella
   cheese

Spread olive oil over prepared pizza dough. Cover with tomato slices. Sprinkle with garlic, basil, pepper and 5 cheeses. Bake as directed in pizza recipe. (Makes topping for one pizza)

Very gourmet and very delicious! When grating cheese in the processor, use light pressure for fine shreds; hard pressure for coarser shreds.

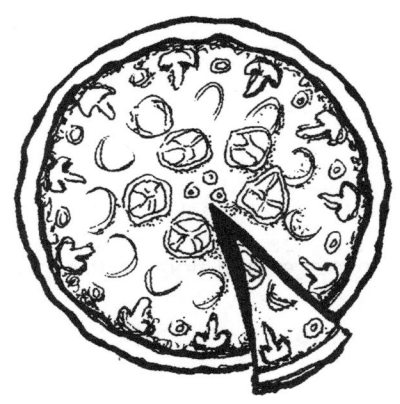

MEDITERRANEAN PIZZA

UNCOOKED TOMATO SAUCE:
1 (1 lb) can whole peeled tomatoes
2 Tablespoons tomato paste
1/2 teaspoon sugar
1/4 teaspoon salt
1/2 teaspoon basil
1/2 teaspoon oregano
1/4 teaspoon hot red pepper flakes

With metal blade in place, process all ingredients until blended, about 15 seconds. (Makes 1 cup)

TOPPING:
1/4 cup uncooked tomato sauce
1/2 cup slivered ham
1/2 cup sliced mushrooms
1/2 cup sliced artichoke hearts
1/2 cup sliced black olives
1/2 teaspoon basil
1/2 teaspoon oregano
1/4 cup grated Parmesan cheese
1/2 cup grated mozzarella cheese

Spread tomato sauce over prepared pizza dough. Cover with ham, mushrooms, artichoke hearts and black olives. Top with basil, oregano and cheeses. Bake as directed in pizza recipe. (Makes topping for one pizza)

 *A nice departure from take out pizzas! Any leftover tomato sauce can be frozen or tossed with cooked pasta for a quick supper.*

APPLE KUCHEN

CRUST:
1 1/4 cups flour
1/4 teaspoon salt

1/2 cup cold butter, cut up
2 Tablespoons sour cream

Preheat oven to 375°. With metal blade in place, process flour, salt and butter until crumbly. Add sour cream and process only until dough starts to form a ball. Transfer dough to a greased 9" tart or pie pan. Press out dough with fingers to cover the bottom and sides of the pan evenly. Place a piece of foil under the pan to catch any drippings. Bake for 20 minutes. Cool slightly.

FILLING:
4 medium red delicious apples, peeled & cored
Juice of 1/2 lemon
3 egg yolks
1/3 cup sour cream

1 cup sugar
1/4 cup flour
1/4 teaspoon salt
1 egg white

Wipe out processor work bowl with a paper towel. Cut apples in half (top to bottom) to fit feed tube and pack tightly, with slicing blade in place. Slice apples and place in another bowl; sprinkle with lemon juice.

Wipe out processor bowl again and with metal blade in place, add egg yolks, sour cream, sugar, flour and salt. Process until combined, about 15 seconds.

After crust cools slightly, brush with lightly beaten egg white to seal the crust.

Arrange apple slices in concentric circles in crust and cover with filling. Bake at 375° for about 45 minutes or until custard is set and top is lightly browned. Allow to cool and refrigerate to set custard and for easier slicing.

Fresh peaches can be substituted for apples.
Always use very cold butter when using a food processor since the heat generated by the speed of the processor tends to warm foods more than usual. Also, cut butter into pieces and it will process more evenly. Stop the machine as soon as the pastry dough forms a ball; don't overprocess or the pastry will be tough.

FRENCH

MENUS

SWISS BROCCOLI SOUP
BRAISED RICE & VEGETABLES
ROASTED CORNISH HENS AMANDINE
FROZEN ORANGE CREAM
IN TULIP COOKIE CUPS

SHRIMP BISQUE PROVINCIAL
POULET AU VIN
ALMOND RICE PILAF
APPLES CRÈME ANGLAISE

CHEESE PUFFS WITH
MUSHROOM DUXELLES
ROQUEFORT SALADE
TROUT AU BEURRE LEMON
SAUTÉED VEGETABLE STRIPS
STRAWBERRY ALMOND TART

FRENCH ONION SOUP
SPINACH SALAD VINAIGRETTE
SEAFOOD EN CROÛTE
FLOATING ISLANDS AMANDINE

ROASTED GARLIC SOUP
POTATOES GRATINÉE
PORK MEDALLIONS WITH
DRIED CRANBERRIES
CHOCOLATE PECAN GÂTEAU

SALADE DE FROMAGE
ROASTED POTATO WEDGES
PORK NORMANDY
PECAN APPLE TART

SHRIMP IN CHAMPAGNE SAUCE
BRIE & WALNUT SALAD
BEEF WELLINGTON
BERRIES & ALMOND CREAM

French cuisine is one of the most elegant of all cuisines. When looking for a menu for a special dinner party, many students turn to their French classes for successful recipes.

SWISS BROCCOLI SOUP
BRAISED RICE & VEGETABLES
ROASTED CORNISH HENS AMANDINE
FROZEN ORANGE CREAM
IN TULIP COOKIE CUPS

SWISS BROCCOLI SOUP

1 bunch fresh broccoli, trimmed
1/4 cup butter or margarine
1/2 onion, chopped
1/2 cup chopped celery
1/4 cup flour

4 cups chicken broth
1 cup half & half cream
1 cup grated Swiss cheese
Salt & pepper to taste
1/8 teaspoon thyme
Dash of nutmeg

In a large saucepan over high heat, bring about 4 cups of water to a boil. Add broccoli, cover and cook 10 minutes. Drain. Cut off florets and set aside. Coarsely chop broccoli stems.

In the same saucepan, melt butter over medium heat. Add onion & celery and sauté until softened. Stir in flour and cook 3 minutes, stirring constantly. Warm chicken broth and add to saucepan with broccoli stems. Stir to combine. Turn heat to medium high and bring mixture to a boil. Cook about 5 minutes. Purée soup in a food processor or blender. Return to saucepan over low heat. Add half & half, Swiss cheese and seasonings. Stir in florets and heat thoroughly. (Serves 6 - 8)

BRAISED RICE & VEGETABLES

1/4 cup butter or margarine
1/4 cup chopped green onion
1/4 cup chopped parsley
1/2 cup finely chopped carrot
1/2 cup finely chopped celery

1 1/2 cups rice
2 cups chicken broth
1 cup water
1/2 teaspoon salt
1/8 teaspoon pepper

Melt butter in a medium saucepan, greased with cooking spray, over medium heat. Sauté all vegetables for about 3 minutes. Stir in rice until well coated. Add chicken broth, water, salt and pepper and bring to a boil over high heat. Cook until most of the liquid has evaporated and craterlike holes appear on the surface. Turn off heat, cover and let steam for about 20 minutes. (Serves 6)

ROASTED CORNISH HENS AMANDINE

6 Cornish game hens
3 Tablespoons butter, softened
1/2 cup chopped green onion
1/2 cup chopped parsley
1 teaspoon thyme
Salt & pepper to taste

3 Tablespoons butter
1/2 cup fresh orange juice
1/2 cup honey
1 Tablespoon cornstarch
2 teaspoons water
1 cup sliced almonds, toasted

Preheat oven to 375°. Wash hens and remove giblets. Blot dry with paper towels. In a small bowl, mix together butter, green onions, parsley and thyme. Place seasoned butter in cavity of each hen. Use string to tie legs together on each hen and tuck wings under. Place hens in a greased foil lined roasting pan and season with salt & pepper. Place breast side up and dot with 3 Tablespoons butter. Roast, uncovered, for about 1 hour. Baste hens with pan juices once during roasting.

When hens are cooked, cut strings off legs and remove. Place orange juice and honey in a small saucepan over medium heat. Bring to a boil; stir cornstarch in water and add to sauce. Cook until slightly thickened.

To serve, place whole or half of a hen on plate. Spoon orange and honey sauce on top and sprinkle with almonds. (Serves 6)

FROZEN ORANGE CREAM IN TULIP COOKIE CUPS

TULIP COOKIE CUPS:
1/3 cup butter or margarine
1/2 cup sugar
Pinch of salt
1/2 teaspoon vanilla

3 egg whites
1/2 teaspoon cornstarch
1/2 cup flour

Preheat oven to 375°. Generously grease 2 aluminum foil covered baking sheets and mark off 8 circles, using a 6" bowl as a guide.

With an electric mixer, cream butter, sugar, salt and vanilla until light and fluffy. Add egg whites one at a time. Mix in cornstarch and flour until smooth. Place a large spoonful of batter in each circle and spread with a spatula, trying not to get the edges too thin. Bake for about 10 minutes, until lightly browned. (Edges will brown more than center)

Remove from sheet while still hot and immediately place each cookie inside a custard cup to mold, using a small greased glass to gently press cookie down into cup. Cool and store loosely covered with aluminum foil to maintain crispness. (Makes 8) *(continued on next page)*

 *If cookies harden before shaped, return to oven briefly to soften.*

FROZEN ORANGE CREAM:
- 2 eggs
- 3/4 cup sugar
- 2 cups heavy cream
- 1 cup milk
- 1 (6 oz) can frozen orange juice concentrate, thawed
- 2 teaspoons vanilla

In a large bowl, whisk eggs for 1 minute. Beat in sugar, a little at a time, until blended. Mix in cream and milk. Stir in orange juice and vanilla. Freeze in an ice cream freezer according to manufacturer's directions. Serve in tulip cookie cups and garnish with a sprig of mint, if available. (Makes about 1 quart)

A small hand cranked ice cream freezer works best.
A very lovely and refreshing dessert!

CHEESE PUFFS WITH MUSHROOM DUXELLES
ROQUEFORT SALADE
TROUT AU BEURRE LEMON
SAUTÉED VEGETABLE STRIPS
STRAWBERRY ALMOND TART

CHEESE PUFFS WITH MUSHROOM DUXELLES

CHEESE PUFFS:
- 6 Tablespoons butter
- 1 cup water
- 1 teaspoon salt
- 1 cup flour
- 1/2 teaspoon Tabasco
- 4 eggs
- 1/2 cup grated Parmesan cheese

Preheat oven to 400°. Place butter, water and salt in a medium saucepan over medium heat. Bring to a boil and stir until butter is melted. Reduce heat to low; add flour all at once and stir vigorously for 1 minute. Remove from heat and stir in Tabasco. Let cool 2 minutes. Beat in eggs, one at a time, until dough is smooth. Stir in Parmesan cheese.

Place dough in a pastry bag fitted with a 1/2" round tip. Squeeze 2" mounds onto a greased foil lined baking sheet. Bake until puffed and golden, about 25 minutes. Remove from oven and cut a slit in the side of each puff to release steam. Let cool on baking sheet. (Makes about 30)

(continued on next page)

MUSHROOM DUXELLES:

1/4 cup butter
2 Tablespoons flour
3 Tablespoons chopped green onion
1/2 cup chopped ham
8 oz. fresh mushrooms, coarsely chopped
1 Tablespoon minced parsley
1/2 cup heavy cream, heated
1/2 teaspoon lemon juice
1/4 teaspoon dry mustard
Dash of Tabasco
Salt & pepper to taste
1/4 cup grated Parmesan cheese

Melt butter in a small saucepan over medium heat. Stir in flour and cook, stirring constantly, for 3 minutes. Add green onion, ham, mushrooms and parsley. Cook for 2 minutes. Stir in remaining ingredients and remove from heat.

To serve, fill cheese puffs with mushroom duxelles. Place on a baking sheet and heat in a 350° oven for about 5 minutes or until hot. Serve immediately.

Cheese puffs and duxelles can be made ahead and reheated separately before serving.

ROQUEFORT SALADE

1 (8 oz) pkg. cream cheese
1 (3 oz) pkg. Roquefort cheese
1/3 - 1/2 cup milk
1/4 cup chopped green onion
1 Tablespoon minced parsley
3 Tablespoons lemon juice
1/4 teaspoon tarragon
Dash of Tabasco
Salt & pepper to taste

Combine all ingredients in a food processor or blender. Mix until smooth. Chill.

Serve on individual salads of romaine lettuce, cherry tomatoes and cucumbers. (Makes about 1 1/2 cups)

Can also be served as a dip with fresh vegetables; just add more milk.

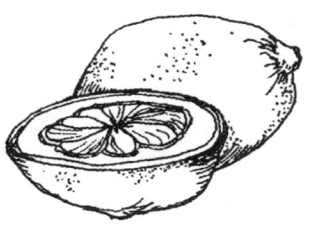

TROUT AU BEURRE LEMON

6 trout fillets
Salt & pepper
3 Tablespoons butter
3 Tablespoons vegetable oil
Flour

1/4 cup fresh lemon juice
1/2 cup butter
Chopped parsley for
   garnish

     Season trout with salt and pepper on both sides. Melt butter and oil in a large skillet over medium high heat. Dredge half of trout with flour and sauté until golden brown on each side. Keep warm in a low heated oven. Repeat with remaining trout.
     Meanwhile, in a small saucepan, bring lemon juice to a boil and reduce to 1 Tablespoon. Lower heat and whisk in butter, 1 Tablespoon at a time; beating constantly so butter does not separate and mixture forms an emulsion.
     Serve trout topped with Beurre Lemon Sauce and garnish with chopped parsley.

Always flour any food to be sautéed just before placing in oil, otherwise the flour tends to be absorbed.

SAUTÉED VEGETABLE STRIPS

2 carrots, peeled
2 zucchini, scrubbed
2 yellow squash, scrubbed

2 Tablespoons butter
Salt & pepper to taste

     Cut carrots, zucchini and squash in strips with a vegetable peeler (don't include seeds).
     Melt butter in a skillet over medium high heat. Sauté vegetable strips about 1 minute, just to heat. Salt & pepper and serve immediately. (Serves 6)

A different presentation of basic vegetables!

STRAWBERRY ALMOND TART

PASTRY:
1/3 cup slivered almonds
3/4 cup flour
2 Tablespoons powdered sugar
1/2 cup cold butter, cut up

Preheat oven to 425°. Place almonds in a food processor and grind until fine. Add other ingredients and process just until mixture resembles coarse meal. Press into a greased 9" tart pan. Bake for 10 minutes. Cool.

ALMOND FILLING:
1/2 cup almond paste
1/4 cup powdered sugar
2 Tablespoons butter, softened
1 egg yolk

Mix all ingredients in food processor to combine. Spread over cooled pastry shell.

STRAWBERRIES:
1 qt. fresh strawberries, washed, hulled & sliced
1/4 cup apricot preserves
1 cup heavy cream
1 teaspoon vanilla
2 Tablespoons sugar

Arrange sliced strawberries in an overlapping pattern on top of almond filling, working from an outside circle inward. Warm the apricot preserves, strain if necessary, and brush over strawberries to glaze. Chill.

Whip heavy cream with vanilla and sugar until stiff. Chill. When ready to serve, place whipped cream in a pastry bag with a star tip. Place a slice of strawberry tart on a dessert plate and garnish with whipped cream along the side of each slice. (Serves 8)

ROASTED GARLIC SOUP
POTATOES GRATINÉE
PORK MEDALLIONS WITH DRIED CRANBERRIES
CHOCOLATE PECAN GÂTEAU

ROASTED GARLIC SOUP

1 large head (bulb) of garlic
1/2 teaspoon olive oil
1/4 cup butter or margarine
1/2 onion, chopped
1/4 cup flour
2 medium baking potatoes, peeled & chopped (1 lb)

3 cups chicken broth
1 cup heavy cream
Salt & white pepper to taste
Chopped parsley for garnish

Preheat oven to 325°. Cut a small slice off the top of the whole garlic head to expose garlic cloves. Place in a garlic roaster or small baking dish, drizzle with olive oil, cover and roast for 30 minutes. Remove cover and roast 30 minutes more. When cool enough to handle, squeeze garlic pulp from peel.

In a large saucepan, heat butter over medium heat. Add onion and sauté until tender. Add flour and cook, stirring constantly, for about 2 minutes, until lightly browned. Add roasted garlic, potatoes and chicken broth. Bring to a boil, cover and lower heat. Cook for 15 - 20 minutes, stirring occasionally. Purée soup in food processor or blender until smooth. Return to saucepan and stir in cream, salt and white pepper. Heat thoroughly and taste for seasonings. Add more chicken broth if soup is too thick. Serve garnished with a little chopped parsley. (Serves 6 - 8)

Roasted garlic becomes sweeter and milder as it cooks, adding a subtle flavor to this rich soup.
Try roasted garlic on hot French bread or in mashed potatoes for variation.

POTATOES GRATINÉE

4 baking potatoes, peeled & sliced,
   about 2 (lbs)
Salt & pepper

1 cup milk
1 cup heavy cream
1 cup shredded Swiss cheese

    Preheat oven to 375°. Grease a medium size baking dish. Layer potatoes, slightly overlapping, and sprinkle with salt and pepper. In a small saucepan over medium heat or in the microwave, bring milk and cream to a boil. Pour over potatoes and top with Swiss cheese. Bake 45 - 50 minutes until potatoes are tender and browned. (Serves 6 - 8)

Swiss cheese gives these potatoes a nutty flavor that really compliments the pork.

PORK MEDALLIONS WITH DRIED CRANBERRIES

1 1/2 lbs. boneless pork tenderloin,
   cut into 3/4" slices
Salt, pepper, flour
2 Tablespoons butter or margarine
2 Tablespoons vegetable oil
1 clove garlic, minced
1 cup chicken broth

2 teaspoons Dijon mustard
2 Tablespoons maple syrup
2 Tablespoons balsamic
   vinegar
1/2 cup chopped green
   onion
1/2 cup dried cranberries
Salt & pepper

    Preheat oven to 375°. Season pork with salt and pepper. Heat butter and oil in a large skillet over medium heat. Flour pork lightly and sauté until browned on both sides. Place in an ovenproof baking dish.
    Meanwhile, add garlic to the same skillet and sauté lightly. Whisk in chicken broth and mustard. Boil for 5 minutes to reduce slightly. Add syrup, vinegar, green onions and dried cranberries. Cook 2 minutes more. Pour sauce over pork and cook in oven for about 10 minutes to heat thoroughly. (Serves 6)

One of the best company dishes you can serve! Can be prepared ahead and finished in the oven just before serving. Chicken breasts can be substituted for pork.

CHOCOLATE PECAN GÂTEAU

1 cup semisweet chocolate chips
1/4 cup butter or margarine
1 cup light brown sugar
2 eggs, lightly beaten
1 teaspoon vanilla
1/2 teaspoon salt
1/2 teaspoon baking powder
1 cup flour
1/2 cup chopped pecans

GLAZE:
1/2 cup semisweet chocolate chips
1 Tablespoon butter
1 Tablespoon light corn syrup
1 Tablespoon water

Vanilla ice cream

Preheat oven to 350°. Grease a 9" round cake pan, line with wax paper and grease again. In a medium saucepan over low heat, melt chocolate chips and butter, stirring until smooth. Remove from heat. Add brown sugar and stir to combine. Mix in eggs and vanilla. Add salt, baking powder and flour. Pour into prepared pan and cover top of batter with pecans.

Bake for 25 - 30 minutes. Cool in pan for 20 minutes. Loosen sides of cake with a knife. Place a piece of aluminum foil over cake to catch pecans and turn out on a rack. Turn pecan side up and cool completely.

Make glaze by melting chocolate chips, butter, corn syrup and water together in a small saucepan over low heat or in the microwave. Place cake on a plate and arrange wax paper just under edges to catch drips. Drizzle glaze over cake in a crisscross pattern. Remove wax paper and let glaze dry before cutting. Serve with vanilla ice cream and decorate serving plates with any leftover glaze.

Like a dressed up brownie; so easy, yet elegant!

SHRIMP BISQUE PROVINCIAL
POULET AU VIN
ALMOND RICE PILAF
APPLES CRÈME ANGLAISE

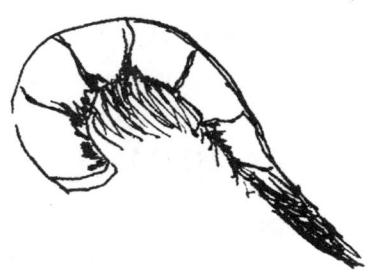

SHRIMP BISQUE PROVINCIAL

1 lb. medium shrimp
1 carrot
1 rib of celery
1 onion
1 teaspoon crab boil

1/4 cup butter or margarine
1 small onion, chopped
1 clove garlic, minced

1/4 cup chopped green onion
1/4 cup chopped parsley
1/4 cup flour
3 cups reserved stock
1 cup sliced mushrooms
Salt, pepper, cayenne to taste
1 cup heavy cream, warmed
Chopped parsley for garnish

 Peel shrimp and refrigerate. Place shrimp shells in a large stock pot along with cut up carrot, celery, onion and crab boil and enough water to cover (about 1 1/2 qts). Bring to a boil over high heat and skim off any residue. Lower fire to a simmer a cook for about 1 hour. Strain and reserve 3 cups of stock for bisque. Freeze any extra.
 In a large saucepan over medium heat, melt butter and sauté onion, garlic, green onion and parsley until softened. Add flour and cook about 3 minutes, stirring constantly. Stir in warm shrimp stock and bring to a boil. Add shrimp, mushrooms, salt, pepper and cayenne. Simmer about 10 minutes.
 Purée soup in food processor or blender, in batches, and place in a clean saucepan. Return to low heat and stir in warmed cream. Taste for seasonings and heat thoroughly. Serve garnished with chopped parsley.
(Serves 6)

POULET AU VIN

6 - 8 chicken breasts, skinned & deboned
Salt, pepper, flour
1/4 cup butter or margarine
2 Tablespoons vegetable oil
1/2 cup chopped onion
1/2 cup julienned ham

2 cloves garlic, minced
1 cup sliced mushrooms
1/2 cup chopped green onion
2 Tablespoons flour
Salt, pepper & cayenne
1/4 cup dry white wine
1 cup chicken broth

Preheat oven to 350°. Season chicken with salt and pepper and dust with flour. Melt butter and oil in a large skillet over medium high heat. Sauté chicken until golden brown on both sides, in two batches, if necessary. Remove and place in an ovenproof baking dish.
Lower heat to medium and sauté onion, ham and garlic in skillet for a few minutes. Add mushrooms and green onions and cook for 1 minute. Stir in flour, salt, pepper and cayenne; cook for 2 minutes, stirring constantly. Add wine and broth. Bring to a boil and cook about 3 minutes. Pour sauce over chicken and bake, uncovered, for about 20 minutes. (Serves 6 - 8)

A very simple dish with a sauce that makes it very special!

ALMOND RICE PILAF

1/4 cup butter or margarine
1/2 cup chopped onion
1 1/2 cups rice
1/3 cup almond slices

1/4 cup chopped parsley
2 cups chicken broth
1 cup water
Salt & pepper to taste

Grease a medium size saucepan and melt butter over medium heat. Add onion and sauté until softened. Stir in rice, almonds and parsley. Sauté for 3 minutes. Add chicken broth, water, salt and pepper. Turn heat to high and bring to a boil. Cook until most of the liquid has evaporated. Turn off heat, cover and let steam for about 20 minutes. (Serves 6)

A wonderful accompaniment to Poulet au Vin!

APPLES CRÈME ANGLAISE

CRÈME ANGLAISE:
6 egg yolks
1 cup heavy cream, warmed
1 cup milk, warmed

1/2 cup sugar
2 teaspoons vanilla

In top of a double boiler over simmering water, whisk together egg yolks, cream, milk and sugar. Cook about 30 minutes, stirring frequently, until sauce thickens enough to coat the back of a spoon. Remove from heat, strain and stir in vanilla. Transfer to a bowl, place plastic wrap directly on the surface of the sauce and refrigerate for several hours to chill.

APPLES:
3 medium red delicious apples
1 teaspoon lemon juice
6 Tablespoons butter
1/3 cup sugar

1/2 teaspoon cinnamon
Freshly grated nutmeg

Toasted chopped pecans

Peel, core and cut apples in half. Cut into thin slices, place in a bowl and toss with lemon juice.
In a large skillet, melt butter over low heat. Stir in sugar and cinnamon. Add apple slices and sauté until softened but not mushy, about 15 minutes. Add fresh grated nutmeg.
To serve, spoon warm sautéed apples in dessert dishes, top with chilled Crème Anglaise and sprinkle with chopped pecans. (Serves 6)

Apples can be sautéed in advance, refrigerated, then reheated gently before serving.
Crème Anglaise makes this dessert anything but ordinary.

FRENCH ONION SOUP
SPINACH SALADE VINAIGRETTE
SEAFOOD EN CROÛTE
FLOATING ISLANDS AMANDINE

FRENCH ONION SOUP

4 onions, preferably red
1 Tablespoon olive oil
2 Tablespoons butter
1 teaspoon sugar

4 cups chicken broth
Salt & pepper to taste
Small slices of toasted
 French bread
Grated Parmesan cheese

Chop onions into large pieces. Heat olive oil and butter over low heat and sauté onions, very slowly, until softened and translucent. Add sugar, chicken broth, salt and pepper. Let simmer about 20 minutes.
To serve, place a slice of French bread in each soup bowl. Spoon soup over bread and top with Parmesan cheese. (Serves 4 - 6)

Red onions give a sweet and mild flavor to this classic soup.

SPINACH SALADE VINAIGRETTE

DRESSING:
1 cup vegetable oil
2/3 cup red wine vinegar
1/4 cup sugar
1 teaspoon salt
1 teaspoon pepper
1 teaspoon dry mustard
1 teaspoon Worcestershire
1/2 teaspoon Tabasco
1 clove garlic, minced

1 or 2 pkgs. fresh spinach,
 cleaned
Sliced fresh mushrooms
Halved cherry tomatoes

Combine all ingredients for dressing and mix well. Refrigerate.
Make individual salads or toss spinach, mushrooms and tomatoes with dressing in a large bowl and serve. (Serves 6 - 8)

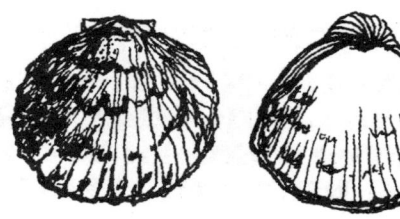

SEAFOOD EN CROÛTE

PASTRY SCALLOP SHELLS:
6 oz. cream cheese, cut up
1 cup cold butter or margarine, cut up
2 cups flour

Place cream cheese, butter and flour in a food processor and process just until dough forms a ball. Remove, wrap in plastic wrap and chill for 30 minutes or until ready to use.

Roll out dough on a lightly floured surface. Cut out 8 pieces to fit around the outside of 8 scallop sea shells. Grease the outside of each shell and mold dough to cover the shell, trimming to fit. Place on a baking sheet and chill 30 minutes.

Preheat oven to 400°. Prick shells with a fork. Bake for about 15 minutes or until golden brown. Cool on a wire rack for 15 minutes. Gently loosen and remove scallop shells. Cool completely.

SEAFOOD FILLING:
1/4 cup butter or margarine
1 lb. medium shrimp, peeled
 (or shrimp & crab meat)
1/2 cup sliced mushrooms
1/2 cup chopped green onion
2 Tablespoons flour
Salt & pepper to taste
1/2 cup dry white wine
1 cup heavy cream
1 Tablespoon tomato paste
1 Tablespoon lemon juice
Parsley for garnish

Melt butter in a large skillet over medium heat. Add shrimp and sauté until pink. Add mushrooms and green onions and sauté about 2 minutes. Stir in flour, salt and pepper. Cook for 1 minute, stirring frequently. Gradually add wine and cream. Cook, stirring constantly, until sauce thickens and bubbles. Add tomato paste and lemon juice and stir to combine. If using crab meat, gently stir in and simmer until heated through.

Serve seafood filling in warmed pastry shells and garnish with a sprig of parsley.

The pastry scallop shells make for a very different and elegant presentation.

FLOATING ISLANDS AMANDINE

MERINGUES:
4 egg whites, room temperature
Pinch of salt
1/2 cup sugar
1/2 teaspoon vanilla

Preheat oven to 275°. Grease six ovenproof glass custard cups (3 1/2"). Coat cups lightly with sugar, shaking out excess.

Beat egg whites and salt with an electric mixer until soft peaks form. Add sugar, 1 Tablespoon at a time, beating until whites are stiff. Beat in vanilla. Gently spoon into prepared cups, filling about 2/3 full. Arrange cups in a large roasting pan. Add enough hot water to the pan to come halfway up sides of custard cups and carefully transfer to the oven. Bake until meringues are set, about 25 minutes. Cool on racks. Refrigerate.

CUSTARD SAUCE:
4 egg yolks, room temperature
1/2 cup sugar
1 cup milk, scalded
3/4 cup heavy cream
Pinch of salt
3 Tablespoons Amaretto
1/2 teaspoon vanilla
Toasted slivered almonds for garnish

Beat eggs yolks with a wire whisk in the top of a non-aluminum double boiler, over simmering water, until pale yellow. Gradually beat in sugar. Stir in scalded milk, cream and salt. Cook, stirring frequently, until mixture coats the back of a wooden spoon, about 25 minutes. Stir in Amaretto and vanilla. Cool, cover with plastic wrap directly on the surface and chill.

To serve, divide custard sauce evenly among 6 dessert bowls or champagne glasses. Unmold meringues into each bowl and sprinkle with toasted almonds. (Serves 6)

A rich yet light as air dessert---one of the best!
Scald milk by heating to just below the boiling point.

SALADE DE FROMAGE
ROASTED POTATO WEDGES
PORK NORMANDY
PECAN APPLE TART

SALADE DE FROMAGE

1 cup olive oil
1/4 cup red wine vinegar
1/2 teaspoon dry mustard
1/4 teaspoon dried basil
1/4 teaspoon dried oregano
1/4 teaspoon dried thyme
1/4 teaspoon celery seed
1/4 teaspoon salt
1/4 teaspoon pepper

1/4 teaspoon Tabasco
1/4 teaspoon Worcestershire

Red leaf or green leaf lettuce, cherry tomatoes, mushrooms, etc.
Crumbled bleu cheese or Roquefort cheese

Whisk together all ingredients for dressing until combined. Chill.
To serve, make individual salads of leaf lettuce, cherry tomatoes, mushrooms, etc. Top with cheese and dressing. (Serves 6 - 8)

ROASTED POTATO WEDGES

3 white baking potatoes
2 sweet potatoes

1/4 cup butter, melted
Salt & pepper

Preheat oven to 400°. Scrub baking potatoes clean and cut in half lengthwise. Cut each half into 4 pieces. Peel sweet potatoes and cut in wedges also. Place in a large pot with just enough water to cover and bring to a boil over high heat. Boil 5 minutes, remove and drain.
Line a large baking sheet with foil and grease. Arrange potatoes on sheet and brush with melted butter. Sprinkle with salt and pepper. Bake about 30 - 40 minutes until browned. (Serves 6 - 8)

A different and tasty version of a simple potato dish.

PORK NORMANDY

12 boneless pork loin medallions
Salt & pepper
1 Tablespoon vegetable oil
2 cups apple cider
Pinch of thyme

1 clove garlic, minced
1/2 cup heavy cream
1/2 teaspoon Dijon mustard
Chopped parsley for garnish

Season pork with salt and pepper. Heat oil in a large skillet over medium high heat. Add pork and brown on both sides. Stir in apple cider, thyme and garlic. Bring to a boil and cook for about 20 minutes until tender. Remove pork and place in a large casserole or serving dish. Place in a warm oven while making sauce.

Slowly whisk heavy cream into cider and cook until mixture reduces and thickens slightly. Remove from heat and stir in mustard. Pour sauce through a strainer over pork. Garnish with parsley. (Serves 6 - 8)

   ***Apples and pork always work well together!***

PECAN APPLE TART

CRUST:
2 1/4 cups flour
1/2 teaspoon salt
1 teaspoon sugar
3/4 cup cold butter
1/3 cup ice water

Place flour, salt and sugar in a food processor with the metal blade in place. Add cut up butter and process just until mixture is crumbly. With processor running, add water through feed tube, just until dough forms a ball. Remove and divide into 2 pieces and wrap in plastic wrap. Chill while preparing other ingredients.

TOPPING:
1/4 cup butter, softened
1/2 cup coarsely chopped pecans
1/2 cup light brown sugar

Combine butter, pecans and sugar in a bowl and mix together with fingers until blended. Place mixture in a greased 9" pie pan and spread evenly on bottom of pan.

FILLING:
3 green apples (Granny Smith)
1/3 cup sugar
2 Tablespoons flour
1 teaspoon cinnamon
Zest of 1 lemon
1 Tablespoon lemon juice

Peel, core and slice apples 1/4" thick. Place in a bowl and combine with other ingredients until coated.

Preheat oven to 425°. Roll out one half of dough between two sheets of wax paper into a 10" circle. Place dough in pie pan on top of pecan mixture. Roll out second piece of dough. Pour apple mixture over dough in pie pan. Brush edge of dough with water and top with second half of dough. Trim edges of dough and crimp with fingers to form a border. Make steam cuts in top of dough and bake on a foil lined pan for 20 minutes. Lower heat to 350°, cover edges of crust with foil, and bake about 30 minutes more until golden. Remove and cool for 2 minutes. Invert tart on a serving plate and cool before serving.

FRENCH

```
SHRIMP IN CHAMPAGNE SAUCE
BRIE & WALNUT SALAD
BEEF WELLINGTON
BERRIES & ALMOND CREAM
```

SHRIMP IN CHAMPAGNE SAUCE

1 lb. medium shrimp, peeled
1 cup champagne (brut)
1/2 cup chopped green onion
Salt & pepper to taste

1/2 cup heavy cream
1/2 cup butter cut in 1" pieces
Chopped parsley
Toasted French bread slices

In a large skillet, place shrimp, champagne, green onions, salt and pepper. Bring to a boil over high heat; reduce to low. Simmer about 5 minutes or until shrimp are tender. Remove shrimp with a slotted spoon and arrange in individual serving dishes. Add cream to skillet, place heat on medium high and boil vigorously until liquid is reduced by half and sauce starts to thicken. Lower heat to low and whisk in butter, one piece at a time, until combined. Spoon sauce over shrimp, garnish with parsley and serve immediately with toasted bread slices. (Serves 6)

Butter is whisked in slowly so an emulsion forms and the sauce thickens yet doesn't separate.
Brut champagne is very dry.

BRIE & WALNUT SALAD

1/2 cup olive oil
2 Tablespoons lemon juice
1 teaspoon Dijon mustard
1/2 teaspoon sugar
1/4 teaspoon salt

1/4 teaspoon pepper
Small wedges of Brie cheese
Leaf lettuce
Coarsely chopped toasted walnuts

Combine olive oil, lemon juice, mustard, sugar, salt and pepper and mix well. Keep at room temperature.
Place Brie wedges either in oven or microwave to warm and soften slightly (don't melt). Place lettuce in a large bowl and toss with dressing.
To serve, place lettuce on chilled salad plates, top each salad with a piece of Brie and sprinkle with walnuts. Serve immediately. (Serves 6 - 8)

BEEF WELLINGTON

BEEF:
2 - 2 1/2 lbs. beef tenderloin
Salt & pepper to taste

2 Tablespoons butter

Season beef with salt and pepper. Melt butter in a skillet warmed over medium high heat. Quickly sear beef on all sides to brown and seal in juices. Remove to a plate to cool. Reserve pan for sauce.

DUXELLES:
2 Tablespoons butter
1/2 lb. fresh mushrooms, chopped
1/2 cup chopped green onion

1/2 cup chopped ham
1/4 cup chopped parsley
Salt & pepper to taste

In another skillet over medium heat, melt butter and sauté all ingredients until liquid completely evaporates. Remove and cool.

PASTRY:
3 cups flour
1/2 teaspoon salt
6 Tablespoons butter

1 egg, lightly beaten
1 cup sour cream

Place flour and salt in a large mixing bowl. Cut in butter until it resembles small peas. Mix in egg and sour cream and work dough until combined. Cover with plastic wrap and chill at least 30 minutes.

ASSEMBLY:
1 egg

1 Tablespoon water

Preheat oven to 400°. Beat egg and water together until combined. Set aside. Roll dough out on a lightly floured surface. Spread duxelles in center of dough. Place beef, top side down, on top of duxelles. Trim off excess pastry and fold tightly over meat, envelope style. Brush seams with egg wash to seal. Turn over and place in a greased foil lined baking dish, seam side down. Cut designs from excess pastry and decorate top. Brush with egg wash and cut vents in dough to let steam escape.

Bake about 45 minutes until golden brown. Cover with foil if getting too brown. While beef cooks, prepare sauce and vegetables.

(continued on next page)

MADEIRA SAUCE:
2 Tablespoons butter
2 Tablespoons flour
1 cup beef broth, heated
1 teaspoon Kitchen Bouquet
1 teaspoon Madeira wine
Salt & pepper to taste
Pinch of thyme
Chopped parsley for garnish

In the same skillet meat was browned, melt butter over medium heat and stir in flour. Cook for 5 minutes, stirring constantly. Add broth, Kitchen Bouquet, Madeira, salt, pepper and thyme. Lower heat and cook until thickened.

VEGETABLES:
New potatoes, baby carrots, green beans, snow peas, squash, zucchini; select vegetables of your choice. Precook potatoes and carrots in boiling salted water until tender. Sauté vegetables in butter until tender and season with salt and pepper to taste.

To serve, let beef stand 10 minutes before cutting. Slice and serve each piece topped with sauce and vegetables on the side. Sprinkle some chopped parsley on top of beef to garnish. (Serves 6 - 8)

What could be more special than Beef Wellington? It's definitely worth the effort!

BERRIES & ALMOND CREAM

1 (3 oz) pkg. cream cheese, softened
1/2 cup powdered sugar
3 Tablespoons Amaretto
1/2 cup whipping cream
Fresh strawberries,
   raspberries, blueberries, etc.

Beat cream cheese, sugar and Amaretto with an electric mixer until smooth. While beating, very slowly pour in cream until combined. Cover and refrigerate.

Prepare berries of your choice. Serve almond cream sauce over berries. (Makes 1 cup sauce)

One of the easiest and most delicious ways to serve fresh berries.

GIFTS OF FOOD

MENUS

CINNAMON CANDY CANE TWISTS
SUN DRIED TOMATO HERBED CHEESE
SUGAR & SPICE APPLE LOAVES
HEAVENLY HOT CHOCOLATE
AMARETTI
CARAMEL PECAN CLUSTERS

HOLIDAY PUNCH
PEPPERED CHEESE
APRICOT NECTAR BREAD
ORANGE APRICOT JAM
CANDY CANE COOKIES
CRANBERRY PECAN TART

SALMON CHEESE SPREAD
CAFÉ AU LAIT DIP
SNOWFLAKES
AMARETTO QUICK BREAD
CANDIED AMARETTO CRANBERRIES
CHRISTMAS COOKIE ORNAMENTS

RED HOT JELLY
SUGAR & SPICE DIP
ORANGE CARROT BREAD
CANDY APPLE COOKIES
FESTIVE CRANBERRY BRAID

APRICOT COFFEECAKE
LOUISIANA PEPPER JELLY
LIME VEGETABLE DIP
CRANBERRY BISCOTTI
CHOCOLATE PEPPERMINT FUDGE

CRANBERRY CHEER
VEGIE CHRISTMAS TREE
HERBED VEGETABLE DIP
CHOCOLATE CHIP COFFEECAKE
CARAMEL POPCORN CRUNCH
SUGAR LUMP BREAD

CINNAMON ORNAMENTS
COCONUTTY BREAD
SAUCY CRANBERRIES
BRITTLEBREAD
SWEET ROLL CHRISTMAS TREE

CHEESE PINEAPPLE
CRANBERRY COFFEECAKE
PICKLED PINEAPPLE
CHRISTMAS PINWHEELS
MICRO NUT BRITTLE

One of the most popular classes through the years has been Gifts of Food. Every year a different menu is presented to give new and exciting ideas for Christmas gift giving as well as for holiday entertaining. Almost everyone appreciates a gift of food, especially during the holidays. So if gift giving becomes a real decision making chore, give one of the nicest gifts of all, the gift of food.

CINNAMON CANDY CANE TWISTS
SUN DRIED TOMATO HERBED CHEESE
SUGAR & SPICE APPLE LOAVES
HEAVENLY HOT CHOCOLATE
AMARETTI
CARAMEL PECAN CLUSTERS

CINNAMON CANDY CANE TWISTS

1 1/2 cups unbleached flour
1 Tablespoon sugar
1 teaspoon salt
1 envelope quick rise yeast
   (2 1/4 teaspoons)
2/3 cup hot water (125-130°)

1/4 cup melted butter
2 eggs, slightly beaten
2 cups unbleached flour
2 Tablespoons melted
   butter or margarine
1/2 cup sugar
1 teaspoon cinnamon

Combine flour, sugar, salt and yeast in large bowl of an electric mixer. Mix in hot water and butter. Add eggs and beat until combined. Mix in flour to make a soft dough and beat for 2 minutes to knead. Turn dough out on a lightly floured surface and knead by hand until smooth. Divide in half and let rest 5 minutes. Roll each half into a 12" x 12" square, keeping ends even. Brush dough with some melted butter. Combine sugar & cinnamon and sprinkle generously over dough, reserving about 2 Tablespoons. Fold 1/3 of dough over center third. Brush with butter and top with remaining cinnamon sugar. Fold remaining third of dough over center. Cut each square into 12 strips. Twist strips tightly, about 4 times, and pinch ends together. Place on 2 greased foil lined baking sheets, shaping into canes. Let rise in a warm spot about 10 - 15 minutes.
   Preheat oven to 400°. Pinch ends together again, since they tend to come apart. Bake each sheet about 12 - 14 minutes, until golden brown. Cool. (Makes 24)

GLAZE:
1 1/4 cups powdered sugar
2 Tablespoons water

Red sugar crystals

Mix together powdered sugar and water to make a glaze. Drizzle over cinnamon twists and immediately sprinkle with sugar crystals.

SUN DRIED TOMATO HERBED CHEESE

1 (8 oz) pkg. cream cheese, cut up
2 Tablespoons butter or margarine
1 small clove garlic, finely minced
1/4 cup chopped parsley
1 Tablespoon chopped green onion
1 teaspoon basil
1/8 teaspoon black pepper
6 or more sun dried
   tomatoes, chopped

Mix all ingredients in a food processor or with an electric mixer until combined. Store in refrigerator. Serve with crackers.

 *A delicious variation of a Boursin (herb flavored) cheese.*

SUGAR & SPICE APPLE LOAVES

2 medium red delicious apples
1/2 cup butter or margarine
1 cup sugar
2 eggs
1 1/2 teaspoons baking powder
1/2 teaspoon baking soda
1 teaspoon cinnamon
1/4 teaspoon nutmeg
1/4 teaspoon ginger
1 Tablespoon vanilla
2 cups flour
1/2 cup orange juice
1 cup chopped pecans
2 Tablespoons sugar

Preheat oven to 350°. Peel, core and chop apples. Beat butter & sugar with an electric mixer until combined, about 2 minutes. Mix in eggs. Add baking powder, soda, cinnamon, nutmeg, ginger and vanilla. Mix in flour and orange juice. Stir in apples and pecans. Spoon into 6 greased mini loaf pans, filling about half full. Sprinkle with sugar and bake about 25 minutes, until tested done. Cool in pans 10 minutes. Remove and cool completely. (Makes 6 mini loaves)

 *Very moist and flavorful; these mini loaves make ideal gifts!*

HEAVENLY HOT CHOCOLATE

1 (14 oz) can sweetened condensed milk
1 (4 oz) bar German's sweet chocolate, broken up
1 (8 oz) carton Cool Whip, thawed
Milk

Place condensed milk and chocolate in a small saucepan over low heat. Stir constantly until chocolate melts. Remove, transfer to a bowl and cool. Fold in Cool Whip. Store in refrigerator.

For each serving, spoon 2 Tablespoons chocolate mixture into 6 oz. milk. Whisk to combine. Heat in microwave or in saucepan over medium heat until hot.

 *A great hot drink to have on hand during the holidays!*

AMARETTI

1 (8 oz) can almond paste
2 egg whites
1/2 cup sugar
1/2 cup powdered sugar
1/8 teaspoon salt
1/4 cup flour
1/3 cup slivered almonds, chopped
Red & green candied cherries, halved

Place almond paste in the mixing bowl of an electric mixer and break up with a fork. Add egg whites and beat until smooth and combined, about 1 minute. Mix in sugar, powdered sugar, salt and flour until smooth. Chill for easier handling.

Preheat oven to 300°. On a greased foil lined baking sheet, spoon about 1 teaspoon dough, for each cookie, into a small mound. Sprinkle each cookie with some chopped almonds and press a cherry half into the center of each cookie. Bake about 25 minutes, until golden. Cool on baking sheet. (Makes about 3 dozen)

 *A perfect gift for "almond lovers"!*

CARAMEL PECAN CLUSTERS

72 pecan halves
24 caramels

4 oz. semisweet chocolate
Powdered sugar

Preheat oven to 300°. On a greased foil lined baking sheet, arrange pecans in a clusters of 3 pecans each. Flatten caramels with fingers and place on top of pecan clusters. Place in oven for about 5 minutes, to soften caramels. Cool slightly. Press caramels down on pecans to cover.

Melt chocolate in a double boiler over simmering water. Spoon chocolate over clusters to cover. Place in refrigerator to set chocolate, about 30 minutes. Remove and sprinkle with powdered sugar. Store at room temperature. (Makes 24)

**SALMON CHEESE SPREAD
CAFÉ AU LAIT DIP
SNOWFLAKES
AMARETTO QUICK BREAD
CANDIED AMARETTO CRANBERRIES
CHRISTMAS COOKIE ORNAMENTS**

SALMON CHEESE SPREAD

2 (8 oz) cartons soft cream cheese
1 (12 1/2 oz) can skinless, boneless
  pink salmon, drained well
2 teaspoons horseradish

Juice of 1 lemon
1 teaspoon liquid smoke
Crackers or tortilla chips

Place cream cheese in a mixing bowl and stir until smooth. Mix in salmon, horseradish, lemon juice and liquid smoke. Refrigerate. Serve with crackers or tortilla chips.

CAFÉ AU LAIT DIP

8 oz. cream cheese, cut up
3/4 cup light brown sugar
1 cup sour cream

1/4 cup Kahlúa
1 cup Cool Whip, thawed
Toasted chopped pecans

Place cream cheese, brown sugar, sour cream and Kahlúa in a food processor. Process just until smooth. Remove and fold in Cool Whip. Top with pecans and chill. Serve with fruits (apples, bananas, strawberries, grapes, etc.).

Give in a pretty glass jar, along with a basket of fresh fruits. Also great to serve at a brunch.

SNOWFLAKES

1 (12 oz) pkg. semisweet chocolate
  chips (2 cups)
1 (12 oz) jar creamy peanut butter

1/2 cup butter or margarine
1 (12.3 oz) box Crispix cereal
1 (1 lb) box powdered sugar
  (3 3/4 cups)

Place chocolate chips, peanut butter and butter in a heavy saucepan over low heat. Stir until melted and smooth.
Place cereal in 2 large baking pans. Pour chocolate mixture over cereal and toss gently until covered.
Place about half of powdered sugar in a brown paper bag and add half of chocolate coated cereal. Shake gently until coated with powdered sugar. Repeat with remaining half. (Makes a lot!)

A wonderful treat, especially enjoyed by kids. Snowflakes are absolutely addicting!

AMARETTO QUICK BREAD

1/2 cup butter or margarine
1 cup sugar
2 eggs
1 cup sour cream
2 Tablespoons Amaretto
1 Tablespoon almond extract
1 teaspoon baking powder
1 teaspoon baking soda

1/2 teaspoon salt
Zest of 1 lemon
2 cups flour
1/2 cup chopped almonds

2 Tablespoons Amaretto
1/4 cup toasted sliced
   almonds
Sugar

Preheat oven to 350°. In the large bowl of an electric mixer, cream butter and sugar until light and fluffy, about 3 minutes. Beat in eggs, sour cream, Amaretto and almond extract. Add baking powder, baking soda, salt, lemon zest and flour. Mix in chopped almonds.
Pour into a greased 9" x 5" x 3" loaf pan and smooth top. Bake about 55 - 60 minutes, until tested done. Cool in pan 15 minutes and remove to a rack.
Brush top of bread with 2 Tablespoons Amaretto. Sprinkle with toasted sliced almonds and sugar. Cool completely before wrapping. (Makes 1 loaf)

A quick bread with lots of flavor!

CANDIED AMARETTO CRANBERRIES

12 - 16 oz. fresh cranberries
2 cups sugar

1/4 cup Amaretto
Sugar

Preheat oven to 350°. Grease a 9" x 13" glass baking dish. Pour in cranberries and pick over to remove any stems or imperfect berries. Sprinkle 2 cups sugar over berries. Cover tightly with heavy duty aluminum foil. Bake for 1 hour. Cool. Stir in Amaretto and sprinkle lightly with sugar. Store in refrigerator.

Package in a decorative jar and give with a loaf of Amaretto Quick Bread.

CHRISTMAS COOKIE ORNAMENTS

1 cup butter or margarine
1/2 cup powdered sugar
1/2 cup sugar
1/8 teaspoon salt
1 egg
1 teaspoon vanilla

1/2 teaspoon baking soda
1/2 teaspoon cream of tartar
2 1/2 cups flour
2 egg yolks
Food coloring
Ribbon

In the large bowl of an electric mixer, cream butter, powdered sugar, sugar and salt until light and fluffy. Mix in egg and vanilla until combined. Add soda, cream of tartar and flour. Divide dough in half, wrap in plastic wrap and place in the freezer for 15 minutes.

Preheat oven to 350°. Remove half of dough from freezer and roll out on a floured surface, using as much flour as necessary to keep from sticking. Cut out large and small shapes with cookie cutters. Place large shapes on a greased foil lined baking sheet and top with a small shape. Use a plastic straw to make a hole near the top of each cookie.

Bake about 15 minutes, until lightly browned. Repeat with remaining dough. While cookies are warm, reopen holes with straw, if necessary. Cool on pans. To decorate, divide egg yolks between small bowls and tint with food coloring, to make an edible paint. Paint as desired. When paint is dry, run ribbons through the holes and tie in bows. (Makes about 18)

 *Small and large shapes can be alike or different.*
Cookies can be eaten right off the Christmas tree!

APRICOT COFFEECAKE
LOUISIANA PEPPER JELLY
LIME VEGETABLE DIP
CRANBERRY BISCOTTI
CHOCOLATE PEPPERMINT FUDGE

APRICOT COFFEECAKE

STREUSEL:
1/2 cup light brown sugar
2 Tablespoons butter or margarine
2 Tablespoons flour
1 teaspoon cinnamon

CAKE:
3/4 cup butter or margarine
1 1/2 cups sugar
4 eggs
1 teaspoon vanilla
1 teaspoon almond extract
1/4 teaspoon salt
1 teaspoon baking soda
1 1/2 teaspoons baking powder
3 cups flour
1 cup sour cream
1 cup coarsely chopped dried apricots (6 oz. pkg.)
Powdered sugar

Preheat oven to 350°. Grease a 10" tube pan with a removable bottom.

Measure ingredients for streusel in a small bowl and combine with your fingers or with a fork.

Beat butter with an electric mixer until light and fluffy. Add sugar and beat until creamy. Mix in eggs, one at a time. Add vanilla, almond, salt, baking soda and baking powder. Mix in flour, alternately with sour cream, until combined. Add apricots.

Spoon about 1/3 batter into prepared pan, spreading evenly. Sprinkle with 1/3 streusel. Repeat twice. Bake for 50 - 55 minutes, until tested done. Let cake cool in pan for 15 minutes. Turn out on a rack to cool completely. Sift powdered sugar on top before serving.

Dried apricots add a wonderful tart flavor to this moist coffeecake, but other dried fruits can be used.

LOUISIANA PEPPER JELLY

1 medium size red bell pepper, finely chopped
1 cup cider vinegar
3 cups sugar

1 teaspoon Tabasco or more
3 oz. liquid pectin
6 drops red food coloring

In a large saucepan, combine chopped pepper, vinegar, sugar and Tabasco. Bring to a boil over medium high heat and boil for 5 minutes. Remove from heat, stir in pectin and food coloring. Return to heat and boil 1 minute more. Pour into 3 half pint jars. Cool completely. Cover tightly and store in the refrigerator. Serve on cream cheese with crackers. (Makes approximately 3 half pints, plus a little extra.)

 *A very simple pepper jelly without ever handling the peppers*

LIME VEGETABLE DIP

1 cup mayonnaise
1 cup sour cream
1 lime
2 Tablespoons horseradish
2 Tablespoons Dijon mustard
1/2 teaspoon salt

Broccoli, cherry tomatoes, cauliflower, baby carrots

Stir mayonnaise and sour cream together in a medium size bowl. Remove the zest from the lime and reserve. Squeeze juice from lime and add to the mixing bowl along with horseradish, Dijon mustard and salt. Stir to combine. Sprinkle zest on top for garnish.
Serve dip with a mixture of vegetables. Broccoli can be arranged in a wreath shape around a bowl of dip and decorated with cherry tomatoes, cauliflower and carrots.

 *A very tangy and different vegetable dip!*

CRANBERRY BISCOTTI

3 eggs
1/2 cup vegetable oil
1 cup sugar
1 teaspoon almond extract
1 Tablespoon baking powder
3 cups flour
1/2 cup dried cranberries
1/2 cup sliced almonds

ICING:
1 cup powdered sugar
1/4 teaspoon almond extract
1 - 1 1/2 Tablespoons water

Preheat oven to 350°. Grease a large baking sheet. Beat eggs with an electric mixer for about 2 minutes. Add oil, sugar and almond extract. Beat until combined. Mix in baking powder and flour until a stiff dough is formed. Stir in dried cranberries and sliced almonds.

Spoon dough onto baking sheet, shaping into 2 separate logs, each about 2" wide. Bake for 25 minutes. Remove from oven and carefully cut dough into 3/4" slices using a serrated knife. Turn slices on their sides and bake again for 12 - 15 minutes, until lightly toasted. Cool in pan.

Make icing by combining powdered sugar, almond and water until smooth. Drizzle on biscotti slices in a wavy pattern. Let icing dry before storing. (Makes about 3 dozen)

Try substituting different extracts, nuts, fruits and even chocolate chips for variations of this popular Italian cookie that means "twice baked."
Makes a great gift along with a bag of fresh ground coffee!

CHOCOLATE PEPPERMINT FUDGE

2 cups semisweet chocolate chips
1 (14 oz) can sweetened condensed milk
2 teaspoons vanilla extract

1 cup vanilla chips
1 Tablespoon peppermint extract
1/4 cup crushed peppermint candy

Place chocolate chips in a microwave proof bowl along with about 1 cup sweetened condensed milk. Melt in microwave, about 1 minute. Add vanilla and stir to combine. Pour half of chocolate mixture into a greased 8" x 8" pan and spread evenly. Place in freezer for 5 minutes. Melt vanilla chips and remaining condensed milk in microwave for about 30 seconds. Add peppermint extract and stir to combine. Spread over chocolate layer. Spread remaining chocolate mixture on top and sprinkle with crushed peppermint candy. Place in freezer for about 20 minutes until firm. Cut into 1" squares. Place in individual paper candy cups. (Makes 64 pieces)

GIFTS OF FOOD

**CINNAMON ORNAMENTS
COCONUTTY BREAD
SAUCY CRANBERRIES
BRITTLEBREAD
SWEET ROLL CHRISTMAS TREE**

CINNAMON ORNAMENTS

1/4 cup prepared applesauce   **6 Tablespoons cinnamon**

In a small bowl, mix together applesauce and cinnamon until a stiff dough forms. Divide in half and roll out into a thin layer. Cut out shapes with cookie cutters. Make a hole in the top of each ornament with a toothpick and place on a wax paper lined baking sheet to dry. Let dry completely (24 - 48 hours), before handling. String with thin ribbon to make ornaments. (Makes about 1 dozen)

These are not for eating, but for decorating presents or hanging on the tree---a unique combination of ingredients that really works.

COCONUTTY BREAD

1 cup grated coconut (frozen)   **1 teaspoon vanilla**
1 egg   **1 Tablespoon baking powder**
1 cup sugar   **2 cups flour**
1/4 cup vegetable oil   **1/4 teaspoon nutmeg**
1 cup milk   **1/2 cup chopped pecans**

Preheat oven to 350°. Place coconut on a baking sheet and toast, stirring occasionally to brown evenly.
In a large mixing bowl, beat egg with an electric mixer until light. Slowly beat in sugar, oil, milk and vanilla. Mix in baking powder, flour and nutmeg. Stir in pecans and toasted coconut.
Pour into a greased 9 x 5 x 3 inch loaf pan and bake for 50 - 60 minutes. Let cool in pan 10 minutes. Remove and cool completely on a rack.
GLAZE:
1 cup powdered sugar   **1 - 2 Tablespoons milk**
1/4 teaspoon almond extract

Mix all ingredients together in a small bowl and drizzle over bread.

SAUCY CRANBERRIES

1 (12 -16 oz) bag fresh cranberries
1 orange & 1 Tablespoon zest
1 green apple (Granny Smith)
1 cup sugar

1/2 cup water
1 small cinnamon stick
Dash of nutmeg

Rinse cranberries and remove any stems. Place in a medium saucepan. Remove 1 Tablespoon zest from orange. Peel, seed and remove membrane from orange; chop pulp and add to cranberries with zest. Peel and core apple. Dice and add to saucepan. Mix in sugar, water, cinnamon and nutmeg. Place on medium high heat and bring to a boil. Lower heat and simmer about 40 minutes, stirring occasionally. Remove cinnamon stick and cool. Store in a tightly covered jar and refrigerate. (Makes 3 cups)

A terrific cranberry sauce to serve with turkey or pork!

BRITTLEBREAD

2 3/4 cups flour
1/4 cup sugar
1/2 teaspoon salt
1/2 teaspoon baking soda

1/2 cup butter or margarine
1 cup sour cream
1 egg white
Sweet or savory topping

Preheat oven to 400°. In a food processor with metal blade in place, add flour, sugar, salt and soda. Pulse to combine. Add cut up butter and pulse to mix. Add sour cream and process to form a soft dough. (By hand, mix dry ingredients in a large bowl. Cut in butter until crumbly. Mix in sour cream until combined.)

Divide dough in half and roll out smooth and thin on a lightly floured surface. Cut out in any shape desired (bars, circles, squares, rectangles, etc.).

Place on a greased foil lined baking sheet. Brush with 1 egg white beaten with 1 Tablespoon water and top with a sweet or savory topping, or bake plain. Bake for 12 - 15 minutes until browned. Remove and let cool on baking sheet to crisp. (Makes 3 - 4 dozen)

SWEET TOPPINGS: sugar, cinnamon sugar, powdered sugar, sugar and chopped pecans or almonds, melted chocolate, frosting, etc.

SAVORY TOPPINGS: salt, sesame seeds, poppy seeds, Parmesan cheese, cheddar cheese, herbs, etc.

Tastes like a cookie or a cracker, depending on your choice of toppings.

SWEET ROLL CHRISTMAS TREE

2 pkgs. yeast (4 1/2 teaspoons)
1/2 cup warm water (110°)
1 teaspoon sugar
1 cup milk
1/2 cup butter or margarine

3 eggs
1/2 cup sugar
1 teaspoon salt
5 - 6 cups unbleached flour

    Dissolve yeast in warm water and add sugar. Let stand 5 minutes. Meanwhile, heat milk and butter until butter melts. Let cool. Place eggs in a large mixing bowl and whisk until beaten. Add sugar, salt, milk and butter. Stir in yeast mixture and 2 cups flour. Mix until smooth. Add 3 or more cups flour to make a stiff, yet sticky, dough. Place in a greased bowl or Ziploc, cover and refrigerate for 2 - 48 hours.

FILLING:
1/2 cup butter, softened
1/2 cup sugar

1 Tablespoon cinnamon
1/2 cup chopped pecans

    In a small bowl, mash butter with a fork. Mix in sugar, cinnamon and pecans to form a paste.
    Divide dough into 2 parts. Place on a lightly floured surface and roll out each piece to a 12" x 12" square. Spread filling on dough with fingers. Roll up jelly roll style and cut into 10 slices. On a greased foil lined baking sheet, place smallest pieces at top in a tree shape, in rows of 1, 2, 3 and 4 rolls. Leave a little space (about 1 inch) between rolls for rising. Repeat with other half of dough. Place in a warm spot and let rise 1 hour.
    Preheat oven to 375°. Bake rolls for 25 minutes. Alternate shelves half way through for even browning. Remove from oven and cool on sheet.

GLAZE:
3 cups powdered sugar
5 Tablespoons milk

Candied cherries, red & green
or colored sugars

    Mix powdered sugar and milk together to form a glaze. Spread on rolls and top with candied cherries or sugars while icing is moist. Let dry before wrapping. (Makes 2 trees)

 *A very pretty presentation of the traditional cinnamon roll!*

HOLIDAY PUNCH
PEPPERED CHEESE
APRICOT NECTAR BREAD
ORANGE APRICOT JAM
CANDY CANE COOKIES
CRANBERRY PECAN TART

HOLIDAY PUNCH

1 (64 oz) bottle cranberry juice cocktail
1 (46 oz) can unsweetened pineapple juice
1/4 cup lemon juice
1/2 cup light brown sugar
1/2 teaspoon ground cloves
1/2 teaspoon ground allspice
1/2 teaspoon cinnamon
1/2 teaspoon ground nutmeg

Mix all ingredients together in a large pot. Place over medium high heat until heated through. Lower heat to low and simmer about 30 minutes. Serve hot. Refrigerate to store and reheat as needed. (Makes 1 gallon)

 *Can be served from a large coffee urn.*

PEPPERED CHEESE

1 (8 oz) pkg. cream cheese, cut up
1 cup grated cheddar cheese
1 cup grated Monterey Jack cheese
1 teaspoon Worcestershire sauce
2 - 3 teaspoons seasoned pepper
Parsley for garnish
Assorted crackers

Combine cream cheese, cheddar cheese, Monterey Jack cheese and Worcestershire sauce in a food processor until smooth. Remove and place on a piece of plastic wrap. Form into a ball and flatten slightly.
Spread seasoned pepper on a sheet of wax paper and roll cheese ball in pepper until covered on top and sides. Refrigerate until ready to serve. Serve garnished with parsley and crackers.

APRICOT NECTAR BREAD

2 1/2 cups flour
2 teaspoons baking powder
1 teaspoon baking soda
1 teaspoon salt
1/2 cup sugar
1/2 cup chopped dried apricots

1 egg
2 Tablespoons butter, melted
1 (12 oz) can apricot nectar
1/2 teaspoon vanilla
1 Tablespoon orange marmalade

Preheat oven to 350°. Grease an 8" x 4" loaf pan. In a large bowl, combine flour, baking powder, baking soda, salt, sugar and apricots. In another bowl beat egg. Stir in butter, nectar and vanilla. Stir flour mixture into egg mixture, only until dry ingredients are moistened. Pour into prepared pan and smooth top.

Bake for 40 - 45 minutes or until tested done. Cool in pan for 10 minutes, then remove to a rack to cool completely. When cool, spread with orange marmalade to glaze. (Makes 1 loaf)

ORANGE APRICOT JAM

1 medium orange, washed
3/4 cup dried apricots, chopped

1 (12 oz) can apricot nectar
3/4 cup sugar

Cut orange (with peeling left on) into quarters and remove seeds. Chop into small pieces. Place orange, apricots and nectar in a medium saucepan. Bring to a boil over medium high heat. Reduce heat to medium and boil for 15 minutes until fruit is tender. Stir in sugar, reduce heat to low and cook for 15 minutes, stirring occasionally until syrupy. Remove from heat. Cool slightly and pour into jars. Cool. Cover and store in refrigerator. (Makes 2 1/2 cups)

CANDY CANE COOKIES

1 cup butter or margarine, softened
1 1/4 cups sugar
2 eggs
2 teaspoons vanilla
1/4 teaspoon salt
2 teaspoons baking powder
3 1/2 cups flour
10 drops each of red & green food coloring

In the large bowl of an electric mixer, cream butter and sugar until light and fluffy. Add eggs and beat to combine. Add vanilla, salt and baking powder. Mix in flour until blended.

Divide dough in half. Add red coloring to half and green to the other half. Mix each thoroughly. Wrap each ball of dough in plastic wrap and chill about 30 minutes.

Preheat oven to 350°. Roll a 1" ball of pink dough and a 1" ball of green dough into ropes, about 6" long. Cross pink and green ropes in the middle and spiral them together from the middle to the ends. Press ropes together at ends.

Place cookies on a greased foil lined baking sheet and shape into candy canes.

Bake for 12 - 15 minutes, until just barely browned. Cool on sheet.
(Makes 3 dozen)

GIFTS OF FOOD

CRANBERRY PECAN TART

PASTRY:
- 2 cups flour
- 1/2 cup sugar
- 1/3 cup cocoa
- 1/4 teaspoon salt
- 3/4 cup cold butter or margarine, cut up
- 2 eggs
- 1 teaspoon vanilla
- 1 Tablespoon cold water

Place flour, sugar, cocoa and salt in a food processor and pulse to combine. Add butter, eggs, vanilla and cold water. Process just until mixture forms a ball. Remove and press into a greased 9" or 10" tart pan with a removable bottom. Chill while making filling.

FILLING:
- 2 eggs
- 1 cup light brown sugar
- 2 Tablespoons butter or margarine, melted
- 2 Tablespoons flour
- 1 teaspoon vanilla
- 1 cup coarsely chopped pecans
- 1 cup hand chopped fresh cranberries
- 8 pecan halves

Preheat oven to 375°. Place eggs in a medium size bowl and beat with a whisk. Mix in brown sugar, butter, flour, vanilla, pecans and cranberries.
Pour filling into pastry crust and arrange pecan halves on top of filling. Place a piece of foil under tart pan, to catch any drippings. Bake 40 - 45 minutes until firm and golden. Cool before serving.

 *A festive Christmas dessert to bring to a holiday gathering!*

RED HOT JELLY
SUGAR & SPICE DIP
ORANGE CARROT BREAD
CANDY APPLE COOKIES
FESTIVE CRANBERRY BRAID

RED HOT JELLY

2 cups apple juice
4 cups sugar

1/3 cup Red Hots (cinnamon candies)
6 oz. liquid pectin

Combine juice, sugar and candies in a large saucepan, stir well and place over high heat. Bring to a boil, stirring frequently. Add liquid pectin, stir constantly, and boil 1 minute. Remove from heat and let stand until all candies are melted, stirring occasionally. Let cool slightly and skim any foam off the top. Pour into 5 half pint jars and cover with lids. Store in refrigerator. (Makes 5 half pints)

A pretty jelly with lots of cinnamon flavor!

SUGAR AND SPICE DIP

1 (8 oz) container soft cream cheese
3 Tablespoons light brown sugar
1 teaspoon cinnamon
1/2 teaspoon nutmeg

1 teaspoon vanilla
2 Tablespoons milk
Assorted fresh fruits or cookies

In a small bowl, combine all ingredients for dip, stirring until smooth. Cover and refrigerate. Serve with fruits or cookies (Makes 1 cup)

ORANGE CARROT BREAD

4 carrots,
 (2 cups shredded)
4 eggs
2 cups sugar
1 1/4 cups vegetable oil
1/2 teaspoon baking soda
2 teaspoons baking powder
1/2 teaspoon salt
1 teaspoon nutmeg
1 teaspoon cinnamon
3 cups flour
2 teaspoons orange zest
1 (11 oz) can mandarin
 oranges, drained & chopped

Preheat oven to 350°. Peel carrots and shred in food processor. In a large mixing bowl, beat eggs and sugar with an electric mixer until fluffy. Slowly add oil, while beating, until combined. Mix in baking soda, baking powder, salt, nutmeg, cinnamon and flour. Add orange zest, mandarin oranges and shredded carrots. Pour batter into 2 greased 9 x 5 x 3 inch loaf pans. Bake 45 - 50 minutes, until tested done. Remove from pans and cool completely on wire racks. Sift powdered sugar on top. (Makes 2 loaves)

CANDY APPLE COOKIES

1/2 cup butter or margarine
1/2 cup powdered sugar
1/2 cup light brown sugar
1 egg
1 teaspoon vanilla
2 cups flour
1 (14 oz) bag caramels
1/4 cup milk
8 drops red food coloring
Toothpicks
1 cup chopped pecans

Preheat oven to 350°. Cream butter with an electric mixer until smooth. Add powdered sugar and brown sugar. Mix well. Beat in egg and vanilla. Mix in flour. Shape into 1 inch balls and place on a greased foil lined baking sheet. Bake about 18 - 20 minutes. Remove from oven and immediately insert a toothpick in each cookie, while still warm. Let cool.

In the top of a double boiler, over simmering water, melt caramels with milk. Stir until smooth. Add red food coloring. Dip cookies, one at a time, into caramel mixture, then roll bottom in chopped pecans. Place in small paper muffin cups. Store in an airtight container. (Makes about 3 dozen)

 *Cookies that look like candied apples---kids will love them!*

FESTIVE CRANBERRY BRAID

FILLING:

1 (12 - 16 oz) pkg. fresh cranberries
1 cup sugar
1 Tablespoon cornstarch
1/4 cup fresh orange juice
 (remove zest & save)

Rinse cranberries and discard any stems. Combine sugar and cornstarch in a large saucepan. Add orange juice and cranberries. Bring to a boil over medium high heat, stirring frequently. Lower heat and cook until thickened, about 10 minutes. Remove and cool. Refrigerate until cold.

DOUGH:

1 1/2 cups water
3/4 cup butter or margarine
7 cups unbleached flour
2 pkgs. rapid rise yeast
 (4 1/2 teaspoons)
2/3 cup sugar
2 Tablespoons reserved
 orange zest
1 teaspoon salt
4 eggs

Heat water and butter in a small saucepan over medium heat or in microwave just until butter melts (125 - 130°). In a large bowl, combine 2 cups flour, yeast, sugar, zest and salt. Beat in warm water and butter mixture with a whisk or mixer. Beat in 3 eggs and 1 egg yolk (reserve 1 egg white). Stir in enough flour (about 5 cups) to make a stiff but not dry dough. Turn dough out on a lightly floured surface and knead until smooth, about 5 minutes. Place in a greased bowl, cover and let rise in a warm spot until doubled, about 1 hour.

Grease 2 foil lined baking sheets. Punch dough down and turn out on a lightly floured surface. Cut in half. Roll out each half to a 14 x 10 inch rectangle. Place each piece on baking sheets. Brush dough lightly with slightly beaten reserved egg white. Spread half the cranberry filling down the center of each rectangle, about 3" wide to within 1" of ends of dough. Cut dough crosswise on each side of filling into 1" strips. Fold strips alternately across bread. Let rise about 20 minutes.

Preheat oven to 350°. Brush braids again with egg white. Bake about 35 - 40 minutes until browned. Cool.

To make glaze, mix powdered sugar and water to a smooth consistency. Drizzle glaze over braids. (Makes 2 loaves)

A very impressive gift for Christmas morning! Stock up on fresh cranberries when in season and store in the freezer to use throughout the year.

```
┌─────────────────────────────────┐
│      CRANBERRY CHEER            │
│    VEGIE CHRISTMAS TREE         │
│    HERBED VEGETABLE DIP         │
│   CHOCOLATE CHIP COFFEECAKE     │
│   CARAMEL POPCORN CRUNCH        │
│       SUGAR LUMP BREAD          │
└─────────────────────────────────┘
```

CRANBERRY CHEER

1 lb. fresh cranberries
2 qts. water
6 cinnamon sticks
4 whole cloves
Zest of 1 orange

1 1/2 cups sugar
1 (12 oz) can frozen orange juice
3 cans water
1 (6 oz) can frozen lemonade
Orange slices for garnish

Combine cranberries, water, cinnamon sticks, cloves and orange zest in a large saucepan over medium high heat. Bring to a boil and cook until berries pop. Strain liquid into a large pitcher or container. Add sugar, orange juice, water and lemonade, stirring until sugar dissolves. Serve hot or cold. Float thin slices of orange in pitcher or cups when serving. (Makes 12 - 15 servings)

A nice departure from the traditional spiced cider!

VEGIE CHRISTMAS TREE

1 tall styrofoam cone
Green leaf lettuce

Assorted vegetables: cherry tomatoes, broccoli, carrots, cauliflower, celery, zucchini, cucumbers, radishes, mushrooms, etc.

Attach lettuce to cone, starting from the bottom, with toothpicks. Decorate the tree with assorted vegies. Arrange extra vegies around the bottom of the tree. Keep refrigerated until serving time. Serve with Herbed Vegetable Dip.

A great centerpiece for your Christmas food table!

HERBED VEGETABLE DIP

1 (8 oz) pkg. cream cheese
1 cup sour cream
1 Tablespoon tarragon vinegar
1 teaspoon salt
1/4 teaspoon pepper

1 clove garlic, minced
1/4 cup chopped green onion
1/4 cup chopped parsley
1/2 ripe avocado
1 Tablespoon lemon juice

Combine all ingredients in a food processor until mixed. Chill until ready to serve. (Makes 2 cups)

CHOCOLATE CHIP COFFEECAKE

3/4 cup butter or margarine
1 cup sugar
2 eggs
1 teaspoon baking soda
1 1/2 teaspoons baking powder
2 cups flour
1 cup buttermilk

1 teaspoon vanilla
1 cup semisweet chocolate
 chips
TOPPING:
1/2 cup chopped pecans
2 Tablespoons sugar
1 teaspoon cinnamon

Preheat oven to 350°. Cream butter in a large mixing bowl with an electric mixer until light and fluffy. Slowly add sugar and mix until blended. Add eggs, one at a time, and mix in baking soda and baking powder. Add flour alternately with buttermilk, blending well after each addition. Mix in vanilla and fold in chocolate chips.

In a small bowl, combine pecans, sugar and cinnamon. Pour 2/3 of the batter into a greased tube or bundt pan and top with half of topping mixture. Pour the remaining 1/3 batter into the pan and sprinkle with remaining half of topping.

Bake for about 45 - 50 minutes or until tested done. Cool in the pan for 15 minutes. Place a piece of aluminum foil under a cake rack (to catch any topping that might fall off). Turn cake out onto rack and flip it over again, along with foil, onto another rack, so the topping side is up. Cool or serve warm.

 *A perfect gift for chocolate lovers!*

CARAMEL POPCORN CRUNCH

8 quarts popped corn
1 cup dry roasted peanuts (optional)
2 cups light brown sugar
1/2 cup light corn syrup

1 cup butter or margarine
1/2 teaspoon baking soda
Pinch of salt
1/2 teaspoon vanilla

Preheat oven to 225°. Place popped corn and peanuts into 2 large greased baking pans. In a medium saucepan over medium high heat, combine sugar, syrup and butter. Bring to a boil and let boil for 5 minutes. Remove from heat and stir in baking soda, salt and vanilla. Pour mixture over popcorn and mix well, using two spoons.

Bake for 1 hour, stirring every 15 minutes. Cool and store in an airtight container.

Be careful when stirring popcorn and sauce together, as it is very hot. Also, be careful when eating this, as it is very addicting!

SUGAR LUMP BREAD

1 1/2 cups milk
1/2 cup butter or margarine
1/2 cup sugar
1 teaspoon salt
2 pkgs. yeast (4 1/2 teaspoons)
1 Tablespoon vanilla
1 egg
5 1/2 - 6 cups unbleached flour

1/4 cup butter or margarine, softened
1 Tablespoon cinnamon
48 sugar cubes

ICING:
1 cup powdered sugar
1 - 2 Tablespoons milk

Heat milk and butter in the microwave or a small saucepan over medium high heat, just until butter melts. Pour milk into a large mixing bowl and whisk in sugar and salt. Cool to lukewarm ($110°$). Stir in yeast. Whisk in vanilla and egg. Mix in 3 cups flour until combined. Then, using a wooden spoon or spatula, add enough remaining flour to form a stiff dough. Turn out on a floured surface and knead for a few minutes until smooth. Place in a greased bowl, cover with a towel or plastic wrap and place in a warm spot until doubled, about 1 hour.

Punch dough down and divide in half. On a lightly floured surface, roll out each half to a 10 x 7 inch rectangle. Spread both portions with softened butter and sprinkle with cinnamon. Place sugar cubes in 6 rows of 4 each on each piece of dough. Starting from the short side, roll up dough, pinching ends under to seal. Place seam side down in 2 greased 9 x 5 x 3 inch loaf pans. Cover and let rise about 30 minutes.

Preheat oven to $375°$. Bake loaves for 30 - 35 minutes. Remove from pans and place on wire racks to cool.

Make icing by mixing powdered sugar and milk until smooth. Spread over loaves and let cool completely before storing. (Makes 2 loaves)

 **The sugar cubes melt into a delicious filling!**

GIFTS OF FOOD

CHEESE PINEAPPLE
CRANBERRY COFFEECAKE
PICKLED PINEAPPLE
CHRISTMAS PINWHEELS
MICRO NUT BRITTLE

CHEESE PINEAPPLE

2 (8 oz) pkgs. cream cheese, softened
3/4 lb. sharp cheddar cheese, grated
1/4 cup butter, softened
1 teaspoon Worcestershire sauce
1 teaspoon lemon juice

Dash of salt
1/8 teaspoon cayenne pepper
Pimiento stuffed olives
1 leafy crown from a fresh pineapple
Parsley for garnish

Combine cream cheese, cheddar cheese, butter, Worcestershire, lemon juice, salt and cayenne in a large bowl with an electric mixer and beat until smooth.
Shape cheese mixture into a standing pineapple, flatten top and cover with plastic wrap. Chill until firm.
To assemble, mark cheese with a toothpick to resemble a pineapple, with diagonal criss-crossing lines forming diamonds. Place an olive slice in the center of each diamond. Place the leafy crown on top of cheese and secure with toothpicks. Surround with parsley and serve with crackers.

Recipe can be doubled for a larger cheese pineapple or can be shaped into a ball or roll, covered with chopped parsley, pecans or paprika.

CRANBERRY COFFEECAKE

1/2 cup butter or margarine
1 cup sugar
2 eggs
1/2 teaspoon salt
1 teaspoon baking powder
1 teaspoon baking soda
1 teaspoon almond extract
2 cups flour
1 cup sour cream
1 (1 lb) can whole berry
  cranberry sauce
1/2 cup chopped pecans

Preheat oven to 350°. Grease a tube pan. Cream butter and sugar with an electric mixer until light and fluffy. Add eggs, one at a time, and beat well. Mix in salt, baking powder, baking soda and almond extract. Add flour, alternately with sour cream until well blended.

Place about 1/3 of batter into the tube pan. Stir cranberry sauce to recombine. Spoon half the sauce over the batter and swirl through. Put another 1/3 of batter into pan. Spoon on sauce and top with remaining batter. Sprinkle with pecans.

Bake for about 50 minutes or until tested done. Cool thoroughly in pan before removing.

FROSTING:
1 cup powdered sugar
2 Tablespoons warm water
1/4 teaspoon almond extract

Combine all ingredients until smooth. Drizzle over coffeecake.

PICKLED PINEAPPLE

2 (20 oz) cans unsweetened
  pineapple chunks
3/4 cup reserved juice
3/4 cup sugar
3/4 cup white vinegar
10 whole cloves
1 cinnamon stick, broken
6 whole allspice
Pinch of salt

Drain pineapple chunks and reserve 3/4 cup juice. Place chunks in a 1 quart jar, 2 pint jars or 4 half pint jars.

Place reserved juice and all other ingredients in a small saucepan over medium heat. Cook for 15 minutes. Pour over pineapple. When cool, cover and refrigerate at least 3 days before serving. Keep refrigerated for about 2 months.

 *An interesting condiment that makes a nice addition to a holiday meal!*

CHRISTMAS PINWHEELS

1 cup butter or margarine
1 1/2 cups sugar
1 egg
1 1/2 teaspoons baking powder
1/2 teaspoon salt

1 teaspoon vanilla
2 1/2 cups flour
8 drops red food coloring
8 drops green food coloring
Powdered sugar

Beat butter in a large bowl with an electric mixer until creamy. Add sugar until combined. Mix in egg, baking powder, salt, vanilla and flour. Beat for 3 minutes. Divide dough into 3 equal parts on pieces of wax paper. Place 8 drops of red food coloring on 1 part, green on 1 part and leave the last part plain. To mix in food coloring, place dough back in mixing bowl and beat with mixer. Wrap each piece with plastic wrap and place in refrigerator for 1 hour.

Divide each piece in half, making 6 parts. Working with one piece at a time, sprinkle powdered sugar on a piece of wax paper and roll out a piece of the green dough into a 10 x 6 inch rectangle. Try to keep as even as possible. Repeat with plain dough and red dough. Invert the plain dough on top of the green and peel off the wax paper. Then top with the red dough. Starting with one long side, roll up dough tightly, jelly roll style, using wax paper as an aid. Wrap up dough in wax paper and refrigerate for 1 hour. Repeat with remaining 3 pieces of dough for form another roll.

Preheat oven to 350^0. Cover a baking sheet with foil and grease with cooking spray. Remove one roll of cookie dough and slice into 1/4" slices. Place on foil about an inch apart and bake for 12 - 14 minutes. Repeat with second roll. Cool on racks and store in an airtight container. (Makes 5 dozen)

MICRO NUT BRITTLE

1/2 cup light corn syrup
1 cup sugar
1 cup dry roasted salted peanuts

1 Tablespoon butter
2 teaspoons vanilla
1 teaspoon baking soda

Grease a baking pan and a metal spatula with cooking spray. Stir corn syrup and sugar together in a 4 cup glass measuring cup. Microwave on high for 2 minutes, until bubbling. Using a wooden spoon, stir in peanuts. Micro on high for 3 minutes, just until light brown. Stir in butter and vanilla. Micro on high for 2 minutes, until syrup turns a deep golden brown (like peanut butter).

Stir in soda and immediately pour into baking pan and quickly spread thin with the metal spatula (be very careful as candy, measuring cup and baking pan get extremely hot). Cool completely, then break into pieces. Store in an airtight container. (Makes about 1 lb.)

Soak utensils in hot water to clean.

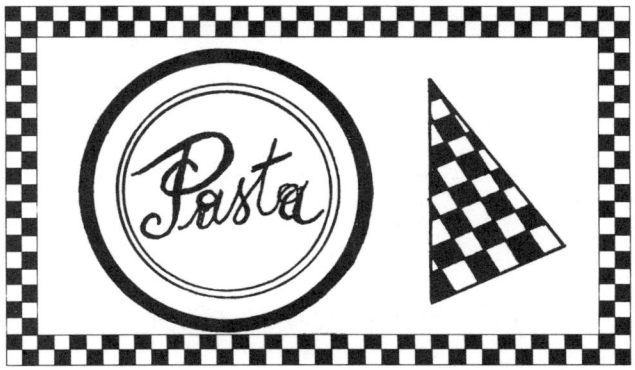

ITALIAN

MENUS

SUPPA DI POMODORI
RISOTTO
CHICKEN SALTIMBOCCA
CASSATA ALA SICILIANO

CROSTINI
PARMESAN VINAIGRETTE SALAD
SEAFOOD CANNELLONI
LEMON TORTA

SUN DRIED TOMATO CROUSTADES
PASTA CARBONARA
VEAL WITH ARTICHOKE SAUCE
AMARETTO BREAD PUDDING

ANTIPASTA
BAKED GNOCCHI WITH
SUN DRIED TOMATOES
POLLO LIMONESE
CHOCOLATE AMARETTO DOLCI

SUPPLI DI RISO
SALSA CRUDO
HOMEMADE EGG PASTA
PASTA WITH PEPPERS & OIL
POLLO D'OLIVE
TIRAMISU

FRIED MOZZARELLA MARINARA
ITALIAN VEGETABLE SALAD
CHICKEN MELANZANA WITH
ANGEL HAIR PASTA
ZABAGLIONE

CREAMY ITALIAN SALAD
CAPONATA
FETTUCCINE ALFREDO
VEAL FLORENTINA
SPUMONI CREMA

STUFFED ARTICHOKE LEAVES
SALSA DI POMODORI
VEAL MOZZARELLA
CIOCCOLATA CREMA

Italian cuisine has always been a favorite of food lovers. Flavors are very direct, not subtle. Although many pasta dishes are offered in Italian classes, we also prepare a variety of interesting recipes, not related to pasta. So be adventurous, you and your guests will be delighted with the results!

ZUPPA DI POMODORI
RISOTTO
CHICKEN SALTIMBOCCA
CASSATA ALA SICILIANO

ZUPPA DI POMODORI

2 Tablespoons olive oil
1 small onion, chopped
1/2 cup chopped celery
1/4 cup chopped carrot
1 clove garlic, minced
1 (15 oz) can tomato purée
3 cups beef broth

1 teaspoon basil
Salt & pepper to taste
1 cup dried tortellini pasta
  with cheese
1 cup heavy cream
2 teaspoons Anisette
  or Pernod

Heat oil in a large saucepan over medium heat. Sauté onion, celery, carrot and garlic until tender. Add tomato purée, broth, basil, salt and pepper. Bring to a boil and stir in tortellini. Cover, lower heat and cook for 20 minutes. Stir in cream and Anisette. Heat thoroughly before serving. (Serves 6 - 8)

Not just any "tomato soup", this recipe will become a favorite. Don't omit the Anisette---it makes a difference!

RISOTTO

1/4 cup butter or margarine
1/2 cup chopped onion
1 1/2 cups Arborio rice
4 cups hot chicken broth

Salt & pepper to taste
2 Tablespoons chopped
  parsley
Grated Romano cheese

Melt butter in a medium saucepan over medium heat. Sauté onion until tender. Stir in rice to coat. Add 2/3 cup hot broth. Cook, stirring frequently, until broth is almost absorbed. Keep adding 1/3 cup chicken broth at a time, stirring until absorbed before adding more. Cook until all the broth is absorbed and the risotto becomes thick and creamy, about 25 - 30 minutes. Add parsley and stir constantly towards the end of cooking, so the risotto doesn't stick. Serve garnished with grated Romano cheese. (Serves 6 - 8)

Patience is needed when preparing Risotto.
Don't add the broth too fast or the rice won't be cooked.
Arborio is an Italian short grain rice, high in starch.

CHICKEN SALTIMBOCCA

6 - 8 boneless, skinless chicken breasts
Salt & pepper
Thin slices of ham
Thin slices of provolone cheese
1 pkg. frozen chopped spinach, cooked & drained well
2 Tablespoons olive oil
2 Tablespoons butter or margarine
2 Tablespoons flour
1/4 cup dry white wine
1/4 cup lemon juice
1 cup chicken broth
1/8 teaspoon basil
1/8 teaspoon oregano
1/4 cup chopped parsley
Salt & pepper to taste
Lemon zest for garnish

Preheat oven to 375°. Pound chicken breasts to flatten slightly. Season with salt and pepper. Place a small slice of ham and cheese on one side of each breast, lengthwise. Top with a layer of spinach, fold in half lengthwise and secure with toothpicks, laid sideways.
Heat oil and butter in a large skillet over medium high heat. Brown chicken on both sides. Cook in two batches if necessary. Place in a large ovenproof dish and remove toothpicks. Add flour to skillet and cook, stirring constantly, for 1 minute. Whisk in wine, lemon juice, broth, basil, oregano and parsley. Bring to a boil and cook about 2 minutes. Pour sauce over chicken and place in oven, uncovered, for 20 minutes. Garnish with lemon zest. (Serves 6 - 8)

A pair of needlenose pliers makes for easy removal of toothpicks. This dish is traditionally prepared with sage and prosciutto and means "jump in the mouth".

CASSATA ALA SICILIANO

CAKE:
3 eggs
1 cup sugar
1/4 teaspoon salt
1 teaspoon baking powder
1 cup flour
1/2 cup milk
1 teaspoon vanilla

Preheat oven to 375°. Grease a 15 1/2" x 10 1/2" x 1" jelly roll pan. Line with wax paper and grease again.
Beat eggs with an electric mixer for 5 minutes at medium speed. Lower speed and gradually add sugar. Mix in salt and baking powder. Add flour alternately with milk. Stir in vanilla. Batter will be very thin. Spread evenly into the prepared pan and bake about 15 minutes, until very lightly browned. Remove from oven and cool in pan for 5 minutes. Remove cake to a rack to cool completely. Keep cake right side up for easier handling. Peel paper off when cooled.

FILLING:
1 (15 oz) carton ricotta cheese
1/4 cup powdered sugar
1/4 teaspoon almond extract
1/4 cup mini chocolate chips

Stir together ricotta cheese, powdered sugar, almond and chocolate chips until combined.

FROSTING:
1/4 cup butter or margarine
2 1/2 cups powdered sugar
1/2 cup cocoa
1/4 cup hot water
Chopped pecans for garnish

Make frosting by beating butter, powdered sugar, cocoa and enough water with an electric mixer to achieve a smooth consistency.
Cut cake into 4 rectangles (10 1/2" x 3 3/4"). Spread filling between 3 layers and top with cake. Frost entire cake with frosting, decorate with an icing comb and top with chopped pecans, if desired. Chill. (Serves 12)

A lovely cake that makes a very nice finale to a grand meal.

SUN DRIED TOMATO CROUSTADES
PASTA CARBONARA
VEAL WITH ARTICHOKE SAUCE
AMARETTO BREAD PUDDING

SUN DRIED TOMATO CROUSTADES

12 small slices French bread
12 small slices mozzarella cheese
6 sun dried tomatoes, packed in oil, chopped
Fresh ground pepper
Fresh or dried basil, chopped

Preheat oven to 400°. Place slices of French bread on a greased foil lined baking sheet. Top each slice with a piece of cheese. Sprinkle a few pieces of tomato on each slice and season with pepper and basil.

When ready to serve, toast croustades in oven for about 5 - 10 minutes until browned and bubbly. Recipe can be easily doubled. (Serves 4 - 6)

PASTA CARBONARA

6 slices bacon
1/4 cup butter or margarine
1 clove garlic, minced
1 cup sliced mushrooms
1/4 cup chopped parsley
1 cup heavy cream
1 (1 lb) pkg. vermicelli or thin pasta
1 egg, beaten
1/2 cup grated Romano or Parmesan cheese
Salt & pepper to taste

Cook bacon in the microwave or a skillet until crisp. Drain, crumble and set aside.

Melt butter in a medium skillet over medium heat. Sauté garlic and mushrooms for a few minutes. Stir in parsley and cream. Lower heat to keep warm.

Meanwhile, bring a large pot of salted water to a boil. Add pasta and cook al dente (tastes done). Drain.

Place beaten egg in a large bowl. Add hot pasta and toss with egg to coat. Stir in sauce, cheese, bacon, salt and pepper. (Serves 6 - 8)

When pasta is added to boiling water, stir immediately for at least 1 minute to keep pasta from sticking. Taste test is the best way to determine when pasta is done.

VEAL WITH ARTICHOKE SAUCE

3 fresh artichokes	2 Tablespoons butter
Salt & pepper	1 small onion, chopped
Juice of 1/2 lemon	1 clove garlic, minced
1 Tablespoon olive oil	1 cup chicken broth
	1/4 cup chopped parsley
	1/8 teaspoon basil
6 - 8 veal cutlets	1/8 teaspoon oregano
Salt, pepper & flour	2 Tablespoons tomato paste
Vegetable oil	1/2 teaspoon sugar
	Salt & pepper to taste

Cut stems off artichokes and snip off thorny tops of the leaves with kitchen shears. Rinse under cold water and drain. Salt and pepper artichokes and place in a large saucepan. Add water to come half way up artichokes. Top with lemon juice and olive oil. Place over high heat, cover and bring to a boil. Cook for about 45 minutes, until a leaf pulls off easily. Drain and let cool. Remove all leaves and discard fuzzy choke. Coarsely chop artichoke hearts. Set aside.

Pound veal cutlets and pat dry with paper towels. Season with salt and pepper. Heat a very thin layer of oil in a large skillet over medium high heat. Coat half the veal with flour and sauté until golden brown on both sides. Remove to a large baking dish and keep warm in a low heated oven. Repeat with remaining veal. Pour off any remaining oil.

In the same skillet, lower heat and melt butter. Add onion and garlic; sauté until softened. Stir in chopped artichokes and remaining ingredients; bring to a boil. Cover and simmer about 10 minutes. Serve sauce over veal. (Serves 6)

Veal and sauce can be made ahead and reheated separately when ready to serve.
Artichoke leaves can be eaten with a vinaigrette, as an appetizer.

AMARETTO BREAD PUDDING

12 pieces of sliced bread
4 cups milk
1/4 cup butter
3 eggs
1 1/2 cups sugar
1 teaspoon almond extract
1/2 cup sliced almonds

SAUCE:
1/2 cup butter
1 cup powdered sugar
1 egg
1/4 cup Amaretto

    Preheat oven to 350°. Tear up bread into medium size pieces and place in a large greased baking dish. Heat milk and butter in a large saucepan over low heat until butter melts. Pour over bread. Beat eggs; add sugar and almond extract. Pour over bread and gently stir in. Sprinkle with almonds. Bake about 40 minutes until set.
    To make sauce, melt butter and powdered sugar in a small saucepan over low heat. Remove from heat and quickly whisk in 1 egg. Stir in Amaretto and beat until smooth.
    To serve, cut bread pudding into squares and top with sauce. Serve warm, even if made ahead. (Can be reheated in microwave) (Serves 12)

Bread pudding tends to deflate once it starts to cool. Better than the average bread pudding---don't pass this one by!

ITALIAN

```
SUPPLI DI RISO
SALSA CRUDO
HOMEMADE EGG PASTA
PASTA WITH PEPPERS & OIL
POLLO D'OLIVE
TIRAMISU
```

SUPPLI DI RISO

1 cup long grain white rice
2 cups chicken broth
1 Tablespoon butter
1/4 cup grated Parmesan cheese
Salt & pepper

2 eggs, beaten
1 cup Italian seasoned
  bread crumbs
Mozzarella cheese,
  cut into 1/2" cubes
Vegetable oil for frying

    Grease a small saucepan with cooking spray and add rice, chicken broth and butter. Bring to a boil over high heat and let boil until most of the liquid has evaporated and small craterlike holes appear in the surface. Cover with lid and let steam for about 20 minutes. Let cool completely or refrigerate.
    When ready to cook, stir Parmesan cheese into rice and season with salt and pepper. Beat eggs in a large bowl and stir in rice. Add bread crumbs and stir to combine. Brush hands with a small amount of oil (or cooking spray). Place about 2 Tablespoons rice mixture into palm of hand and make an indentation in the center. Put a mozzarella cheese cube in the depression and cover with more rice mixture. Form into an egg shape, covering the cheese cube completely. Repeat until all rice mixture is used.
    Heat enough vegetable oil for frying in a large saucepan over medium high heat. When hot, add a few croquettes and fry until golden brown on both sides. Remove and drain on paper towels. Keep warm in a low oven. Serve as appetizers with Salsa Crudo. (Makes about 2 dozen)

Suppli di Riso are deep fried rice croquettes with mozzarella cheese inside that draws out into long "wires" when pulled apart.

SALSA CRUDO

1 (1 lb) can whole peeled tomatoes
2 Tablespoons tomato paste
1/2 teaspoon sugar
1/4 teaspoon salt

1/2 teaspoon basil
1/2 teaspoon oregano
1/4 teaspoon hot red pepper flakes

Place all ingredients in a food processor and mix until combined. Pour sauce in a small saucepan and cook over medium heat until hot.

A quick, uncooked tomato sauce for pasta and pizzas.

HOMEMADE EGG PASTA

1 1/2 cups all purpose flour
2 large eggs
1/4 teaspoon salt
2 teaspoons olive oil
Water as needed
(Makes 10 oz.)

2 1/4 cups flour
3 eggs
1/2 teaspoon salt
1 Tablespoon olive oil
Water as needed
(Makes 1 lb.)

By hand: Place flour in a mound on the countertop or in a large bowl. Make a well in the center and add eggs, salt and oil. Start beating eggs with a fork, gradually working in flour towards the center; first with the fork, then with fingers until all the flour is incorporated. Add a teaspoon of water at a time, if necessary, to obtain a stiff but dry dough. Knead for about 5 minutes until smooth. Let stand 15 minutes to rest.

By food processor: Place eggs, salt and oil in processor fitted with the metal blade. Process for a few seconds to combine. Add flour and process until dough looks crumbly, adding water if necessary. Remove and knead lightly. Let rest 15 minutes.

Divide dough in half and run through the largest setting of a manual pasta machine, sprinkling with flour as necessary. Fold over and run through one or two more times until smooth. Change setting down 2 turns and repeat rolling. If pieces get too long, cut in half. Stop at next to last setting. Run through cutter of your choice.

To cook, bring a large pot of water to a boil over high heat. Add about 1 Tablespoon salt and stir in pasta with a long fork. Cook until al dente (tastes done) and drain. Mix with sauce immediately or toss with butter to keep from sticking.

Homemade pasta cooks very fast compared to dried pasta, so start tasting after a few minutes of cooking. It's not difficult to make, it just takes time.

PASTA WITH PEPPERS AND OIL

1/2 cup olive oil
2 cloves garlic, minced
1/2 green pepper and 1/2 red pepper cut into very thin strips about 1" long
1/4 teaspoon hot red pepper flakes
1 lb. thin pasta
Salt & pepper to taste
Grated Parmesan cheese

Heat oil in a small saucepan or skillet over medium heat. Sauté garlic and peppers until softened. Add red pepper flakes and keep warm while cooking pasta. When pasta is done, drain and toss with oil and peppers. Season with salt, pepper and cheese. (Serves 6)

A very colorful and simple dish to prepare!

POLLO D'OLIVE

6 - 8 boneless chicken breasts
Salt & pepper
1/3 cup flour
1/3 cup Italian seasoned bread crumbs
2 Tablespoons olive oil
2 Tablespoons butter or margarine
1/2 cup whole black olives
1 teaspoon olive oil
2 Tablespoons grated Parmesan cheese
1 clove garlic, minced
Grated mozzarella cheese

Preheat oven to 350°. Season chicken breasts with salt and pepper. Mix flour and bread crumbs together in a small bowl.

Heat olive oil and butter in a large skillet over medium high heat. Dredge chicken in flour mixture and sauté until browned on both sides. Place in a greased baking dish.

Make olive paste by combining olives, oil, Parmesan cheese and garlic in a food processor until smooth. Spread each chicken breast with a thin layer of olive paste. Top with grated mozzarella cheese. Bake in oven for about 5 minutes, just until cheese is melted. (Serves 6)

TIRAMISU

CAKE:
- 2 eggs
- 1/2 cup sour cream
- 1 cup sugar
- 1 teaspoon vanilla
- 1 teaspoon baking powder
- 1/4 teaspoon baking soda
- Pinch of salt
- 1 cup flour

Preheat oven to 350°. Grease a 9" round cake pan. With an electric mixer, beat eggs and sour cream until mixed, about 2 minutes. Add sugar and beat 2 minutes more. Add vanilla, then mix in dry ingredients until blended.

Bake about 25 minutes, until tested done. Cool in pan 5 minutes. Cool completely on a rack.

FILLING:
- 1 (8 oz) pkg, cream cheese, cut up
- 1/4 cup sugar
- 1 teaspoon vanilla
- 2 Tablespoons sour cream
- 2 Tablespoons heavy cream

Place all ingredients in a food processor and mix until combined.

TO ASSEMBLE:
- 1/2 cup strong hot coffee or espresso
- 1/4 cup sugar
- 1 Tablespoon Amaretto
- 1 oz. semisweet chocolate, grated
- Cocoa
- 1/2 pt. heavy cream, whipped

Split cooled cake in half horizontally. Brush both cut sides of cake with a mixture of coffee, sugar and Amaretto. Spread half of cheese filling on bottom cake layer. Top with second layer and spread remaining filling over top and lightly on sides.

Place wax paper strips under cake to catch drippings. Press chocolate shavings around sides of cake. Sift cocoa completely over top of cake. Chill.

When ready to serve, re-sprinkle with cocoa if necessary. Serve slices with whipped cream piped along the side of each piece.

A popular dessert in many Italian restaurants, Tiramisu means "pick me up".
Almond extract can be substituted for Amaretto.
Best served the same day as made.

ITALIAN

**CREAMY ITALIAN SALAD
CAPONATA
FETTUCCINE ALFREDO
VEAL FLORENTINA
SPUMONI CREMA**

CREAMY ITALIAN SALAD

1 small clove garlic
1/4 cup mayonnaise
1/4 cup sour cream
3 Tablespoons red wine vinegar

1/4 teaspoon dried basil
1/2 teaspoon salt
1/4 teaspoon pepper
1/2 teaspoon sugar
1/4 cup vegetable oil

Drop garlic through feed tube of a food processor with the machine running. Stop machine and add other ingredients, except oil. Pulse to combine. Turn machine on and slowly pour in oil through the feed tube. Store in a covered container and refrigerate. (Makes about 3/4 cup)

Serve dressing over individual salads of romaine lettuce, mixed partially cooked vegetables (broccoli, cauliflower, baby carrots, etc.) and chopped black olives.

CAPONATA

1/4 cup olive oil
1 small onion, chopped
2 cloves garlic, minced
1/2 cup chopped celery
1/2 cup chopped green pepper
1 small eggplant, washed & cubed
2 small zucchini, washed & cubed
2 tomatoes, peeled & chopped

1 Tablespoon sugar
3 Tablespoons tomato paste
2 Tablespoons water
3 Tablespoons red wine vinegar
Salt & pepper to taste

Heat olive oil in a large skillet or saucepan over medium heat. Add onion, garlic, celery, green pepper, eggplant and zucchini. Sauté for about 10 minutes, stirring frequently. Add tomatoes, sugar, tomato paste, water, vinegar, salt and pepper. Lower fire, cover and simmer about 20 minutes, stirring occasionally. (Serves 6)

FETTUCCINE ALFREDO

1 lb. fettuccine pasta
1 cup heavy cream
1/2 cup butter
2 Tablespoons chopped parsley

1/2 cup grated Parmesan
　cheese
Salt & pepper to taste

Cook the pasta in a large amount of rapidly boiling salted water just until tender (al dente). While pasta is cooking, heat cream and butter until butter melts and mixture is hot.

Drain pasta well and toss in a large bowl with cream and butter, parsley, cheese, salt and pepper. Serve immediately. (Serves 6)

 *A wonderful traditional dish that is very quick and easy!*

VEAL FLORENTINA

6 veal cutlets, pounded thin
Salt & pepper
3 thin slices ham, halved
3 slices provolone cheese, halved
1 pkg. fresh spinach (or frozen),
　cooked & drained
Flour

2 Tablespoons butter
2 Tablespoons vegetable oil
1 cup sliced mushrooms
1/2 cup chicken broth
1/4 cup chopped parsley
1/4 cup heavy cream
Salt & pepper to taste

Preheat oven to 350°. Salt and pepper veal cutlets. Top each cutlet with a slice of ham, cheese and about 2 Tablespoons spinach. Roll up each piece, secure with toothpicks and dust with flour.

Heat butter and oil in a large skillet over medium high heat. Brown veal rolls on all sides. Place in a baking dish, remove toothpicks and cover to keep warm.

Add mushrooms to drippings, sauté lightly and stir in broth. Bring to a boil, scraping bottom of skillet. Add parsley, cream, salt and pepper. Heat and pour sauce over veal rolls.

Bake uncovered for 15 minutes. (Serves 6)

 *Chicken breast fillets can be substituted for veal.*

SPUMONI CREMA

1 envelope unflavored gelatin
1/4 cup cold water
1 (8 oz) pkg. cream cheese, softened
1 cup sugar
1/2 cup half & half cream
Juice of 1 lemon

1 teaspoon almond extract &
  3 drops green food coloring
2 Tablespoons cherry juice &
  2 drops red food coloring
1 cup heavy cream
1/4 cup powdered sugar

    Soften gelatin in cold water in a small saucepan for about 5 minutes. Place over medium heat and stir until dissolved (don't boil). Set aside to cool.
    With an electric mixer, beat cream cheese until fluffy. Add sugar and beat until smooth. Stir in half & half and gelatin. Divide mixture into 3 bowls (putting a little more in the bowl for cherry; then almond; then smallest amount for lemon). Stir lemon juice into smallest mixture. Add almond and green coloring to the next mixture. Add cherry juice and red coloring to the largest mixture. Chill for about 15 minutes, until slightly thickened.
    Beat heavy cream with powdered sugar in a chilled bowl until stiff. Divide whipped cream among the 3 bowls and lightly fold in. Grease a 1 1/2 qt. bowl or mold with cooking spray and spoon in lemon mixture to cover bottom, spreading out to edges. Top with green almond mixture; then red cherry mixture, spreading to edges, keeping each layer separate. Cover with plastic wrap and chill until firm and ready to serve.
    Dip bottom of bowl or mold in warm water to loosen. Invert on a plate and garnish with a fanned strawberry or cherry on top. To serve, slice in wedges. (Serves 8)

Looks and tastes like real spumoni ice cream!

```
┌─────────────────────────────────┐
│         CROSTINI                │
│  PARMESAN VINAIGRETTE SALAD     │
│      SEAFOOD CANNELLONI         │
│         LEMON TORTA             │
└─────────────────────────────────┘
```

CROSTINI

8 (1/2") slices Italian bread
1/4 cup butter, melted
1 cup chopped Canadian bacon or prosciutto

Sliced black olives
Grated mozzarella cheese
Grated Parmesan cheese

Preheat oven to 350°. Brush slices of bread with melted butter and sauté in a large skillet over medium high heat until browned. Remove and place on a foil lined baking sheet. Lightly sauté bacon in the same skillet and place on bread slices. Top with some sliced black olives, mozzarella and Parmesan cheeses. Bake for about 5 minutes, until cheeses melt. (Serves 8)

A very simple and delicious appetizer!
Recipe doubles easily.

PARMESAN VINAIGRETTE SALAD

1/4 cup white vinegar
1/4 teaspoon sugar
1/2 teaspoon salt
1/8 teaspoon pepper
2 teaspoons Dijon mustard
1 cup olive oil

1/2 cup grated Parmesan cheese
Leaf Lettuce
Sliced black olives
Avocado slices
Shaved Parmesan cheese

Combine vinegar, sugar, salt, pepper and mustard. Whisk in olive oil until smooth. Stir in grated Parmesan cheese. Chill.
Tear leaf lettuce into a large salad bowl. Add some sliced black olives and avocado. Mix in enough dressing to coat, and toss well. Serve individual salads topped with a few pieces of shaved Parmesan cheese. (Serves 6 - 8)

Use a vegetable peeler to shave Parmesan cheese.

SEAFOOD CANNELLONI

TOMATO SAUCE:

1 Tablespoon olive oil	3 Tablespoons tomato paste
1 small onion, chopped	3 Tablespoons sugar
1 clove garlic, minced	1/2 teaspoon basil
3 (1 lb) cans tomatoes, puréed	1/2 teaspoon oregano
	Salt & pepper to taste

Heat oil in a large saucepan over medium heat. Sauté onion and garlic until softened. Stir in remaining ingredients and bring to a boil. Lower heat and simmer, uncovered, for about 1 hour, stirring occasionally.

SEAFOOD FILLING:

1/4 cup butter or margarine	1 lb. crab meat, drained
1 lb. small shrimp, peeled	1/4 cup grated Parmesan cheese
1 cup coarsely chopped mushrooms	
1/2 cup chopped green onion	Salt & pepper to taste

Melt butter in a large skillet over medium high heat. Sauté shrimp until pink. Add mushrooms and green onions and cook for about 2 minutes. Gently stir in crab meat, cheese, salt and pepper. Remove from heat.

CREAM SAUCE:

6 Tablespoons butter or margarine	1/2 cup grated Parmesan cheese
6 Tablespoons flour	
2 cups half & half cream, heated	Salt & pepper to taste

Melt butter in a medium size saucepan over medium heat. Stir in flour and cook, stirring constantly, for 3 minutes. Add warm cream and stir until mixture comes to a boil and thickens. Mix in cheese, salt and pepper. Remove from heat and add half of cream sauce to the seafood filling.

PASTA:

1 (8 oz) pkg. manicotti-cannelloni pasta	1/4 cup grated Parmesan cheese
	1/4 cup chopped parsley

Preheat oven to 350°. Cook pasta in a large pot of boiling salted water until done, about 10 minutes. Drain well and place on paper towels to absorb any excess liquid. Spoon a layer of tomato sauce in the bottom of a large greased casserole. Spoon seafood filling generously into cooked pasta shells and arrange on top of tomato sauce. Spread pasta with remaining cream sauce and top with tomato sauce. Sprinkle with Parmesan cheese and parsley. Bake, uncovered, for about 30 minutes, until hot. (Serves 6 - 8)

The results are worth every minute of the several steps involved in this recipe. One of the best! Can be made ahead and reheated later.

LEMON TORTA

CRUST:
1/4 cup butter or margarine
1 1/2 oz. cream cheese
2/3 cup flour
1/2 teaspoon sugar

Preheat oven to $350°$. Cut up butter and cream cheese into a food processor and add flour and sugar. Process just until mixture forms a ball. Remove and roll out on a lightly floured surface. Press dough into the bottom and up the sides of a greased 9" shallow tart pan with a removable bottom.

FILLING:
2 eggs
3 Tablespoons melted butter
3 Tablespoons lemon juice
2/3 cup sugar
Powdered sugar
Whipped cream
Lemon zest for garnish

Place eggs, butter, lemon juice and sugar in a food processor and process for about 30 seconds. Pour filling into crust and bake for about 30 - 35 minutes until golden brown. Cool completely and chill. Before serving, sprinkle torta with powdered sugar. Serve each slice with a dab of whipped cream and lemon zest for garnish.

Especially for lemon lovers!

ITALIAN

ANTIPASTA
BAKED GNOCCHI
WITH SUN DRIED TOMATOES
POLLO LIMONESE
CHOCOLATE AMARETTO DOLCI

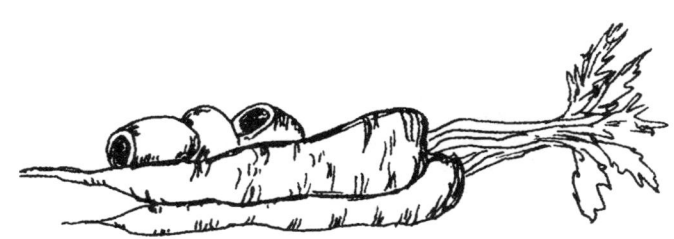

ANTIPASTA

2/3 cup white vinegar
2/3 cup olive oil
3 Tablespoons lemon juice
1/2 cup sugar
Dash of Tabasco
2 teaspoons oregano
1 teaspoon salt
1/2 teaspoon pepper

Mixture of fresh vegetables:
  broccoli, cauliflower,
  carrots, pepperoncini,
  artichoke hearts,
  mushrooms,
  black olives, red onion,
  green pepper, cucumber,
  cherry tomatoes, etc.
Leaf lettuce

Whisk together all ingredients for marinade. Place all vegetables, except tomatoes, in a large glass or plastic bowl and cover with marinade. Cover and refrigerate several hours or overnight, stirring occasionally.

To serve, arrange drained vegetables, including tomatoes, on lettuce leaves on a large platter. Serve with toothpicks or in small salad plates. (Serves 8 - 12)

A great way to serve a variety of vegetables!
Antipasta means "before the pasta".

BAKED GNOCCHI WITH SUN DRIED TOMATOES

4 cups milk
1 cup Farina (Quick Cream of Wheat)
1/4 cup butter or margarine
1 cup grated Romano cheese
1 teaspoon salt
1/4 teaspoon pepper

2 eggs, beaten
1/4 cup chopped sun dried tomatoes
1/4 teaspoon basil
Chopped parsley & slivers of sun dried tomatoes for garnish

Preheat oven to 350°. Heat milk in a large saucepan over medium high heat until hot but not boiling. Lower heat and slowly stir in Farina. Stir with a whisk until thickened, about 5 minutes. Remove from heat and add remaining ingredients, except for garnish.

Pour into a greased medium size baking dish. Bake about 30 minutes until set. To serve, cut into squares and garnish with some chopped parsley and a sliver of sun dried tomato. (Serves 8 - 10)

   *A nice change from pasta!*

POLLO LIMONESE

1/4 cup lemon juice
Zest of 1 lemon
1 clove garlic, minced
1/2 teaspoon salt
1/4 teaspoon pepper
1/2 teaspoon oregano
2 Tablespoons olive oil

6 - 8 boneless chicken breasts
1 pkg. fresh spinach, washed & trimmed

1 cup water
Salt & pepper
6 - 8 slices peeled tomato

2 Tablespoons butter or margarine
2 Tablespoons olive oil
Flour
1/4 cup water
Lemon twists for garnish

Mix marinade ingredients together in a small bowl with a whisk until combined. Place chicken breasts in a glass baking dish and cover with marinade. Cover with plastic wrap and marinate for 1 hour or longer in the refrigerator.

Cook spinach by bringing 1 cup of water to a boil in a medium saucepan over high heat. Add spinach and cook for 5 minutes. Drain well. Chop and season with salt and pepper. Also season tomato slices with salt and pepper. Place tomato slices in a greased baking dish and top with spinach.

Preheat oven to 350°. In a large skillet over medium heat, heat butter and oil. Remove chicken from marinade and reserve. Coat chicken with flour and sauté until browned on each side. Remove from skillet and place on top of spinach and tomato. Deglaze skillet with reserved marinade and 1/4 cup water, until heated through. Spoon glaze over chicken and place in oven for 15 minutes. Serve garnished with lemon twists. (Serves 6 - 8)

A very tangy, lemon flavored sauce---delizioso!

CHOCOLATE AMARETTO DOLCI

CHOCOLATE CREMA:

8 oz. semisweet chocolate
8 oz. cream cheese, softened
1/4 cup sugar
2 egg yolks

1 teaspoon vanilla
2 egg whites
1/4 cup sugar
1 cup heavy cream, whipped

Melt chocolate in top of a double boiler over simmering water.
With an electric mixer, beat cream cheese, sugar and egg yolks until smooth. Mix in vanilla and chocolate.
In another bowl, beat egg whites until soft peaks form. Gradually add sugar and beat until stiff. Gently fold into chocolate mixture. Then fold in whipped cream. Cover with plastic wrap directly on the surface and chill for several hours.

CAKE:

1 1/3 cups flour
1 cup sugar
3 Tablespoons cocoa
1/2 teaspoon baking soda
1/2 teaspoon salt

1 egg
1/3 cup vegetable oil
3/4 cup water
1/2 teaspoon vanilla

Preheat oven to 350°. Place flour, sugar, cocoa, soda and salt in a large mixing bowl. Beat with an electric mixer until combined. Add egg, oil, water and vanilla. Beat well, about 3 minutes, on medium speed. Pour evenly into a greased 9" round cake pan. Bake about 30 minutes until tested done. Cool in pan for 10 minutes. Turn out on a rack to cool completely.

TO ASSEMBLE:

1/4 cup apricot preserves, warmed
1/4 cup Amaretto
1 cup heavy cream

1 Tablespoon sugar
Toasted almond slices

Split cake in half horizontally and spread with warmed apricot preserves on bottom half. Replace top of cake and pierce all over with a fork. Drizzle with half of Amaretto. Turn cake over, pierce with a fork, and drizzle with remaining Amaretto. Cut cake into small bite size pieces.
In a trifle or glass bowl, place half of the chocolate crema in the bottom and up the sides of the bowl. Fill the center with half of the cake pieces. Top with remaining crema and then the cake pieces. Cover the top with whipped cream and place toasted almond slices around the border. Cover with plastic wrap and chill thoroughly before serving. (Serves 8 - 10)

An Italian version of an English Trifle, especially good because its chocolate!

FRIED MOZZARELLA MARINARA
ITALIAN VEGETABLE SALAD
CHICKEN MELANZANA
WITH ANGEL HAIR PASTA
ZABAGLIONE

FRIED MOZZARELLA MARINARA

MARINARA SAUCE:

2 Tablespoons olive oil
1/2 cup chopped onion
1 clove garlic, minced
1 (1 lb) can tomatoes, puréed & strained
1 Tablespoon tomato paste

1 Tablespoon minced parsley
1/2 teaspoon basil
1/2 teaspoon oregano
1/2 teaspoon sugar
1/4 teaspoon salt
Pepper to taste

Heat oil in a medium saucepan over medium heat. Sauté onion and garlic until soft. Add remaining ingredients and simmer uncovered for about 30 minutes.

The food processor can be used to chop onion and garlic; then to purée tomatoes.

FRIED MOZZARELLA:

12 oz. mozzarella cheese
2 eggs, beaten
Flour

Italian seasoned bread crumbs
Vegetable oil for frying

Cut mozzarella into squares or rectangles (3" x 2" x 1/2"). Dip each piece into eggs, then in flour, back in eggs and finally in bread crumbs to coat. Arrange in a single layer on a plate lined with wax paper and place in freezer for about 20 minutes.
To cook, heat oil in a large saucepan or deep fryer to 375°. Fry a few pieces at a time, very quickly, just until browned. Remove and place on paper towels to drain. Keep warm in a low oven until frying is completed.
To serve, place cheese on small plates and top with Marinara Sauce. (Serves 6)

Cheese lovers will adore this dish!

ITALIAN VEGETABLE SALAD

Mixed vegetables: tomatoes, avocado, artichoke hearts, cauliflower, broccoli, celery, carrots, black olives, green olives, etc.

1/4 cup red wine vinegar
3/4 cup olive oil
1/4 teaspoon basil
Leaf lettuce
Grated Romano cheese
Salt & pepper to taste

Chop desired vegetables into small pieces. Combine vinegar, olive oil and basil. Mix vegetables with dressing. Toss with lettuce and Romano cheese. Season with salt and pepper. (Serves 6)

CHICKEN MELANZANA WITH ANGEL HAIR PASTA

4 Tablespoons vegetable oil, divided
1 medium eggplant, peeled & sliced
6 boneless chicken breasts
Salt & pepper to taste
1/2 cup butter or margarine, divided
1 onion, chopped
2 cloves garlic, minced
1/2 green pepper, chopped

2 zucchini, sliced
1 (1 lb) can tomatoes, puréed
1 (8 oz) can tomato sauce
2 Tablespoons chopped parsley
1/4 teaspoon basil
1/4 teaspoon oregano
1/4 teaspoon thyme
1 (1 lb) pkg. angel hair pasta

Grated Romano cheese

Heat 2 Tablespoons oil in a large skillet over medium heat. Sauté eggplant in two batches, using other 2 Tablespoons oil for second batch. Drain eggplant on paper towels and place in a large greased baking dish.

Season chicken breasts with salt and pepper. Melt 1/4 cup butter in a large skillet over medium heat and brown chicken, in two batches, if necessary. Place over eggplant.

Preheat oven to 350°. Heat remaining 1/4 cup butter and sauté onion, garlic and green pepper until softened. Add zucchini, tomatoes, tomato sauce and seasonings. Cook for about 10 minutes. Pour over chicken and eggplant. Cover with foil and bake for about 1 hour.

Cook angel hair pasta in a large pot of salted boiling water until done. Strain and serve immediately with chicken, eggplant and sauce over pasta. Top with Romano cheese. (Serves 6)

Try this dish, even if you don't like eggplant (melanzana), it's a super combination of ingredients!

ZABAGLIONE

5 egg yolks
1 whole egg
2 Tablespoons sugar
1/4 cup Amaretto

1 pt. fresh strawberries, washed, hulled & sliced
1/2 cup whipping cream, whipped with 1 Tablespoon powdered sugar

Combine egg yolks, egg and sugar in top of a double boiler over simmering water. Beat with a wire whisk until pale yellow and creamy, about 5 minutes.

Stir in Amaretto and continue beating until custard becomes thick and starts to hold its shape on a spoon, about 8 - 10 minutes.

Remove from heat and place bowl over ice cubes and beat until cooled. Spoon into wine glasses and chill.

Serve topped with sliced strawberries and whipped cream. (Serves 6)

A delicious custard sauce usually made with Marsala wine; it's even better with Amaretto!

STUFFED ARTICHOKE LEAVES
SALSA DI POMODORI
VEAL MOZZARELLA
CIOCCOLATO CREMA

STUFFED ARTICHOKE LEAVES

1 medium artichoke
Salt & pepper
1/4 cup chopped onion
1/4 cup chopped celery
1/4 cup chopped green onion
2 Tablespoons chopped parsley
1/4 cup grated Parmesan cheese
1 clove garlic, minced
1/2 cup Italian seasoned
  bread crumbs
Dash of cayenne pepper
2 Tablespoons olive oil,
  divided
1 Tablespoon lemon juice

Trim tips of artichoke leaves and cut off stem. Rinse well, opening up leaves. Drain. Season with salt and pepper. Combine stuffing ingredients with 1 Tablespoon olive oil and stuff leaves. Place in a medium saucepan and top with 1 Tablespoon olive oil and lemon juice. Add enough water to reach half way up artichoke. Cover and bring to a boil over high heat. Lower fire and cook, basting occasionally, for about 1 hour.

To serve, pull off leaves and arrange on a serving plate. (Serves 6 - 8)

Can be made ahead, covered and reheated in the oven. Makes a great appetizer as well as a light meal!

SALSA DI POMODORI

2 Tablespoons olive oil
1 onion, chopped
2 cloves garlic, minced
2 Tablespoons chopped parsley
1 teaspoon oregano
1 teaspoon basil
4 (14 oz) cans peeled tomatoes
2 (12 oz) cans tomato paste
1 tomato paste can of water
3 Tablespoons sugar,
  or more
Salt & pepper to taste

Heat oil in a large saucepan over medium heat. Sauté onion and garlic until softened. Add all other ingredients. Simmer for 2 - 3 hours, covered, stirring occasionally. Taste for seasonings. (Makes 2 1/2 qts.)

Some canned tomatoes are bitter; add more sugar to compensate.

VEAL MOZZARELLA

4 - 6 veal cutlets
Salt & pepper
1 egg, lightly beaten with
1 Tablespoon water

Italian seasoned bread
 crumbs
Vegetable oil
Slices of mozzarella cheese

Preheat oven to 350°. Season veal with salt and pepper. Dip in egg, then in bread crumbs to coat. Pour a thin layer of oil in a large skillet over medium high heat. Brown veal on both sides. Remove to an ovenproof dish and cover each piece with a slice of mozzarella cheese. Heat in oven until cheese has melted. Serve with Salsa di Pomodori and pasta. (Serves 4 - 6)

Chicken may be substituted for veal.

CIOCCOLATO CREMA

1/2 cup semisweet chocolate chips
3 Tablespoons Amaretto
2 Tablespoons butter
1 cup whipping cream

1/2 cup whipping cream
1 Tablespoon sugar
1 1/2 teaspoons Amaretto
1/4 teaspoon vanilla

Heat chocolate chips, Amaretto and butter in top of a double boiler, over simmering water, until melted. Cool to room temperature; do not let mixture set. Beat 1 cup whipping cream until stiff peaks form and gently fold into chocolate mixture. Spoon into wine glasses and chill.
Beat 1/2 cup whipping cream with sugar, Amaretto and vanilla until stiff peaks forms. Chill.
To serve, top each chocolate mixture with a dollop of whipped cream. (Serves 4)

Better than the average chocolate mousse--- an Italian mousse!

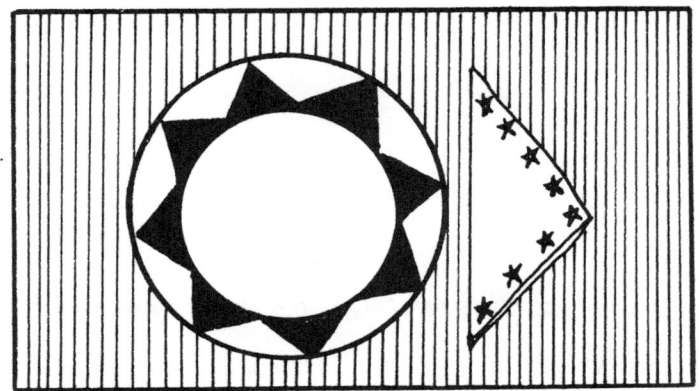

PHYLLO PASTRY

MENUS

**JUMBO SHRIMP PHYLLO
WITH JEZEBEL SAUCE
CHICKEN PHYLLO PIES
PHYLLO CHEESECAKE TARTLETS**

**PHYLLO HORS D'OEUVRES
SEAFOOD STRUDEL
PINEAPPLE CHEESE PIE**

Although phyllo pastry is not difficult to handle, it does take some patience when working with it. The secret is to not let the dough dry out. Try a few of the class recipes and you'll be an expert in no time. All recipes in these classes use phyllo pastry, so you may want to pair them up with other menus for variety.

HANDLING PHYLLO PASTRY

There are about 22 sheets of phyllo in a one pound package (14" x 18") of frozen dough. To use, thaw in the refrigerator overnight. When ready to shape, cut open the short end of the sealed package (save package). Unroll phyllo and place on 2 sheets of wax paper. Lay wax paper on top of a damp towel. Cover exposed phyllo with 2 more sheets of wax paper and lay a damp towel on top. Do not let the damp towel directly touch the phyllo. Remember to always keep phyllo sheets covered after removing any sheets, to keep dough from drying out and tearing. After using desired amount of phyllo, cover completely with wax paper and roll up. Place in original package and return to refrigerator. An opened package will keep in the refrigerator for about 1 week.

JUMBO SHRIMP PHYLLO WITH JEZEBEL SAUCE
CHICKEN PHYLLO PIES
PHYLLO CHEESECAKE TARTLETS

JUMBO SHRIMP PHYLLO WITH JEZEBEL SAUCE

24 jumbo shrimp, peeled & deveined, with tails left on
Salt & pepper
1/2 cup olive oil
2 cloves garlic, minced
1/4 cup lemon juice
6 sheets of phyllo pastry
1/2 cup melted butter or margarine
4 Tablespoons plain bread crumbs

Season shrimp with salt and pepper. Mix olive oil, garlic and lemon juice together and pour over shrimp. Marinate at least 1/2 hour or longer.

Place 1 sheet of phyllo on a work surface and brush with butter. Sprinkle with 1 Tablespoon bread crumbs and top with another sheet, butter, bread crumbs, and a third sheet, brushed with butter (no bread crumbs on top sheet). Cut pastry into 1" wide strips (about 12), using a pizza wheel or paring knife. Remove a shrimp from the marinade and wrap one strip around each shrimp, starting at the tail end, leaving tail exposed. Place on a greased foil lined baking sheet. Repeat layering procedure with 3 more sheets of phyllo, butter and bread crumbs and cut into strips to wrap remaining shrimp. Brush outside of wrapped shrimp with melted butter.

Preheat oven to 375°. Bake shrimp for about 15 minutes, until golden. Serve with Jezebel sauce. (Serves 6 - 8)

(Continued on next page)

JEZEBEL SAUCE

1/2 cup pineapple preserves
1/2 cup apple jelly

1 1/2 teaspoons Dijon
   mustard
1 Tablespoon horseradish

    Stir all ingredients together until combined. Can be heated slightly in the microwave or served at room temperature.

CHICKEN PHYLLO PIES

1/4 cup butter or margarine
4 boneless chicken breasts, cubed
Salt & pepper
1/2 cup chopped onion
1/2 cup chopped celery
1/2 cup chopped carrot
1/2 cup chopped red potato
1/2 cup flour
2 cups chicken broth

1 cup half & half cream
1 teaspoon poultry seasoning
Salt & pepper
1/2 cup frozen green peas,
   thawed
1/4 cup chopped parsley
12 sheets of phyllo pastry
3/4 cup melted butter or
   or margarine
3/4 cup plain bread crumbs

    Melt butter in a large skillet or saucepan over medium high heat. Season chicken with salt and pepper and sauté until no longer pink. Add onion, celery, carrot and potato. Sauté until tender. Stir in flour and cook, stirring frequently, for about 1 minute. Add chicken broth and bring to a boil. Stir in half & half, poultry seasoning, salt, pepper, peas and parsley. Cook until thoroughly heated.
    Place one sheet of phyllo on a work surface, brush with melted butter and sprinkle with 1 Tablespoon bread crumbs. Repeat, using 5 more sheets of phyllo, brushing with butter and bread crumbs between each sheet (no bread crumbs on top sheet). Cut out 4 circles of dough to fit individual ovenproof casseroles. Repeat layering with a stack of 6 more sheets, cutting out 4 more circles of dough, for a total of 8 circles.
    Preheat oven to 375°. Spoon chicken and vegetable filling into 8 individual greased ovenproof casseroles. Top each with cut out phyllo circles. Make 4 slits in the top of each pastry. Bake about 20 minutes. (Serves 6 - 8)

Frozen chicken pot pies never tasted this good!

PHYLLO CHEESECAKE TARTLETS

4 sheets of phyllo pastry
1/4 cup melted butter or margarine
3 teaspoons sugar
8 oz. cream cheese, cut up
1/2 cup sugar

1 egg
1 teaspoon almond extract
Sliced almonds
Powdered sugar

Place one sheet of phyllo on a work surface, brush with melted butter and sprinkle with 1 teaspoon sugar. Repeat with 3 more sheets, butter and sugar (no sugar on top sheet). Using a 3" round cookie cutter, cut out 24 circles and place into greased mini-muffin tins.

Preheat oven to 375°. Make filling by placing cream cheese, sugar, egg and almond extract into a food processor. Process until smooth. Place 1 Tablespoon filling into each tartlet shell. Top with some sliced almonds and bake about 15 minutes. Cool in pan 5 minutes. Remove and cool on paper towels, to absorb any excess butter. Sprinkle with powdered sugar. Chill until ready to serve. (Makes 24)

A different version of the mini-cheesecake!

PHYLLO HORS D'OEUVRES
SEAFOOD STRUDEL
PINEAPPLE CHEESE PIE

PHYLLO HORS D'OEUVRES

FILLINGS:

I. 2 Tablespoons olive oil
1/2 cup chopped onion
1 (10 oz) pkg. frozen chopped spinach, cooked & drained
1/4 cup crumbled feta cheese
1 egg, beaten
Salt & pepper to taste

Heat oil in a small skillet over medium heat. Sauté onion until softened. Combine with spinach, cheese, egg, salt and pepper.

II. 1/2 cup chopped green onion
1/4 cup chopped parsley
1 cup chopped mushrooms
1/2 cup sour cream
1 cup grated Monterey Jack cheese
1/2 cup grated cheddar cheese
Salt & pepper to taste

Stir all ingredients together to combine.

III. 1 cup chopped ham
1 cup grated Swiss cheese
1 teaspoon Dijon mustard
3 Tablespoons mayonnaise
Pepper to taste

Stir all ingredients together to combine.

IV. 1/2 lb. loose pork sausage
6 eggs
1/4 cup milk
Salt & pepper to taste
1/2 cup grated cheddar cheese

Cook sausage in a large skillet over medium heat, until browned. Drain well. Whisk eggs with milk, salt and pepper. Place skillet over medium heat and cook until eggs are scrambled. Mix sausage, scrambled eggs and cheese together.

(Continued on next page)

SHAPES:

Triangles - use 1 sheet of phyllo and cut into 4 strips. Brush with melted butter or margarine. Place 1 teaspoon filling on lower left corner of each strip of dough. Fold right corner over filling, forming a triangle. Continue folding, as if folding a flag, into a triangle.

Spirals - use 1 sheet of phyllo and cut in half. Brush with melted butter and roll each piece up diagonally. Shape into a tight spiral. Place 1 teaspoon of filling in the center.

Kisses - use 1 sheet of phyllo and brush with melted butter. Cover with a second sheet; brush with butter. Cut into 16 squares. Place 1 teaspoon filling in center of each square, pinch corners together on top and twist.

Rolls - use 1 sheet of phyllo and brush with melted butter. Cut into 4 strips. Place 1 teaspoon filling near the bottom of each strip. Roll up as a cigar, folding sides in as you roll.

TO BAKE:

Preheat oven to 375°. As each pastry is filled, place on a greased foil lined baking sheet and brush with melted butter to keep moist.

Bake for about 15 minutes or until golden brown. Remove and place on paper towels to absorb excess butter. Serve warm.

Pastries can be frozen before or after baking and reheated when ready to serve.

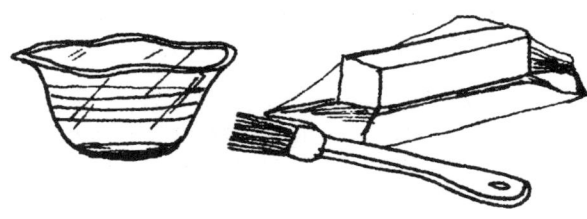

SEAFOOD STRUDEL

1 lb. medium shrimp, boiled & peeled
1/2 lb. crab meat
2 hard boiled eggs, chopped
1 cup sour cream
1/4 cup chopped green onion
1/4 cup chopped parsley
1 clove garlic, minced
Salt & pepper to taste

CRUMB MIXTURE:
1 cup Italian seasoned bread crumbs
1/4 cup grated Parmesan cheese
1/4 teaspoon dry mustard

1/2 lb. phyllo pastry
1 cup melted butter or margarine

MORNAY SAUCE:
3 Tablespoons butter
3 Tablespoons flour
2 cups half & half, heated
1 cup grated Swiss cheese
Salt & white pepper to taste

Parsley for garnish

Reserve 8 shrimp for garnish. Mix together remaining shrimp, crab, eggs, sour cream, green onions, parsley, garlic, salt and pepper for filling.

In another bowl, mix together bread crumbs, Parmesan cheese and dry mustard.

To prepare strudel, place a damp towel on counter and cover with wax paper. Unfold phyllo sheets onto wax paper. Fold towel, wax paper and phyllo in half like a book. Turn back the first sheet of phyllo, brush with butter and sprinkle with crumb mixture. Continue brushing and sprinkling with one half of the "book". Close book and start with last sheet of phyllo, working toward the center, brushing and sprinkling.

Preheat oven to 375^0. Place filling on the lower third of dough, tuck in ends and roll up jelly roll style using the towel to help roll. Place seam side down a greased foil lined baking sheet and brush entire roll with melted butter.

Bake for 10 minutes. Remove from oven and cut diagonal slices through strudel with a serrated knife. Push slices back together, return to oven and bake 30 minutes more.

Make mornay sauce by melting butter in a small saucepan over medium heat. Stir in flour and cook about 3 minutes. Add the heated cream and stir until smooth and thickened. Remove from heat, add Swiss cheese and stir until melted. Season with salt & white pepper.

Serve each slice of strudel with mornay sauce; top with a shrimp and a sprig of parsley. (Serves 8 - 10)

Cutting the strudel before it gets too crisp makes it easier to handle.

PHYLLO PASTRY

PINEAPPLE CHEESE PIE

1/3 cup sugar
1 Tablespoon cornstarch
1 (8 oz) can crushed pineapple, drained
1 (8 oz) pkg. cream cheese, softened
1/2 cup sugar

1/2 teaspoon salt
2 eggs
1/4 cup milk
1/2 teaspoon vanilla
1/4 cup chopped pecans
12 sheets phyllo pastry
1/2 cup melted butter or margarine

Place sugar, cornstarch and pineapple in a saucepan over medium heat. Cook until thickened and clear. Remove and cool.

Beat cream cheese with an electric mixer or food processor until smooth. Add sugar, salt, eggs, milk and vanilla. Mix until combined.

Preheat oven to 375°. Grease a 9" pie pan and place 1 sheet of phyllo dough inside pan, letting excess hang over sides of pie pan. Brush lightly with butter and repeat with 5 more sheets, buttering between each sheet.

Pour pineapple mixture into pan, top with cream cheese mixture and sprinkle with chopped pecans. Cover with 6 more sheets of phyllo, brushing with butter between each sheet and on top. Trim excess dough to fit to the edge of the pie pan. Bake for 30 minutes until golden brown. Cool and refrigerate until firm before cutting. (Serves 8 - 10)

Phyllo gives this pie an interesting crust and the pineapple cream cheese mixture is an added bonus.

QUICK & EASY

MENUS

EASY SPINACH SOUP
THOUSAND ISLAND SALAD WEDGES
CHICKEN DIJON PASTA
PEANUT BUTTER FUDGED ICE CREAM

CREAM OF ASPARAGUS SOUP
ORANGE ALMOND SALAD
FETTUCCINE WITH
ARTICHOKE SAUCE
VEAL LIMONE
BANANAS FOSTER

CREAMY GARLIC SALAD
SCHNITZEL HOLSTEIN
POTATO SAUTÉ
APPLE CRISP

ZUCCHINI SOUP
SPICY FRENCH DRESSING
SPAGHETTI PIE
HOT FUDGE SAUCE

Every cook looks for new and different, quick & easy recipes when time is of the essence. These classes give you the option of preparing several courses within a reasonable amount of time. All you need are the ingredients and you can present a wonderful, quick & easy gourmet meal!

EASY SPINACH SOUP
THOUSAND ISLAND SALAD WEDGES
CHICKEN DIJON PASTA
PEANUT BUTTER FUDGED ICE CREAM

EASY SPINACH SOUP

- 2 cups chicken broth
- 2 (10 oz) pkgs. frozen chopped spinach
- 1/2 cup chopped onion
- 2 Tablespoons butter or margarine
- 2 Tablespoons flour
- 2 cups milk, warmed
- 1 teaspoon Worcestershire sauce
- Salt & pepper to taste
- Dash of Tabasco
- Grated cheddar cheese

Place broth, spinach and onion in a large saucepan over high heat. Bring to a boil, cover and reduce heat to low. Cook for 10 minutes.

Melt butter in a 2 cup glass measuring cup in the microwave on medium heat. Stir in flour to form a paste. Cook for 1 minute on high. Whisk in warmed milk and add to spinach mixture. Season with Worcestershire, salt, pepper and Tabasco. Bring to a boil. Purée soup for a smoother texture, if desired. Serve garnished with cheddar cheese. (Serves 4 - 6)

THOUSAND ISLAND SALAD WEDGES

- 1 cup mayonnaise
- 1/2 cup sour cream
- 1/2 cup chili sauce
- 3 Tablespoons sweet pickle relish
- 1 teaspoon sugar
- 1 teaspoon Worcestershire sauce
- Dash of Tabasco
- 1 or 2 heads of iceberg lettuce
- Thin slices of red onion

Combine all ingredients for dressing together and chill. (Makes 2 cups)

To serve, cut lettuce into 4 - 6 wedges. Place on a individual salad plates, top with slices of red onion and cover with dressing. (Serves 6)

Class Notes

Just measure, assemble and serve!

CHICKEN DIJON PASTA

1 lb. chicken breast fillets
Salt & pepper to taste
4 teaspoons Dijon mustard
2 Tablespoons butter or margarine
1/2 cup chopped green onion
1 clove garlic, minced
3 - 4 cups of cut up broccoli, cauliflower, carrots, squash, zucchini (any or all)

1 lb. thin pasta or vermicelli
1 cup chicken broth
1 cup heavy cream
Salt & pepper to taste
Grated Romano or Parmesan cheese

Place a large pot of water over high heat and bring to a boil.
Cut up chicken into bite size pieces. Season with salt, pepper and Dijon mustard.
In a large skillet over medium high heat, melt butter. Sauté chicken, stirring frequently, until no longer pink. Lower heat and add green onions and garlic. Sauté about 2 minutes.
Meanwhile, add vegetables to boiling water and cook 5 minutes. Then add pasta and cook until tender.
Add broth and cream to chicken mixture and heat thoroughly.
Drain pasta and vegetables. Mix with chicken and season with salt, pepper and cheese. (Serves 6)

Dijon mustard adds a lot of flavor to this easy pasta dish.

PEANUT BUTTER FUDGED ICE CREAM

1 (8 oz) carton soft cream cheese
1 (14 oz) can sweetened condensed milk
1 cup creamy peanut butter

4 oz. (1/2 carton) Cool Whip, thawed
1 oz. semisweet chocolate
2 Tablespoons milk

In a large bowl, stir together cream cheese, condensed milk and peanut butter until smooth. Fold in cool whip. Pour into a greased 9" square pan.
Melt chocolate and milk in the microwave, on medium heat, for 1 minute. Stir until smooth. Drizzle over peanut butter mixture. Freeze. (Serves 12)

A favorite of peanut butter lovers!

CREAMY GARLIC SALAD
SCHNITZEL HOLSTEIN
POTATO SAUTÉ
APPLE CRISP

CREAMY GARLIC SALAD

1 clove garlic
2 Tablespoons parsley
1/4 cup sour cream
2 Tablespoons sugar
1/2 teaspoon dry mustard

1 teaspoon salt
1/2 teaspoon pepper
1/4 cup red wine vinegar
1 cup vegetable oil
Leaf lettuce, tomatoes, avocado

Using a food processor fitted with the metal blade, turn machine on and drop garlic and parsley through the feed tube until chopped. Turn machine off and add sour cream, sugar, dry mustard, salt, pepper and vinegar. With machine running, slowly pour in oil through feed tube, until combined. Place in a covered jar and refrigerate.

Make individual salads of leaf lettuce, tomatoes and avocado. Top with garlic dressing. (Makes 1 1/3 cups dressing)

SCHNITZEL HOLSTEIN

4 veal cutlets
Salt & pepper to taste
1 egg beaten with 1 Tablespoon water
3/4 - 1 cup Italian seasoned bread crumbs

1/4 cup vegetable oil
1 Tablespoon lemon juice
4 eggs
Salt & pepper

Lay out veal on wax paper and season with salt and pepper. Dip each piece into egg, then coat with bread crumbs. Heat oil in a large skillet over medium high heat. Brown veal on both sides. Top with lemon juice.

While veal is browning on second side, cook eggs, over light, in a separate greased skillet over medium heat. Season with salt and pepper.

Top each piece of veal with an egg. (Serves 4)

 *This recipe becomes Wiener Schnitzel when the eggs are omitted.*

POTATO SAUTÉ

4 medium red potatoes
Salt & pepper to taste
2 Tablespoons vegetable oil
1 small onion, sliced thin

1/4 green pepper, chopped
1 Tablespoon chopped
  pimiento
Salt & pepper to taste
1 Tablespoon butter

Peel and slice potatoes thin. Season with salt and pepper. Heat oil in a large skillet over medium heat. Sauté potatoes, stirring and turning frequently for about 10 minutes. Add remaining ingredients and turn lower heat to low. Cover and cook until tender, stirring frequently, about 15 minutes. Reduce heat if browning too much. (Serves 4 - 6)

 *Can top with grated cheddar cheese for variation.*

APPLE CRISP

3 medium red delicious apples
1 cup flour
3/4 cup light brown sugar
1 teaspoon cinnamon

1/2 teaspoon ground nutmeg
1/4 cup chopped pecans
1/2 cup butter
Vanilla ice cream

Preheat oven to $350°$. Peel, core and cut apples in half. Cut into thin slices. Put in a greased 9" or 10" baking dish.
Place flour, sugar, cinnamon, nutmeg and pecans in a large bowl. Cut in butter until crumbly. Sprinkle over apples.
Bake for 40 minutes until browned. Serve warm with ice cream. (Serves 6 - 8)

CREAM OF ASPARAGUS SOUP
ORANGE ALMOND SALAD
FETTUCCINE WITH ARTICHOKE SAUCE
VEAL LIMONE
BANANAS FOSTER

CREAM OF ASPARAGUS SOUP

1 large bunch fresh asparagus
1/4 cup butter
1 small onion, chopped
2 cups chicken broth
1 Tablespoon lemon juice
1 cup half & half cream
1 teaspoon tarragon
Salt & white pepper to taste

Cut off rough ends of asparagus and steam or boil about 8 minutes. Drain, cut off tips and reserve. Melt butter in a medium saucepan over medium heat. Sauté onion until softened. Add chicken broth and lemon juice. Place soup in a food processor or blender and add cooked asparagus stalks. Purée until smooth. Return to saucepan and add cream and seasonings. Heat thoroughly over low heat.

Serve garnished with asparagus tips on top. (Serves 4 - 6)

ORANGE ALMOND SALAD

3/4 cup sugar
1 teaspoon dry mustard
1 teaspoon salt
1/3 cup cider vinegar
1 cup vegetable oil
Leaf Lettuce
1 (11 oz) can mandarin
  oranges, chilled & drained
1/2 cup chopped green onion
1/2 cup slivered almonds,
  toasted

Combine sugar, mustard, salt and vinegar in a food processor. With machine running, add oil through feed tube until combined. Chill.

To serve, prepare individual plates of lettuce, oranges, green onion and almonds. Spoon dressing over salads. (Serves 6)

A great combination of flavors with a sweet and tangy dressing.

FETTUCCINE WITH ARTICHOKE SAUCE

1/4 cup butter
1 Tablespoon flour
1 clove garlic, minced
1 cup chicken broth
2 teaspoons lemon juice
1 teaspoon paprika

Salt & pepper to taste
1/2 cup slivered ham
1 (14 oz) can artichoke hearts,
   drained & sliced
1/2 cup grated Romano
   cheese
8 oz. fettuccine

Melt butter in a large saucepan over medium heat. Add flour and cook, stirring constantly, for 3 minutes. Add garlic and sauté lightly. Add other ingredients, except pasta and gently simmer until thoroughly heated.
Meanwhile, cook fettuccine in a large pot of salted boiling water until done. Add to sauce and stir to coat. Serve immediately. (Serves 4 - 6)

Sauce can be made ahead and reheated before mixing with pasta.

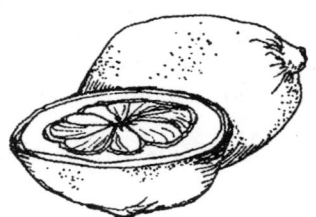

VEAL LIMONE

4 - 6 veal cutlets
Salt & pepper to taste
2 Tablespoons butter
2 Tablespoons oil
Flour

Juice of 1 lemon
2 Tablespoons chopped
   parsley
Lemon twists for garnish

Season veal with salt and pepper. Heat butter and oil in a large skillet over medium high heat. Dredge veal with flour and sauté on both sides until browned. Remove from skillet and add lemon juice to deglaze, scraping up any browned bits. Add chopped parsley, remove from heat and spoon over veal. Serve immediately garnished with a lemon twist. (Serves 4 - 6)

Chicken or fish are also good substitutes.

BANANAS FOSTER

2 Tablespoons butter
3 Tablespoons light brown sugar
1/2 teaspoon cinnamon
2 bananas, sliced lengthwise & in half crosswise

1/4 cup banana liqueur
1/4 cup rum

Vanilla ice cream

Melt butter in a large skillet over low heat. Add sugar and cinnamon and mix well. Add bananas and sauté until they begin to soften. Pour in liqueur and simmer gently. Meanwhile, heat rum in a separate saucepan until it begins to boil. Quickly add to skillet and ignite, very carefully.

When flame dies down, spoon two slices of banana with sauce over inidividual bowls of ice cream. Serve immediately. (Serves 4)

Not just for brunch anymore!

ZUCCHINI SOUP
SPICY FRENCH DRESSING
SPAGHETTI PIE
HOT FUDGE SAUCE

ZUCCHINI SOUP

2 slices bacon, cut up
3 cups zucchini, cubed
2 cups beef broth
1/2 teaspoon basil
Salt & pepper to taste

1 small onion, quartered
1 clove garlic
2 Tablespoons chopped parsley
Grated Parmesan cheese

In a large saucepan, fry bacon over medium heat until crisp. Add zucchini, beef broth, basil, salt and pepper.

Chop onion and garlic in a food processor. Add to saucepan along with parsley. Cook about 15 - 20 minutes.

Pour soup into food processor and purée until smooth. Return to saucepan and reheat. Taste for seasonings and serve with Parmesan cheese. (Serves 4)

SPICY FRENCH DRESSING

3/4 cup vegetable oil
1/4 cup red wine vinegar
1 teaspoon salt
1/4 teaspoon pepper

1/2 teaspoon dry mustard
1/2 teaspoon paprika
1/2 teaspoon Worcestershire
Dash of Tabasco

Combine all ingredients and mix thoroughly. Chill. (Makes 1 cup)
Make a large salad of leaf lettuce, cherry tomatoes, avocado, artichoke hearts, sunflower seeds and grated Romano cheese. Toss with dressing. (Serves 6)

SPAGHETTI PIE

1 lb. lean ground beef
1/2 cup chopped onion
1/4 green pepper, chopped
1 clove garlic, minced
1 (8 oz) can tomato sauce
1 (6 oz) can tomato paste
1 teaspoon sugar
1 teaspoon oregano
1/2 cup water

1/2 cup sliced mushrooms
Salt & pepper to taste
8 oz. thin spaghetti
2 Tablespoons butter
1/3 cup grated Parmesan
  cheese
2 eggs, beaten
1 cup grated mozzarella
  cheese

In a large skillet over medium high heat, brown ground beef. Drain off fat. Add onion, green pepper and garlic. Sauté until tender. Stir in tomato sauce, paste, sugar, oregano, water, mushrooms, salt and pepper. Simmer about 15 minutes.
Preheat oven to 350°. Meanwhile, cook spaghetti in a large pot of boiling salted water until done. Drain and mix with butter, cheese and eggs. Place in a greased 10" baking dish or pie pan, forming a crust.
Ladle the meat mixture into the spaghetti crust. Bake for 20 minutes. Sprinkle mozzarella cheese on top of pie and bake another 5 minutes, until cheese melts. Cut into wedges. (Serves 6)

Kids will love this one!

BEA'S HOT FUDGE SAUCE

2 oz. unsweetened chocolate
1/2 cup water
1/4 cup sugar

1 (14 oz) can sweetened condensed milk

Cook chocolate and water in top of a double boiler over simmering water until melted. Add sugar and condensed milk. Stir occasionally and simmer until thickened. Pour in a jar and store in refrigerator. Can be reheated in microwave before serving over vanilla ice cream. [Adapted from a recipe by Bea Miceli]

This delicious sauce keeps for several weeks, if it lasts that long!

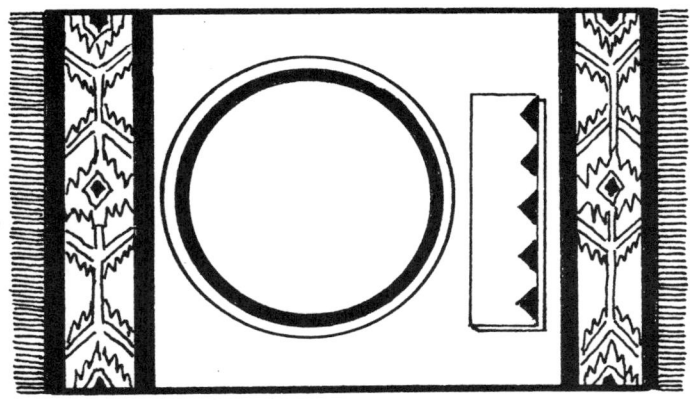

SOUTHWESTERN

MENUS

AVOCADO SALSA
CORN TORTILLA SOUP
SANTA FE CHICKEN & CORNBREAD
SALSA FRESCA
MONTEREY FLAN

SHRIMP GAZPACHO SALAD
FIESTA CORN RELISH
PEPPERED BEEF BRISKET
GREEN CHILIE POTATOES
ADOBE CHOCOLATE CAKE

A combination of regional cuisines gives Southwestern foods a wide appeal. These classes make for great entertaining menus, since most recipes can be prepared in advance.

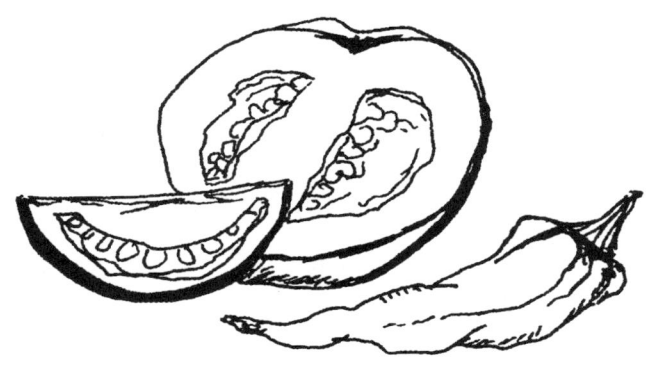

SALSA FRESCA

1 (1 lb) can whole tomatoes
Juice of 1 lime
2 teaspoons cider vinegar
1 clove garlic, minced
1 (4 oz) can green chilies, chopped

1/2 teaspoon cumin
1/4 teaspoon salt
1/4 teaspoon sugar
1 Tablespoon minced parsley
2 teaspoons chopped jalapeño pepper or more

Place tomatoes in a bowl and coarsely chop with a knife and fork. Add all other ingredients and mix together. Store in the refrigerator in a covered container.

Delicious served as a dip with tortilla chips.
Lime juice is the key ingredient!

MONTEREY FLAN

CUSTARD:
2 cups whole milk
1/2 cup heavy cream
1/2 cup whole milk
1/2 cup sugar
3 Tablespoons cornstarch
Pinch of salt
2 egg yolks, lightly beaten
1 teaspoon almond extract

Preheat oven to $325°$. Grease 6 custard cups or ramekins. Scald 2 cups milk and 1/2 cup heavy cream in a medium saucepan over medium heat. Remove from heat, but leave fire on.

In a small bowl, combine remaining 1/2 cup milk, sugar, cornstarch and salt until dissolved. Stir into scalded milk, return to heat and cook, stirring constantly, until mixture boils, about 6 minutes. Remove from heat. Gradually add about 1/3 of hot milk mixture to egg yolks while whisking vigorously. Pour this mixture back into hot milk. Stirring constantly, bring to a boil and cook about 3 minutes. Remove from heat and add almond extract. Fill each custard cup about 2/3 full.

TOPPING:
1 oz. semisweet chocolate
3 Tablespoons heavy cream
2 egg whites
3 Tablespoons sugar
Toasted sliced almonds for garnish

Melt chocolate and cream in top of a double boiler over simmering water. Remove from heat.

Beat egg whites with an electric mixer until frothy. Gradually add sugar and beat to form soft peaks. Stir 1/3 beaten egg whites into melted chocolate, beating rapidly with a whisk. Fold in remaining beaten egg whites until combined. Top each custard with chocolate mixture.

Place filled cups in a large baking pan and pour hot water in pan to come up 2/3 way on cups.

Bake until loosely set, about 45 minutes. Remove cups from water and cool on a rack. Chill.

To serve, turn out custards onto dessert plates and top with some toasted sliced almonds. (Serves 6)

```
╔══════════════════════════════════╗
║   SHRIMP GAZPACHO SALAD          ║
║   FIESTA CORN RELISH             ║
║   PEPPERED BEEF BRISKET          ║
║   GREEN CHILIE POTATOES          ║
║   ADOBE CHOCOLATE CAKE           ║
╚══════════════════════════════════╝
```

SHRIMP GAZPACHO SALAD

1/4 cup olive oil
1/4 cup vegetable oil
Juice of 1 lime
1 clove garlic, peeled & mashed
2 Tablespoons chopped green onion
2 Tablespoons chopped parsley
1/2 teaspoon salt
1/4 teaspoon pepper
1/4 teaspoon cumin
Dash of Tabasco

1 cucumber, peeled, seeded & chopped
1/4 green pepper, slivered
3 tomatoes, peeled & chopped
1 avocado, peeled & chopped
1 cup sliced celery
1 carrot, peeled & slivered
1/2 lb. boiled shrimp, peeled
Leaf lettuce, sliced black olives, tortilla chips

Mix together dressing ingredients and chill. Combine all prepared vegetables in a large bowl. Chill.
When ready to serve, place a layer of leaf lettuce in a large platter. Top with shrimp and mixed vegetables. Remove garlic from dressing and pour over vegetables. Top with black olives and garnish with Tortilla chips around edge of platter. (Serves 6 - 8)

 *All of the ingredients of a traditional Gazpacho make this a super appetizer.*

FIESTA CORN RELISH

2 (11 oz) cans whole kernel corn, drained
2 zucchini, diced
1 small jar chopped pimiento
1/2 cup vegetable oil

1 teaspoon lemon juice
1/2 teaspoon cumin
1/4 teaspoon sugar
Salt & pepper to taste
1 (15 oz) can black beans, drained & rinsed

Mix all ingredients together. Chill at least one hour before serving. (Serves 6)

PEPPERED BEEF BRISKET

1 (4 - 5 lb) beef brisket, market trimmed
Salt, pepper, chili powder
1 (14 oz) can stewed tomatoes
1 (10 oz) can Ro-Tel tomatoes

3 Tablespoons olive oil
1 onion, sliced
1 clove garlic, minced

3 green bell peppers, halved & sliced
2 red bell peppers, halved & sliced
3 tomatoes, peeled & chopped
1/4 cup chopped parsley
1/2 teaspoon sugar
Salt & pepper

Preheat oven to 300°. Trim any excess fat from brisket. Season brisket with salt, pepper and chili powder. Place in a greased foil lined baking pan. Mash tomatoes together and pour over beef. Cover with foil and bake 4 - 5 hours until tender.

Heat oil in a large saucepan over medium heat. Sauté onion, garlic and peppers until softened. Add tomatoes and seasonings. Cover and simmer about 30 minutes, stirring frequently, until tender.

To serve, remove brisket and slice thin. Place in a large serving dish. Spoon some of the pan juices over brisket to keep moist. Top sliced brisket with sautéed peppers and tomatoes. (Serves 8 - 10)

Brisket can be made completely ahead and reheated before serving. A great crowd pleaser!

GREEN CHILIE POTATOES

6 - 8 medium red potatoes
1 cup chicken broth
1 clove garlic, peeled & mashed
1/4 teaspoon cumin
Salt & pepper

1 (4 oz) can chopped green chilies
1 cup grated Monterey Jack cheese
1 Tablespoon butter

Preheat oven to 350°. Peel potatoes and slice 1/8" thick. Heat chicken broth with garlic and cumin until warmed.

In a greased casserole, layer half of the potato slices, salt, pepper, half of green chilies and half of cheese. Repeat with remaining potatoes, salt, pepper, chilies and cheese. Remove garlic from broth and pour over potatoes. Dot with butter.

Bake for about 1 hour, uncovered, until browned and tender. (Serves 8)

ADOBE CHOCOLATE CAKE

1/3 cup butter, softened
1/3 cup light brown sugar
1/3 cup light corn syrup
1/2 cup chopped pecans

1/4 cup butter
1 cup sugar
1 egg

2 oz. unsweetened chocolate, melted
1/4 teaspoon salt
1 Tablespoon baking powder
1 teaspoon vanilla
1 1/4 cups flour
3/4 cup milk

Preheat oven to 350°. Grease a 9" round cake pan, line with wax paper and grease again.
Cream butter and brown sugar with an electric mixer. Beat until fluffy. Add corn syrup and pecans. Spread evenly in bottom of cake pan.
In the same bowl, cream 1/4 cup butter and 1 cup sugar until fluffy. Beat in egg until combined. Add melted chocolate, salt, baking powder and vanilla. Alternately add flour and milk to batter, beating well. Pour batter over topping, spreading evenly. Place a piece of foil under pan to catch any spillovers.
Bake about 40 minutes, until tested done. Cool in pan 15 minutes. Turn out on a serving plate, nut side up. Scrape off any nuts that may have stuck to the pan and add to top of cake. Can be served warm or at room temperature. (Serves 10 - 12)

Can be served with vanilla ice cream, if desired.
A chocolate lovers delight!

SUMMER CUISINE

MENUS

PIÑA COLADA PUNCH
BACON CHEESE TOASTS
WARM CRAWFISH SALAD
LEMON CAKE ROLL

CHILLED AVOCADO SOUP
HERBED FRESH TOMATOES
CRAB PASTA SALAD
ZUCCHINI FRITTATA
STRAWBERRY CREAM TART

BAKED POTATO SKINS
LAYERED SUMMER SALAD
GREEK SHRIMP & PASTA
MISSISSIPPI MUD ICE CREAM PIE

TROPICAL FRUIT COOLER
HUMMUS DIP WITH PITA CRISPS
HONEY MUSTARD SHRIMP
& COUSCOUS SALAD WITH
ROASTED GARLIC VINAIGRETTE
BOSTON ICE CREAM PIE

Summertime means easy, cool, and refreshing meals using lots of fresh fruits and vegetables. Entrée salads, cold summer drinks and ice cream desserts are just some of the recipes featured in summer cuisine.

SUMMER CUISINE

PIÑA COLADA PUNCH
BACON CHEESE TOASTS
WARM CRAWFISH SALAD
LEMON CAKE ROLL

PIÑA COLADA PUNCH

1 can (46 oz) unsweetened pineapple juice, chilled
1 bottle (33.8 oz) club soda, chilled
1 (16 oz) can cream of coconut, chilled
1/2 - 1 cup light rum, optional

Combine all ingredients in a punch bowl or large pitcher. Stir until blended. Serve with Orange Ice Cubes or Ice Ring. (Makes 22 four-ounce servings)

ORANGE ICE CUBES OR RING MOLD:
Half fill an ice cube tray with orange juice and place a cherry in each cube. Freeze to anchor fruit. Fill with more juice and freeze until firm. Can also be made into a ring mold.

A taste of the tropics in this cool summer drink!

BACON CHEESE TOASTS

8 slices bacon
1 egg, lightly beaten
1/2 cup mayonnaise
1 cup grated cheddar cheese
1/4 cup chopped green onion
1/4 teaspoon pepper
1/4 teaspoon dry mustard
1/4 teaspoon Tabasco
1/2 teaspoon Worcestershire
8 slices of bread

Preheat oven to 350°. Cook bacon. Drain and crumble. Mix all ingredients together, except bread. Add crumbled bacon. Cut crusts from bread slices and toast lightly on both sides. Cut each slice into 4 triangles. Spread generously with bacon cheese mixture. Place on a greased foil lined baking sheet. (Can be made ahead, covered with plastic wrap and refrigerated.)
Bake toasts for 10 - 15 minutes, until lightly browned and puffy. Serve hot. (Makes 32 pieces)

WARM CRAWFISH SALAD

VINAIGRETTE:

1 egg, lightly beaten	1/2 teaspoon sugar
1 teaspoon Dijon mustard	1/4 teaspoon salt
2 Tablespoons white wine vinegar	1/8 teaspoon pepper
	1 cup vegetable oil

Mix together all ingredients, except oil, in a small bowl. Slowly whisk in oil until combined. Let stand at room temperature while preparing crawfish.

CRAWFISH:

1 egg, lightly beaten	1 lb. peeled crawfish tails
1/4 cup milk	Vegetable oil for frying
3/4 cup water	
1/2 cup yellow corn meal	Green leaf lettuce
1/2 cup flour	Cherry tomatoes, halved
1 teaspoon salt	Boiled eggs, quartered
1/2 teaspoon pepper	Avocado slices
1 teaspoon cayenne pepper	Whole black olives

Mix together batter ingredients. Rinse off crawfish tails to remove fat, and drain on paper towels. Stir crawfish into batter to coat. Heat oil for frying in a large skillet over medium high heat ($350°$). Drop crawfish individually into hot oil and fry until golden brown. Drain on paper towels and keep warm in a low heated oven.

To serve, place torn lettuce leaves on individual plates. Pile crawfish in center. Garnish with tomatoes, eggs, avocado and black olives. Top with vinaigrette dressing. (Serves 6 - 8)

If crawfish aren't available, shrimp can be substituted.
A popular entrée salad served in many local restaurants.

LEMON CAKE ROLL

CAKE:
4 eggs, separated
1/4 cup sugar
1 teaspoon lemon extract
1 Tablespoon vegetable oil
1/2 cup sugar
1/4 teaspoon salt
1 teaspoon baking powder
2/3 cup cake flour
Powdered sugar

Preheat oven to 375°. Grease a 15" x 10" x 1" jelly roll pan with cooking spray. Line with wax paper. Spray again; dust with flour and shake off excess.
Beat egg yolks with an electric mixer until light and lemon colored, about 4 minutes. Gradually add 1/4 cup sugar, beating constantly. Mix in lemon extract and vegetable oil.
In another bowl, beat egg whites until foamy. Gradually add 1/2 cup sugar, beating until stiff. Fold egg yolk mixture into egg whites. Then fold in salt, baking powder and cake flour until combined. Spread batter evenly in prepared pan and bake for 10 - 12 minutes.
Meanwhile, sift some powdered sugar in a 15" x 10" rectangle on a linen towel. When cake is done, immediately loosen from sides of pan and turn out on the powdered sugar towel. Gently peel off wax paper. Starting at long end of cake, roll up cake and towel together. Cool on a wire rack, seam side down.

FILLING:
1 (14 oz) can sweetened condensed milk, chilled
Zest of 1 lemon
1/4 cup lemon juice
4 drops yellow food coloring
1 (8 oz) carton Cool Whip, thawed

Combine condensed milk, lemon zest, lemon juice, and food coloring in a mixing bowl. Fold in Cool Whip. Unroll cake and spread half of filling over cake. Reroll and place on a large platter, seam side down. Place wax paper strips under cake to cake drippings. Frost entire cake with remaining filling.

TOPPING:
1/2 cup frozen flaked coconut, thawed
1/2 teaspoon water
2 drops yellow food coloring
Fresh strawberries for garnish

Combine coconut, water and food coloring in a plastic bag. Shake well to distribute color. Sprinkle topping over cake roll. Refrigerate. Garnish with strawberries (Serves 10 - 12)

A beautiful cake that is really easy to handle.
Garnish with jelly beans for a special Easter dessert.

**BAKED POTATO SKINS
LAYERED SUMMER SALAD
GREEK SHRIMP & PASTA
MISSISSIPPI MUD ICE CREAM PIE**

BAKED POTATO SKINS

4 large baking potatoes
1/4 cup butter, melted
Salt & pepper to taste

1/2 cup chopped green onion
1 cup grated cheddar cheese
4 slices bacon, cooked and crumbled

Scrub potatoes clean and bake at 425° for about 1 hour, until tender. (Can also be cooked in microwave)

Cut potatoes in half lengthwise and scoop out most of the pulp, except for a thin layer. With kitchen scissors or a knife, cut the skins into 3 or 4 lengthwise pieces and place on a greased foil lined baking sheet. Brush each piece generously with butter. Season with salt and pepper and sprinkle with green onions, cheese and bacon.

Bake at 425° for about 10 minutes or until crisp. (Serves 6 - 8)

Other cheeses and toppings can be substituted.

LAYERED SUMMER SALAD

DRESSING:
1 cup mayonnaise
3/4 cup chili sauce
1 teaspoon lemon juice
1 teaspoon horseradish
2 Tablespoons chopped dill pickle
1/4 cup chopped celery
1/2 teaspoon Worcestershire

Combine all ingredients in a small bowl, cover and chill.

SALAD:
In a clear glass bowl (like a trifle bowl), layer the following ingredients and spoon dressing on top when ready to serve. (Serves 6 - 8)

Iceberg lettuce, shredded
Green onions, chopped
Carrots, grated or in strips
Boiled eggs, sliced
Tomatoes, chopped
Broccoli, cut in florets
Mushrooms, sliced
Bacon, cooked & crumbled

Can substitute or add cucumber slices, beet slices, avocado, black or green olives, boiled shrimp or crab meat. A nice departure from the typical tossed green salad.

GREEK SHRIMP & PASTA

1 Tablespoon butter or margarine
1 Tablespoon olive oil
1/2 onion, chopped
1 clove garlic, minced
5 - 6 ripe tomatoes, peeled, seeded & chopped
1/2 cup chicken broth
1/2 teaspoon sugar
1 teaspoon oregano
Salt & pepper to taste
2 lbs. medium shrimp, peeled
1/4 cup chopped parsley
1/2 cup heavy cream
1 lb. vermicelli or thin pasta
4 oz. feta cheese, crumbled

In a large saucepan, melt butter and oil over medium heat. Sauté onion and garlic until soft. Stir in tomatoes, broth, sugar, oregano, salt and pepper. Bring to a boil, lower heat and simmer for 15 minutes. Add shrimp and parsley and cook for 5 minutes. Stir in cream and cook 5 minutes more.
Meanwhile, cook pasta in a large pot of salted boiling water until done (taste test is best).
Mix shrimp mixture with pasta. Sprinkle with feta cheese and let stand for a few minutes for pasta to absorb the sauce. (Serves 6 - 8)

MISSISSIPPI MUD ICE CREAM PIE

CRUST:
21 Oreos (1 3/4 cups crumbled)   1/4 cup butter, melted

Place Oreos in a food processor and process until fine. Add butter and mix to combine. Press into a greased 9" pie pan. Freeze until firm.

FILLING:
1 qt. Pralines & Cream ice cream (or other favorite flavor)

Soften slightly and spoon into crust. Freeze until firm.

CHOCOLATE GLAZE:
1 oz. unsweetened chocolate   2 Tablespoons corn syrup
2 oz. semisweet chocolate   2 Tablespoons butter
2 Tablespoons water   Powdered sugar

Chop chocolate into small pieces or soften slightly in microwave (about 30 seconds).
Place water, corn syrup and butter in a small saucepan over medium heat. Stir occasionally, until mixture comes to a boil. Remove from heat and add chocolate. Stir until chocolate is melted and smooth. Cool to room temperature.
Pour glaze over frozen ice cream to cover top completely. Freeze until firm. Sprinkle with powdered sugar just before serving. Cover completely with foil to store in freezer. (Serves 8)

 *A great "do ahead" dessert to have on hand during the summer.*

SUMMER CUISINE

**CHILLED AVOCADO SOUP
HERBED FRESH TOMATOES
CRAB PASTA SALAD
ZUCCHINI FRITTATA
STRAWBERRY CREAM TART**

CHILLED AVOCADO SOUP

**2 - 3 ripe avocados
2 cups chicken broth, cold
1 cup sour cream
2 teaspoons lemon juice
Salt & white pepper to taste
Dash of Tabasco
Chopped tomato & crumbled, cooked bacon for garnish**

Peel, seed and mash avocados with a fork. Whisk together all ingredients, except garnish. Chill thoroughly.
Serve in small bowls garnished with chopped tomato and crumbled bacon. (Serves 8)

If you like avocados, you will enjoy this unusual cold soup.

HERBED FRESH TOMATOES

**1 cup vegetable oil
1/4 cup balsamic vinegar
1 clove garlic, mashed
1/4 cup chopped parsley
1/4 cup chopped fresh basil
1/4 cup chopped green onion
6 ripe tomatoes, peeled
Salt & pepper to taste**

Mix dressing ingredients and chill. Slice tomatoes and place on a serving plate. Season with salt and pepper. Spoon dressing over tomatoes. Chill until ready to serve. (Serves 6)

Home grown tomatoes really make this dish special!

SUMMER CUISINE

CRAB PASTA SALAD

DRESSING:
1 Tablespoon white wine vinegar
2 teaspoons Dijon mustard
1/4 teaspoon dill
1 teaspoon basil
1/4 teaspoon Tabasco
1/4 teaspoon salt
1/8 teaspoon pepper
1/4 cup olive oil

1/2 lb. spiral pasta (Rotini)
2 Tablespoons vegetable oil
1/2 cup chopped green onion
1 clove garlic, minced
1/2 cup chopped green pepper
1/4 cup chopped parsley
1 lb. white or lump crab meat
1 carrot, peeled & sliced
1 cup frozen green peas

Combine all ingredients for dressing, except oil. Whisk in oil very slowly. Cook pasta until done and drain. Combine pasta and dressing in a large bowl.
Heat oil in a skillet over medium heat. Sauté green onion, garlic, green pepper and parsley until softened. Gently stir in crab meat. Add mixture to pasta.
In a small saucepan, cook carrot and peas in boiling water for about 5 minutes. Add to salad. Cover and refrigerate until ready to serve. (Serves 6)

Can substitute shrimp, ham, chicken or other vegetables, if desired.

ZUCCHINI FRITTATA

1/2 onion
1 clove garlic
2 Tablespoons olive oil
1/2 lb. zucchini, scrubbed
Salt & pepper to taste
10 eggs
1 teaspoon basil

1 teaspoon salt
Pepper to taste
2 Tablespoons Italian seasoned bread crumbs
1 tomato, peeled & sliced
1 cup grated cheddar cheese
1/4 cup grated Parmesan cheese

Preheat oven to 350°. Chop onion and garlic in a food processor. Heat oil in a large skillet over medium heat. Sauté onion and garlic until softened. Meanwhile, shred zucchini in food processor and add to onion mixture. Cook about 2 minutes. Season with salt and pepper.
Beat eggs in a large bowl. Add basil, salt, pepper and bread crumbs. Stir in onion mixture. Pour into a greased 9" or 10" quiche dish or pie pan. Arrange tomato slices on top and sprinkle with cheddar and Parmesan cheese.
Bake for 20 - 25 minutes or until set. Let cool slightly before cutting. (Serves 8)

STRAWBERRY CREAM TART

CRUST:
1 cup flour
2 teaspoons sugar
Dash of salt
1/2 cup cold butter
1/4 cup cold water

In a large bowl, mix flour, sugar and salt. Cut in butter until crumbly. Slowly add just enough water until dough holds together. (Can be made in a food processor.) Wrap in plastic wrap and chill 15 minutes.

Turn dough out on a lightly floured surface and roll out into a 12" circle. Roll up on a rolling pin and place in a shallow greased 9" tart pan. Cut off excess dough leaving a 1" border and fold edge over inside. Chill for 15 minutes.

Preheat oven to $400°$. Place a greased piece of foil inside pastry shell and fill with pie weights or dried beans. Bake for 20 minutes. Remove foil and weights and bake 15 minutes more. Cool in pan.

PASTRY CREAM:
1/4 cup sugar
1 Tablespoon flour
2 teaspoons cornstarch
1 egg
1 cup milk
3 Tablespoons butter, softened
1 teaspoon vanilla

Mix dry ingredients together in a small bowl. Add egg and beat with a whisk until combined. Place milk in a saucepan over medium high heat and bring to a boil. Whisk milk into egg mixture very slowly, then pour mixture back into saucepan. Cook, whisking constantly, until bubbly and very thick. Remove from heat; add butter and vanilla. Stir until combined. Pour in a bowl, cover with plastic wrap directly on the surface and chill.

TO ASSEMBLE:
1 pint fresh strawberries
2 Tablespoons apricot or currant jam

Wash, hull and slice strawberries vertically. Spread pastry cream in crust. Cover with strawberries in an overlapping design. Melt jam and strain if necessary. Brush jam lightly over berries to glaze. Chill.

TROPICAL FRUIT COOLER
HUMMUS DIP WITH PITA CRISPS
HONEY MUSTARD SHRIMP
& COUSCOUS SALAD WITH
ROASTED GARLIC VINAIGRETTE
BOSTON ICE CREAM PIE

TROPICAL FRUIT COOLER

6 oz. frozen orange juice
6 oz. frozen lemonade
6 oz. frozen limeade

12 oz. frozen pineapple juice
1 cup water
3 (1 liter) bottles ginger ale, chilled

In a large pitcher, mix orange juice, lemonade, limeade, pineapple juice and water, stirring until melted.
For individual servings, mix 1/4 cup fruit juice mixture with 3/4 cup ginger ale and serve over ice. For a pitcher or punch bowl, mix fruit juice mixture with ginger ale and serve over ice. (Serves 6 - 8)

A refreshing drink; perfect for the summertime!
Rum, champagne or vodka can also be added.

HUMMUS DIP

1 (15 oz) can chick peas, drained
1 clove garlic, minced
1/3 cup lemon juice
1 Tablespoon olive oil
1/2 teaspoon cumin
1/2 teaspoon salt
Pepper & cayenne to taste
1/4 cup Tahini (sesame seed paste)
Paprika & parsley for garnish

Mix all ingredients together in a food processor until smooth and combined. Chill in a covered container.
Garnish with paprika and parsley. Serve with pita crisps.

Chick peas are also known as garbanzo beans.
A very easy dip to prepare; everyone will enjoy this one!

PITA CRISPS

4 pita breads
1/4 cup melted butter or margarine

Preheat oven to 425°. Cut pita bread in half, separating top from bottom. Cut into triangular pieces. Place in a single layer on a large greased foil lined baking sheet. Brush each piece with melted butter and toast for about 6 - 8 minutes, until golden brown. When cool, store in an airtight container.

These can also be baked plain, without butter, for a great "no fat" snack.

HONEY MUSTARD SHRIMP & COUSCOUS SALAD WITH ROASTED GARLIC VINAIGRETTE

ROASTED GARLIC VINAIGRETTE:
1 large bulb (head) garlic
1/2 teaspoon olive oil
1/3 cup balsamic vinegar
1 1/4 cups olive oil
1 Tablespoon Dijon mustard
Salt & pepper to taste

Preheat oven to $325°$. Cut a small slice off the top of the bulb of garlic to expose cloves. Place in a garlic roaster or small baking dish and drizzle with 1/2 teaspoon olive oil. Cover and bake for 30 minutes. Remove cover and bake 30 minutes more. When cool enough to handle, squeeze garlic from skin.

Place remaining ingredients in a food processor, along with roasted garlic. Process until combined. Chill in a covered container.

COUSCOUS SALAD:
2 1/4 cups water
1 1/2 cups (10 oz. pkg.) couscous (Moroccan pasta)
1/2 teaspoon salt
1/2 cup chopped green onion
1/2 cup chopped parsley

Bring water to a boil in a medium saucepan over high heat. Remove from heat and stir in couscous and salt. Cover and let stand for 5 minutes. Uncover, stir and let stand for 5 minutes more. Stir in chopped green onions and parsley. Place in a bowl, cover and refrigerate until ready to serve.

SHRIMP:
1 1/2 - 2 lbs. large shrimp, peeled
Salt & pepper to taste
2 Tablespoons lemon juice
1 Tablespoon olive oil
2 Tablespoons honey
2 Tablespoons Dijon mustard

Season shrimp with salt and pepper. Mix together lemon juice, olive oil, honey and mustard in a bowl. Add shrimp, stirring to coat, and marinate for about 30 minutes.

Heat an outdoor grill or stove top grill until hot. Grill shrimp until browned, about 3 - 4 minutes on both sides. Shrimp can be served warm or cold.

(Continued on next page)

TO SERVE:
Leaf lettuce
Tomatoes, peeled & cut into wedges
Avocado, peeled & cut into slices
Cucumber, peeled & cut into chunks
Baby carrots, slivered
Black olives
Feta cheese, crumbled
Sunflower seeds

Make salads by placing lettuce leaves on individual plates. Mix about 1/2 cup vinaigrette into the couscous. Season with salt and pepper. Spoon couscous onto lettuce. Top with grilled shrimp and garnish with tomatoes, avocado, cucumber, carrots, black olives, feta cheese and sunflower seeds. Spoon vinaigrette over salads. (Serves 6)

A beautiful presentation and a super combination of flavors! Entire salad can be made ahead and assembled just before serving. Another pasta can be substituted for couscous. Shrimp can be placed on skewers for easier handling. Chicken can be substituted for shrimp.

BOSTON ICE CREAM PIE

ICE CREAM:
1 qt. Pralines 'n Cream ice cream, vanilla or other favorite.

Mold ice cream by spreading evenly into a 9" round cake pan that has been greased and lined with plastic wrap. Cover with plastic wrap and freeze.

CAKE:
1 egg white
1/4 cup sugar
1 cup flour
1 1/2 teaspoons baking powder
1/2 teaspoon salt

1/2 cup sugar
1/2 cup milk
2 Tablespoons vegetable oil
1 egg yolk
1 teaspoon vanilla

Preheat oven to 350°. In a small bowl, beat egg white with an electric mixer until frothy. Gradually add 1/4 cup sugar, beating until stiff peaks form.

In another bowl, stir together flour, baking powder, salt and sugar. Mix in milk, oil, egg yolk and vanilla. Beat 1 minute at medium speed. Scrape bowl down and beat 1 minute more. Fold in egg white mixture and spread batter into a greased 9" round cake pan.

Bake about 18 - 20 minutes, until tested done. Cool in pan for 10 minutes. Remove from pan and cool on a wire rack. Make glaze and icing.

CHOCOLATE GLAZE:
1 oz. unsweetened chocolate
1 Tablespoon butter or margarine

1 cup sifted powdered sugar
1/2 teaspoon vanilla
About 2 Tablespoons water

Carefully melt chocolate and butter in the microwave. Stir to check melting. Add powdered sugar, vanilla and enough water to obtain a spreading consistency.

VANILLA ICING:
1/2 cup sifted powdered sugar

About 1 Tablespoon milk

In a small bowl, combine powdered sugar and enough milk to obtain a drizzling consistency.

(continued on next page)

TO ASSEMBLE:

When cake is cool, mark with toothpicks as a guide and split cake horizontally into 2 layers, using a long serrated knife. Place bottom layer on a plate and unmold ice cream on top. Place top cake layer on ice cream and spread chocolate glaze over cake. Immediately drizzle with vanilla icing in a spiral pattern, starting from the center. Before icing has set, draw the dull edge of a knife through icing, starting from the center, at regular intervals, to produce a spider web effect. Freeze. (Makes 8 servings)

After splitting cake, mark top layer with a toothpick and just underneath it mark the bottom layer. This makes it easier to line up the layers when putting the cake back together.
Place icing in a plastic mustard or ketchup dispenser to make drizzling easier.
Instant vanilla pudding mix can be prepared and used as a filling, instead of ice cream, to create the traditional Boston Cream Pie. Store in refrigerator.

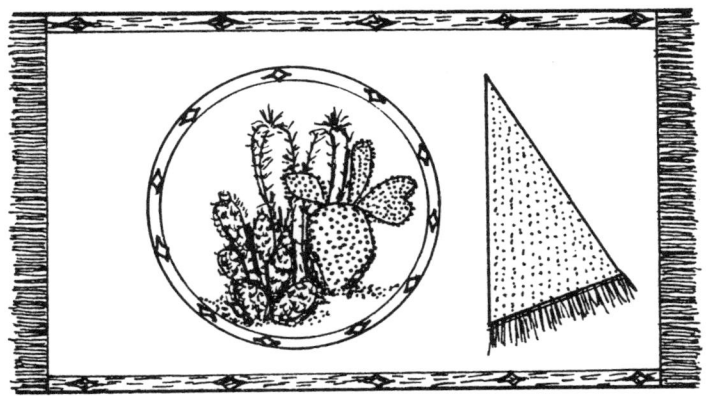

TEX-MEX

MENUS

FRIJOLES TOSTADITAS
FIESTA MEXICAN RICE
CHICKEN ENCHILADAS RANCHEROS
MOCHA ICE CREAM TOSTADAS

SOPA DI LIMA
CHICKEN CORN TORTILLAS
BEEF & CHEESE ENCHILADAS
SALSA ROJA
MEXI RICE
KAHLÚA MOUSSE

Everyone loves Tex-Mex food with its robust flavors and ingredients. These are great crowd pleasing recipes that you will use often. Enchilada dishes are easily prepared in advance and reheated when ready to serve. Use lots of colorful garnishes when preparing Tex-Mex recipes and serve in your most festive dishes.

TEX-MEX

**FRIJOLES TOSTADITAS
FIESTA MEXICAN RICE
CHICKEN ENCHILADAS RANCHEROS
MOCHA ICE CREAM TOSTADAS**

FRIJOLES TOSTADITAS

1 Tablespoon vegetable oil
1/4 cup chopped onion
1 clove garlic, minced
1 (10 oz) can diced Ro-Tel
   tomatoes & green chilies

1 (16 oz) can refried beans
1 cup grated cheddar cheese
Tortilla chips
Cheddar cheese for garnish

Heat oil in a large skillet over medium heat. Add onion and garlic and sauté until tender. Drain tomatoes well and add to skillet. Cook for a few minutes to evaporate any excess liquid. Stir in beans. Reduce heat to low and add cheese, stirring until melted.

Preheat oven to 350°. Place tortilla chips individually on a greased foil lined baking sheet. Spread frijole mixture over each tortilla and top with cheddar cheese. Heat until cheese melts. Let cool slightly before serving. (Serves 6 - 8)

 *Delicious appetizers that will disappear fast!*

FIESTA MEXICAN RICE

2 Tablespoons butter or margarine
1 small onion, chopped
1 clove garlic, minced
1/2 cup chopped green pepper
1/2 cup chopped red pepper
1 1/2 cups rice

3 cups chicken broth
1/2 teaspoon salt
1/8 teaspoon pepper
1/2 teaspoon cumin
1/4 teaspoon oregano
1/4 teaspoon turmeric

Melt butter in a greased 2 1/2 quart saucepan over medium heat. Add onion, garlic, green and red peppers and sauté until tender. Stir in rice. Add chicken broth and seasonings. Stir to combine. Raise heat to high and bring to a boil. Let boil until most of the liquid has evaporated and craterlike holes appear on the surface. Cover, turn off heat and let steam for about 20 minutes. Toss before serving. (Serves 6 - 8)

CHICKEN ENCHILADAS RANCHEROS

1 Tablespoon vegetable oil
5 - 6 boneless chicken breasts,
  cut into cubes
Salt & pepper
1 teaspoon chili powder
1 teaspoon cumin
1 (4 oz) can chopped green chilies

12 flour tortillas (7")
1 (8 oz) pkg. Monterey Jack
  cheese with jalapeño,
  cut into small strips
Shredded lettuce
Chopped tomatoes
Chopped avocado

Heat oil in a large skillet over medium high heat. Add chicken and cook, stirring occasionally, until no longer pink. Season with salt, pepper, chili powder and cumin. Add chopped green chilies and stir to combine. Remove from heat and prepare sauce.

SAUCE:
1/2 cup butter or margarine
1/2 cup flour
2 cups chicken broth, heated
2 cups milk, heated
2 cups grated cheddar cheese

1/4 teaspoon salt
1/8 teaspoon pepper
1 teaspoon dry mustard
1/8 teaspoon cayenne pepper
1/2 teaspoon Worcestershire
1 cup sour cream

Melt butter in a large saucepan over medium heat. Add flour and cook, stirring constantly, for 3 minutes. Stir in heated broth and milk until combined. Cook, stirring frequently, until mixture comes to a boil and sauce thickens. Mix in cheese and seasonings and stir until cheese melts. Remove from heat and add sour cream.

Preheat oven to 350°. Fill each tortilla with chicken mixture and strips of Monterey Jack cheese. Roll up tightly and place side by side in a large greased casserole. Pour cheese sauce over enchiladas. Bake, uncovered, for about 30 minutes. Serve garnished with lettuce, tomatoes and avocado. (Serves 6 - 8)

Baking this dish uncovered helps to thicken the sauce.

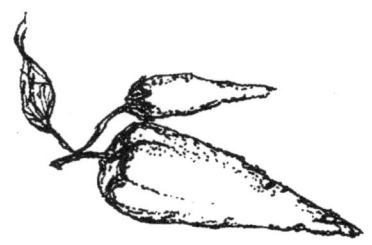

MOCHA ICE CREAM TOSTADAS

MOCHA SAUCE:
3/4 cup sugar
1/2 cup cocoa
1 cup cold strong brewed coffee
2 Tablespoons butter or margarine

In a small saucepan, stir together sugar and cocoa. Add cold coffee and stir until smooth. Place over medium heat and bring to a boil. Turn heat to low and cook, stirring frequently, for 3 minutes. Add butter and cook 3 minutes more. Remove from heat and cool before serving.

6 - 8 flour tortillas (7")
Vegetable oil
Powdered sugar
Vanilla ice cream
Toasted sliced almonds

In a deep 2 qt. saucepan, heat 1 1/2" vegetable oil over medium heat to 375° or until hot. Place one tortilla in oil and immediately press down the center of the tortilla with a metal ladle. Hold in oil until lightly browned, turning to brown all over. Remove with tongs and place on paper towels to drain. Sprinkle with powdered sugar and let cool. Repeat with remaining tortillas.

When ready to serve, place a tostada shell in a dessert bowl. Spoon a scoop of ice cream in each shell. Drizzle with mocha sauce and top with toasted almonds.

A delightful presentation for such an easy dessert!

SOPA DE LIMA
CHICKEN CORN TORTILLAS
BEEF & CHEESE ENCHILADAS
SALSA ROJA
MEXI RICE
KAHLÚA MOUSSE

SOPA DE LIMA

4 cups chicken stock
1 cup cooked chicken, cut up
1/2 cup chopped onion
1/2 cup chopped green pepper

1 tomato, peeled, seeded & chopped
Juice of 2 limes
Salt & pepper to taste
Lime slices & crumbled tortilla chips for garnish

    Combine all ingredients in a saucepan over medium high heat. Bring to a boil. Reduce heat and simmer for about 20 minutes.
    Place a slice of lime in each bowl. Ladle soup into bowls and top with tortilla chips. (Serves 6)

CHICKEN CORN TORTILLAS

2 Tablespoons vegetable oil
4 - 5 boneless chicken breasts, cut into cubes
1 small onion, chopped
1 clove garlic, minced
1 cup chicken broth
1 (8 oz) can tomato sauce
1 (4 oz) can diced green chilies

Salt & pepper to taste
1 cup heavy cream
10 - 12 corn tortillas
1 cup grated Monterey Jack cheese
1 avocado, peeled & sliced
Chopped black olives

    In a large saucepan, heat oil and sauté chicken until no longer pink. Add onion and garlic, cooking until tender. Mix in broth, tomato sauce, green chilies, salt and pepper. Simmer for 10 minutes.
    Heat cream and dip tortillas into cream to soften. Fill each tortilla with chicken mixture. Roll up and place seam side down in a large greased baking dish. Pour remaining cream over tortillas and top with cheese.
    Bake at 350° for about 20 minutes until hot. Serve garnished with avocado slices and black olives. (Serves 8)

BEEF & CHEESE ENCHILADAS

1 1/2 lbs. lean ground beef
1 onion, chopped
2 cloves garlic, minced
1/2 green pepper, chopped
Salt & pepper to taste
6 Tablespoons butter
6 Tablespoons flour
3 cups chicken broth, warmed
2 Tablespoons chili powder
1/2 teaspoon oregano
1/4 teaspoon sage
1/2 teaspoon cumin
Salt & pepper to taste
8 - 10 flour tortillas
3 cups grated cheddar cheese
2 tomatoes, peeled & chopped
Shredded iceberg lettuce, sour cream & Salsa Roja

In a large skillet over medium high heat, brown ground beef, spooning off any excess grease. Add onion, garlic and green pepper. Sauté until softened and season with salt and pepper.

In a large saucepan over medium heat, melt butter. Stir in flour and cook for 3 minutes. Whisk in broth and seasonings. Cook until sauce thickens slightly. Pour 2/3 of the sauce into the beef mixture and reserve 1/3 of the sauce.

Soften tortillas in microwave. Fill each tortilla with meat mixture and top with cheese and tomato. Roll up and place seam side down in a large greased baking dish. Spoon remaining sauce over middle of enchiladas and top with cheese. Cover with foil and bake at 350° for about 20 minutes or until hot.

Serve garnished with lettuce, sour cream and Salsa Roja. (Serves 8)

SALSA ROJA

1 (14 1/2 oz) can stewed tomatoes
1 (10 oz) can Ro-Tel tomatoes & green chilies
1 (7 1/2 oz) can jalapeño relish

Place all ingredients in a food processor and pulse until combined. Refrigerate in a tightly covered container.

Salsa Roja can also be served with tortilla chips as a dip.

MEXI RICE

2 Tablespoons butter
1 small onion, chopped
1/2 green pepper, chopped
1 cup rice
1 tomato, peeled & chopped

2 cups chicken broth, warmed
1/2 cup frozen green peas
1/4 teaspoon cumin
Salt & pepper to taste

    In a large saucepan over medium high heat, melt butter and sauté onion and green pepper until softened. Stir in rice, tomato, broth, peas, cumin, salt & pepper. Raise heat to high and bring to a boil. Cook until most of the liquid has evaporated. Turn off heat, cover and let rice steam for about 20 minutes. (Serves 6 - 8)

KAHLÚA MOUSSE

1 egg white
1 Tablespoon sugar
1 cup heavy cream

1/2 teaspoon instant coffee powder
1/4 cup Kahlúa
2 Tablespoons sugar
1 oz. semisweet chocolate

    Beat egg white in a small bowl, with an electric mixer, to soft peaks. Gradually add 1 Tablespoon sugar and beat until stiff.
    In a small chilled bowl, combine heavy cream with coffee powder. Beat until stiff. Add Kahlúa and 2 Tablespoons sugar and beat until very stiff.
    Fold beaten egg white into whipped cream. Spoon into tall wine glasses or dessert dishes. Run a vegetable peeler over semisweet chocolate to make shavings. Sprinkle chocolate shavings on top of each serving and chill. (Serves 4 - 6)

 ***Best if made same day as served.***

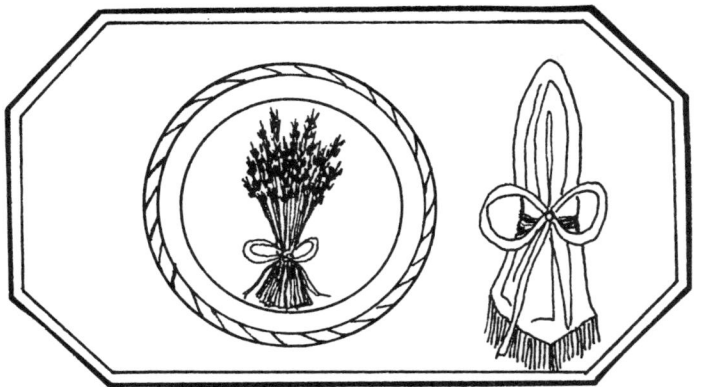

THANKSGIVING

MENU

SAUSAGE STUFFED MUSHROOMS
SWEET POTATO SOUP
SPINACH STUFFED SQUASH
APRICOT GLAZED CHICKEN
WITH CORNBREAD DRESSING
BLACK FOREST TORTE

Thanksgiving dinner is a meal to be shared with family and friends. This class is a nice departure from some of the more traditional recipes, yet uses most of the distinctive foods of the season.

THANKSGIVING

**SAUSAGE STUFFED MUSHROOMS
SWEET POTATO SOUP
SPINACH STUFFED SQUASH
APRICOT GLAZED CHICKEN
WITH CORNBREAD DRESSING
BLACK FOREST TORTE**

SAUSAGE STUFFED MUSHROOMS

1 lb. large fresh mushrooms
1/2 lb. ground pork sausage
1/4 cup chopped green pepper
1/4 cup chopped green onion

1/4 cup Italian seasoned bread crumbs
1 egg, slightly beaten
1/2 cup grated mozzarella cheese

Wipe mushrooms off with a damp paper towel. Remove stems and chop stems coarsely.

Cook sausage in a large skillet over medium high heat until browned. Drain off grease and save 2 Tablespoons drippings. Sauté green pepper, green onion and mushroom stems in drippings until softened.

Preheat oven to 375°. Combine all ingredients in a large bowl and fill mushroom caps with stuffing. Place in a greased baking dish, cover with foil and bake for about 15 minutes. (Serves 6)

Recipe can easily be doubled.

SWEET POTATO SOUP

1/4 cup butter or margarine
1/2 onion, chopped
1/2 cup chopped celery
1 1/2 lbs. sweet potatoes, peeled & sliced thin

4 cups chicken broth
Salt & white pepper to taste
1/8 teaspoon cayenne pepper
1 cup heavy cream

Melt butter in a large saucepan over medium heat. Sauté onion and celery until softened. Add sweet potatoes, broth & seasonings. Raise heat to medium high and bring to a boil. Lower heat, cover and cook about 15 - 20 minutes.

Purée soup in a blender or food processor and return to saucepan. Stir in cream and heat thoroughly. Serve garnished with Sweet Potato Shoestrings. (Serves 8)

SWEET POTATO SHOESTRINGS:
1/2 sweet potato, peeled

Vegetable oil

Cut sweet potato into matchstick juliennes. Place a thin layer of oil in a small skillet over medium high heat. When hot, cook potatoes in batches until golden. Remove & drain on paper towels.

A beautiful and delicious soup for the fall season. Your guests will be surprised by the taste.

SPINACH STUFFED SQUASH

4 medium yellow squash
Salt & pepper
1 pkg. frozen chopped spinach
1 hard boiled egg, chopped
1/4 cup Italian seasoned bread crumbs

2 Tablespoons butter, melted
1/4 teaspoon Worcestershire
1/8 teaspoon Tabasco
Salt & pepper
1/2 cup grated cheddar cheese

Wash squash and trim ends. Place in a large saucepan and cover with water. Bring to a boil over high heat and cook until tender. Remove and drain well. Cut each squash in half lengthwise and carefully scoop out seeds. Season with salt and pepper.

Preheat oven to 350°. Cook spinach in the microwave until done. Drain thoroughly. Combine with remaining ingredients, except cheese, and stuff squash. Place stuffed squash in a greased baking dish and top with cheese. Cover with foil and heat for about 15 minutes, until hot. (Serves 8)

APRICOT GLAZED CHICKEN WITH CORNBREAD DRESSING

CORNBREAD:
1 cup flour
1 cup yellow cornmeal
1/2 teaspoon salt
1 Tablespoon sugar
1 Tablespoon baking powder
1/2 cup butter or margarine
1 1/2 cups buttermilk
2 eggs, lightly beaten
1/2 teaspoon baking soda

Preheat oven to 425°. Place all dry ingredients in a large mixing bowl. Melt butter and allow to cool slightly. Mix buttermilk with eggs and add baking soda. Stir in butter and mix with dry ingredients, just until moistened. Pour into a greased 9" x 13" pan and bake 15 minutes. Let cool.

DRESSING:
1/4 cup butter or margarine
1 onion, chopped
1/4 green pepper, chopped
1/2 cup chopped celery
1 clove garlic, minced
1/4 cup chopped green onion
1/4 cup chopped parsley
1 cup chicken broth
1 egg, lightly beaten
2 teaspoons poultry seasoning
Salt & pepper to taste

Melt butter in a large saucepan or skillet over medium heat. Sauté onion, green pepper, celery, garlic, green onion & parsley until softened. Crumble cornbread in a large bowl and add vegetables. Mix in chicken broth, egg and seasonings. Place in a large greased baking dish.

GLAZED CHICKEN:
8 boneless chicken breasts
Salt & pepper
2 Tablespoons butter or margarine
1 cup chicken broth
1/2 cup apricot preserves
1 teaspoon Dijon mustard

Preheat oven to 350°. Season chicken breasts with salt & pepper. Melt butter in a large skillet over medium high heat and brown chicken in two batches. Place chicken on top of dressing and cover with chicken broth. Cover dish with foil and bake 30 minutes.

Mix apricot preserves with mustard. Spoon over chicken breasts and return to oven, uncovered, for 10 minutes. (Serves 8)

A nice alternative to turkey at Thanksgiving, especially for a small group.

BLACK FOREST TORTE

CAKE:
1 cup butter or margarine
2 cups sugar
2 eggs
1 teaspoon vanilla
1/3 cup cocoa, sifted
1 teaspoon soda
1/2 teaspoon baking powder
2 cups flour
1 1/2 cups buttermilk

Preheat oven to 350°. Grease three 8" or 9" round cake pans. Line pans with wax paper and grease again.
Beat butter and sugar with an electric mixer until smooth, about 3 minutes. Mix in eggs and vanilla. Add cocoa, soda and baking powder. Mix in flour alternately with buttermilk. Scrape bowl down twice during mixing. Pour into prepared pans and bake about 18 - 20 minutes, until tested done. Cool in pans for 15 minutes. Remove to racks to cool completely.

FILLING:
1 (16 oz) can pitted dark
 sweet cherries
2 Tablespoons sugar
3 Tablespoons cornstarch
1/4 teaspoon almond extract

Drain cherry juice into a small saucepan. Reserve 12 cherries, placing on paper towels to drain excess juice; chill. Mash remaining cherries and add to juice. Stir in sugar and cornstarch until combined. Place over medium heat and cook, stirring constantly, until mixture comes to a boil and thickens. Cook 1 minute. Remove from heat and add almond extract. Cool and refrigerate.

FROSTING:
1 (8 oz) pkg. cream cheese
2 Tablespoons butter or margarine
1/2 teaspoon almond extract
2 cups powdered sugar
1/2 cup toasted sliced
 almonds

Beat cream cheese and butter with an electric mixer until smooth. Add almond extract. Mix in powdered sugar until combined.
To assemble torte, place 1 cake layer, top side down, on a plate and spread a 1" border of frosting around the outer edge of the cake layer. Spread half of the cherry filling inside of the border. Top with second cake layer, top side down, and repeat with frosting and filling. Top with third cake layer, top side up, and spread frosting over top. Sprinkle top with almonds and place reserved cherries around the outer edge of cake. Store in refrigerator.

 *A very pretty cake for any festive occasion!*

YOUNG EVERYDAY GOURMET

MENUS

COCA-COLA CHICKEN
CHEESY POTATO CHUNKS
BOILED CORN ON THE COB
STRAWBERRY ANGEL CAKE

PEANUT BUTTER CRUNCHERS
CHOCOLATE HAYSTACKS
JELL-O CHRISTMAS COOKIES

MEXICAN SPAGHETTI
SESAME CORN BISCUITS
FUDGY ICE CREAM BALLS

CINNAMON APPLE BREAD
CHOCOLATE SNOWBALLS
CRISPY PEANUT BUTTER CANDIES

CRUNCHY BAKED CHICKEN TENDERS
SUGAR BROWNED POTATOES
STEAMED BROCCOLI
HOT FUDGE SUNDAE CAKE

PEANUT BUTTER FUDGE
HOT COCOA MIX
CHRISTMAS COOKIES

MINI PIZZAS
CHOCOLATE CHIP EXTRAVAGANZA
BANANA NUT PANCAKES

Young Everyday Gourmet classes are for kids age 9 and older. The classes are full participation, where everyone lends a hand in completing each recipe. It's a great way for kids to learn to cook!

YOUNG EVERYDAY GOURMET MEALS

In the gourmet meals class, we prepare an entire meal that's always quick and easy. These are recipes that kids can handle and have fun with.

**COCA-COLA CHICKEN
CHEESY POTATO CHUNKS
BOILED CORN ON THE COB
STRAWBERRY ANGEL CAKE**

COCA-COLA CHICKEN

**10 - 12 pieces of chicken
 (legs, thighs, breasts)
Salt & pepper**

**1/2 cup ketchup
1/2 cup Coca-Cola Classic
1 teaspoon Worcestershire
 sauce**

Remove skin from chicken pieces and place on a sheet of wax paper. Season both sides of chicken pieces with salt and pepper.

In a measuring cup, measure ketchup, coke and Worcestershire sauce. Mix with a fork until combined.

Grease a large ovenproof dish with cooking spray. Preheat oven to $350°$.

Grease a large non-stick skillet with cooking spray and place over medium high heat. When skillet is hot, add half of the chicken pieces and cook until browned (about 5 minutes). Turn each piece over with tongs and brown on the other side. Remove chicken with tongs and place in the prepared baking dish.

Repeat the same process to brown remaining chicken and add to baking dish. Pour sauce over chicken and cover with foil. Bake for 40 minutes. Remove from oven and serve chicken with sauce spooned on top. (Serves 6 - 8)

Tastes like bar-b-que chicken without using the grill!

CHEESY POTATO CHUNKS

8 - 10 small new potatoes (red)
Salt & pepper

2 Tablespoons butter or margarine
1/2 cup grated cheddar cheese

Wash and scrub potatoes clean. Cut each potato into 4 pieces. Place pieces in a medium size saucepan and add enough water to cover potatoes. Bring to a boil over high heat and cook until tender, about 10 - 15 minutes (test with a knife).
Remove from heat and pour into a colander to drain off water. Place potatoes in a serving dish and add salt, pepper, butter and cheese. Stir gently to coat potatoes with seasonings. (Serves 6 - 8)

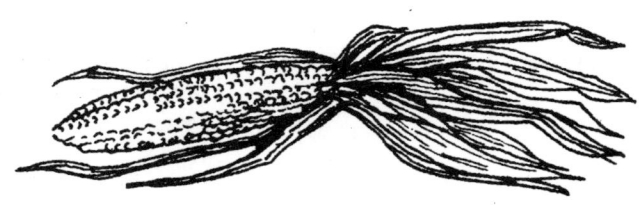

BOILED CORN ON THE COB

3 - 4 ears of fresh corn on the cob
4 cups of water

Salt, pepper & butter

Remove corn husks and silk from each ear of corn and cut off any excess stem. Break each ear in half.
Place 4 cups of water into a medium size saucepan and bring to a boil over high heat. Add corn to boiling water, cover with lid and cook for 5 minutes. Remove corn from water with tongs. Serve with salt, pepper and butter to taste. (Serves 6 - 8)

STRAWBERRY ANGEL CAKE

1 baked angel food cake
1 (3.4 oz) pkg. instant vanilla pudding mix
1 (8 oz) can crushed pineapple
1 (12 oz) carton Cool Whip, thawed
1/2 cup chopped pecans
1 pint fresh strawberries

With a long serrated bread knife, gently cut off the top of the angel food cake about 1" down from the top and reserve. Use a smaller knife to cut a tunnel in the bottom part of the cake, being careful not to cut all the way through the cake's bottom and sides, leaving a shell of at least 1" on sides and bottom. Scoop out cake carefully. (Remember to eat this left over cake!)

In a medium size bowl, mix together dry pudding mix and pineapple with juice. Measure 1 cup Cool Whip and gently stir into bowl. Add pecans.

Remove 6 whole strawberries and set aside. Wash, hull and slice remaining strawberries and add to filling.

Spoon filling into tunnel. Place top of cake back on filled cake. Frost cake with remaining Cool Whip (top first, then outside, then inside). Wash the 6 whole strawberries and remove hulls. Decorate top of cake with the whole strawberries. Refrigerate.

When ready to serve, slice cake with a serrated knife, using a sawing motion. (Serves 10 - 12)

A wonderful summertime dessert!

MEXICAN SPAGHETTI
SESAME CORN BISCUITS
FUDGY ICE CREAM BALLS

MEXICAN SPAGHETTI

1 - 1 1/2 lbs. ground beef
1 (16 oz) jar Thick N' Chunky mild salsa
2 (15 oz) cans tomato sauce
1 teaspoon cumin
1 Tablespoon chili powder
Salt & pepper to taste
1 (11 oz) can corn
1 lb. pkg. thin spaghetti
1 cup grated cheddar cheese

Grease a large pot with cooking spray and place over medium high heat. Add ground beef and cook, stirring frequently, until no longer pink. Spoon off any grease. Stir in salsa, tomato sauce, cumin, chili powder, salt, pepper and corn. Cook until mixture begins to boil. Turn heat to low, cover and cook for 15 minutes.

Meanwhile, bring a large pot of water to a boil over high heat. Stir in 1 Tablespoon salt. Break pasta in half and add to boiling water. Stir constantly for 1 minute, so pasta doesn't stick. Cook for about 10 minutes or until it tastes done. Strain pasta and add to sauce mixture. Stir to combine. Top with cheddar cheese. (Serves 6 - 8)

SESAME CORN BISCUITS

1/2 cup yellow cornmeal
1 1/2 cups flour
1/2 teaspoon salt
4 teaspoons baking powder
1/2 teaspoon cream of tartar
2 Tablespoons sugar
1/2 cup butter or margarine
2/3 cup milk
Milk & sesame seeds

Preheat oven to 425°. Cover a large baking sheet with foil and grease with cooking spray. In a large mixing bowl, measure cornmeal, flour, salt, baking powder, cream of tartar and sugar. Cut butter into small pieces and mix into flour with your fingers, until it resembles fine crumbs. Stir in milk until combined. Place dough on a floured surface and pat into an 8" square, about 1/2" thick. Cut dough into 16 squares with a knife.

Place squares on prepared baking sheet and brush biscuits with a little milk. Sprinkle with sesame seeds. Bake for 15 minutes, until golden brown. Serve hot with butter. (Makes 16)

FUDGY ICE CREAM BALLS

Vanilla ice cream
Chopped pecans, almond slivers
  or slices, toasted

1/2 cup butter or margarine
1 (12 oz) pkg. semisweet
  chocolate chips (2 cups)
1/3 cup evaporated milk

Scoop out ice cream balls and roll in nuts of your choice. Place on a plate lined with wax paper and return to freezer to harden.
To make sauce, place butter, chocolate chips and evaporated milk in a medium size saucepan over low heat. Stir frequently until completely melted. Serve warm over ice cream balls. Store leftover sauce in a covered jar in the refrigerator and reheat in the microwave when ready to serve. (Serves 8)

Nuts have more flavor if lightly toasted under the broiler. These are great when you need a quick dessert!

CRUNCHY BAKED CHICKEN TENDERS
SUGAR BROWNED POTATOES
STEAMED BROCCOLI
HOT FUDGE SUNDAE CAKE

CRUNCHY BAKED CHICKEN TENDERS

18 chicken breast tenders
Salt & pepper to taste
2 1/2 cups cornbread stuffing mix

6 Tablespoons butter or
  margarine
Juice of 1 lemon

Preheat oven to 375°. Pat chicken dry with paper towels. Lay out on a sheet of wax paper and season both sides of chicken tenders with salt and pepper.
Place stuffing mix in a large Ziploc bag and crush with a rolling pin.
Melt butter in the microwave for 1 minute. Remove and stir in lemon juice.
Dip chicken tenders in butter first, then in stuffing mix to coat. Place in a large greased baking dish and bake for 30 minutes, until golden brown. (Serves 6)

Tastes like fried chicken, without all the fuss!

SUGAR BROWNED POTATOES

4 - 5 medium red potatoes
1/4 cup butter or margarine

Salt & pepper to taste
1/4 cup light brown sugar

     Wash potatoes. Peel and cut into chunks. Place in a large saucepan and cover with water. Place over high heat and bring to a boil. Cook for about 10 - 15 minutes, until tender when pierced with a knife. Drain water from potatoes and place in a greased baking dish.
     Preheat oven to 375°. Cut butter into small pieces and place over potatoes. Season potatoes with salt and pepper. Sprinkle with light brown sugar. Place in oven and bake for about 10 minutes, until sugar and butter melts. Toss gently to coat. (Serves 6)

 *Sugar on potatoes? Try it, you'll be surprised!*

STEAMED BROCCOLI

1 bunch of fresh broccoli
Water

2 Tablespoons butter
Salt & pepper to taste
1/2 cup grated cheddar
   cheese

     Cut broccoli into pieces, discarding any heavy stalks. Place about an inch of water in a large saucepan over high heat and bring to a boil. Add broccoli, cover and cook for about 8 minutes. Remove from heat and drain off water. Add butter, salt, pepper and cheese to broccoli. Cover until cheese melts. Serve immediately. (Serves 6)

HOT FUDGE SUNDAE CAKE

**1 cup flour
3/4 cup sugar
2 teaspoons baking powder
1/4 teaspoon salt
2 Tablespoons cocoa
1/2 cup milk
1 teaspoon vanilla
2 Tablespoons butter or margarine,
  melted
1/2 cup chopped pecans**

**1 cup light brown sugar
1/4 cup cocoa
1 3/4 cups hot water**

Vanilla ice cream

Preheat oven to 350°. Measure flour, sugar, baking powder, salt and cocoa into a large mixing bowl. Stir together. Add milk, vanilla and melted butter. Stir in pecans. Grease a 9" square baking pan with cooking spray. Pour batter into pan.

In another bowl, mix together brown sugar and cocoa. Sprinkle over batter. Heat water in microwave and pour on top of cake.

Bake about 40 - 45 minutes. It will be saucy! Serve warm with vanilla ice cream. (Serves 8)

A cake with its own hot fudge sauce!

YOUNG EVERYDAY GOURMET
GIFTS OF FOOD

Gifts of Food classes are a great way to prepare a special gift for teachers, family and friends at Christmas time. Everyone appreciates a gift of food, especially when its made by a Young Everyday Gourmet.

PEANUT BUTTER CRUNCHERS
CHOCOLATE HAYSTACKS
JELL-O CHRISTMAS COOKIES

PEANUT BUTTER CRUNCHERS

1 egg
1 cup sugar
1 cup chunky peanut butter
Semisweet chocolate chips

Preheat oven to $350°$. Grease a foil lined baking sheet with cooking spray.

Break egg into a large bowl and beat with a fork until frothy. Add sugar and peanut butter. Stir with a spoon until smooth.

Pick up about 1 Tablespoon of dough with your hands and roll into a 1inch ball. Place on baking sheet. Repeat rolling out dough to fill cookie sheet. Press each cookie down with a fork. Top each cookie with 1 chocolate chip.

Bake about 20 minutes or until lightly browned. Let cool on baking sheet before removing. (Makes about 3 dozen)

A flourless cookie that bakes up nice and crunchy!

CHOCOLATE HAYSTACKS

1 (12 oz) pkg. semisweet chocolate chips (2 cups)
1 Tablespoon smooth peanut butter
1 (1 3/4 oz) can shoestring potatoes
Powdered sugar

Place chocolate chips and peanut butter in a small saucepan over medium heat. Stir until melted. Remove from heat and gently stir in shoestring potatoes until coated. Pick up a small stack with tongs and drop on a greased sheet of wax paper.

Chill until firm, about 30 minutes. Sprinkle with powdered sugar and store in the refrigerator.

JELL-O CHRISTMAS COOKIES

1 (3 oz) pkg. red or green Jell-O
1 cup butter or margarine
1 cup powdered sugar
2 1/4 cups flour

ICING:
2 cups powdered sugar
3 Tablespoons water
Decorative sprinkles

Preheat oven to 350°. Place 1 pkg. of Jell-O, butter and powdered sugar in a large mixing bowl. Beat with an electric mixer until smooth and creamy. Mix in flour until combined.

Roll out half the dough on a lightly floured surface. Cut out cookies with a cookie cutter (use a candy cane cutter for red Jell-O and a Christmas tree cutter for green Jell-O) Place cookies on a greased foil lined baking sheet and bake for about 10 - 12 minutes, just until set, not browned. Let cool on baking sheet. Repeat with remaining half of dough.

Making icing by placing powdered sugar in a small mixing bowl. Stir in water until smooth. Drizzle icing over cookies and sprinkle with decorative sugar or candies. (Makes about 4 dozen)

 *Jell-O gives these unique cookies color and flavor!*

CINNAMON APPLE BREAD
CHOCOLATE SNOW BALLS
CRISPY PEANUT BUTTER CANDIES

CINNAMON APPLE BREAD

2 eggs
1 cup sugar
1/2 cup vegetable oil
1/4 cup milk
1 cup applesauce
1 teaspoon baking soda
1/2 teaspoon baking powder
1/2 teaspoon cinnamon
1/4 teaspoon salt
1/4 teaspoon nutmeg

2 cups flour
1/2 cup chopped pecans

TOPPING:
1/4 cup sugar
1/4 teaspoon cinnamon

Preheat oven to 350°. Grease a 9 x 5 x 3 inch loaf pan. Break eggs into a large mixing bowl and beat with a whisk for about 30 seconds. Beat in sugar, oil and milk until combined. Mix in applesauce, baking soda, baking powder, cinnamon, salt, nutmeg, flour and pecans.

Pour mixture into greased loaf pan. In a small bowl, mix together sugar and cinnamon. Sprinkle cinnamon sugar over top of loaf. Place in oven and bake for about 1 hour or until tested done.

Remove from oven and let stand for 5 minutes. Cover pan with a piece of aluminum foil and turn bread out. Place right side up on a wire rack, remove foil and cool completely. (Makes 1 loaf)

 *A very moist quick bread that makes a thoughtful gift!*

CHOCOLATE SNOW BALLS

4 (1 oz) squares semisweet chocolate
1/4 cup (1/2 stick) butter
  or margarine
2 cups sugar
4 eggs
1/2 teaspoon salt
2 teaspoons baking powder
3 cups flour
1 cup sifted powdered sugar

Place chocolate squares and butter in a small saucepan over low heat. Stir until melted. Remove from heat and mix in sugar. In a mixing bowl, beat eggs with an electric mixer for about 30 seconds. Stir chocolate mixture into eggs. Add salt, baking powder and flour. Mix until combined. Cover bowl with plastic wrap and place in freezer to chill for 30 minutes to 1 hour.

Preheat oven to 350^0. Shape dough into 1 inch balls and roll in powdered sugar. Place on a greased foil lined baking sheet and bake for about 20 minutes. Bake one sheet at a time. Remove from oven and let cool. (Makes about 6 dozen).

This recipe makes lots of yummy chocolate cookies to share with several friends!

CRISPY PEANUT BUTTER CANDIES

1/2 cup sugar
1/2 cup light corn syrup
1 cup crunchy peanut butter
3 cups Rice Crispies cereal

In a medium size saucepan, stir together sugar and corn syrup. Cook over medium heat, stirring frequently, for about 10 minutes. Mixture will just begin to boil. Stir in peanut butter until melted. Remove from heat and mix in cereal. Drop by the teaspoonful onto greased foil lined baking sheets. Shape into balls when cool enough to handle. Sprinkle with powdered sugar. Place in individual paper candy cups. (Makes about 50)

PEANUT BUTTER FUDGE
HOT COCOA MIX
CHRISTMAS COOKIES

PEANUT BUTTER FUDGE

1 cup semisweet chocolate chips
1 cup peanut butter chips
1 cup chunky peanut butter
1 (14 oz) can sweetened condensed milk

Grease a 9" square baking pan with cooking spray. Place chocolate chips, peanut butter chips and peanut butter in a small saucepan over low heat. Stir often, until chips melt and mixture is smooth. Remove from heat and stir in condensed milk. Mix well. Pour into greased pan and smooth top with a spatula. Cover with plastic wrap and refrigerate until firm, about 2 hours.

When firm, cut into squares by cutting 6 rows across, each way. Store in the refrigerator. (Makes 36 pieces)

HOT COCOA MIX

2 cups nonfat dry milk powder
3/4 cup sugar
1/2 cup powdered non-dairy creamer
1/2 cup cocoa

Measure all ingredients into a medium size bowl and stir with a whisk until smooth. Place cocoa mix in jars and give with the following instructions:
"Mix 3/4 cup boiling water with 1/4 cup Hot Cocoa Mix. Top with marshmellows and enjoy."

CHRISTMAS COOKIES

DOUGH:
1 cup (2 sticks) butter or margarine
3/4 cup sugar
1 egg
2 teaspoons vanilla extract
1 teaspoon almond extract
3 cups flour

FROSTING:
2 cups powdered sugar
2 Tablespoons butter
1/2 teaspoon vanilla
1/2 teaspoon almond
2 - 3 Tablespoons milk
Colored sugars, sugar, cocoa, red & green candied cherries

Preheat oven to 350°. Cover 2 baking sheets with foil and grease with cooking spray.

Place 2 sticks butter and 3/4 cup sugar in a large mixing bowl. Beat with an electric mixer until creamy and light, about 3 minutes on medium speed. Add egg, vanilla and almond and beat for 1 minute. Lower speed of mixer and gradually add flour until combined. Remove dough and place on a lightly floured surface. Divide into 3 equal pieces. Shape into the following cookies:

YULE LOGS:
Take one piece of dough and divide it into 4 pieces. Using your hands, roll dough into a rope, about 1/2" wide. Repeat with each piece. Cut each rope into 3" logs and place on baking sheet.

WREATHS:
Take the second piece of dough and divide into 4 pieces. Using your hands, roll dough into a rope, about 1/4" wide. Repeat with each piece. Cut each rope into 8" lengths and form into circles. Pinch ends together to form a wreath. Place on baking sheet.

TWINKLERS:
Take the third piece of dough and roll out on a lightly floured surface with a rolling pin. Using a small star shaped cookie cutter, cut out twinklers and place on baking sheet. Use a pastry brush to brush each star with a little water and sprinkle with red, green or white sugar.

Bake cookies, one sheet at a time, for about 20 minutes, until cookies are light golden brown. Remove from oven and place on a rack to cool.

Make frosting by beating powdered sugar, butter, vanilla, almond and milk with an electric mixer until smooth. Add more milk only if necessary to make a smooth frosting. Spread frosting on yule logs and wreaths. Sprinkle logs with sifted cocoa and decorate wreaths with candied cherries. Let frosting dry before storing. (Makes about 3 1/3 dozen cookies)

YOUNG EVERYDAY GOURMET
SLUMBER PARTY

Invite friends over for a slumber party and have fun cooking these recipes with everyone's help. Mini Pizzas for supper, Chocolate Chip Extravaganza for dessert and Banana Nut Pancakes for breakfast.

**MINI PIZZAS
CHOCOLATE CHIP EXTRAVAGANZA
BANANA NUT PANCAKES**

MINI PIZZAS

1 pkg. soft flour tortillas or
  1 pkg. pita bread
1 (8 oz) can tomato sauce
1/4 teaspoon oregano
1/4 teaspoon basil

Pepperoni & Canadian bacon,
  cut into small pieces
Grated mozzarella cheese

    Preheat oven to $350°$. Lay 2 tortillas together for each pizza or 1 pita bread out on foil lined baking sheets. Mix tomato sauce with oregano and basil in a small glass bowl. Place sauce in microwave and heat on high for 1 minute.
    Spoon some sauce on each pizza and top with pepperoni, bacon and cheese. Bake about 10 minutes, until cheese is melted and hot. (Makes 5 or 6 mini pizzas)

 **Let everyone create their own mini pizza with their choice of ingredients.**

CHOCOLATE CHIP EXTRAVAGANZA

1/2 cup butter or margarine
1/2 cup sugar
1/2 cup light brown sugar
1/2 teaspoon vanilla
1 egg
1 1/2 cups flour
1/2 cup semisweet chocolate chips

TOPPINGS:
1/4 cup chocolate chips
1/4 cup peanut butter chips
1/4 cup white chocolate chips
1/4 cup mini marshmellows
1/4 cup M & M's

Preheat oven to 375°. Take butter out of refrigerator to soften before using (or heat in microwave on high about 20 seconds, until soft but not melted).
In a large mixing bowl combine butter, sugar, brown sugar, vanilla and egg. Mix well with a wooden spoon. Add flour and stir until a soft dough forms and flour is combined. Stir in chocolate chips.
Grease a 12" pizza pan with cooking spray and press dough evenly in pan, forming a rim along the edge with your fingers.
Bake for 15 minutes. Remove from oven and sprinkle with toppings. Lightly press toppings down into dough with a spatula. Return pan to oven and bake 5 - 10 minutes more, until lightly browned. Remove from oven and let cool completely in pan. Cut into wedges to serve. (Makes 12 servings)

BANANA NUT PANCAKES

1 egg
3/4 cup milk
2 Tablespoons butter or margarine
1 ripe banana
2 teaspoons baking powder

1/2 teaspoon salt
2 Tablespoons sugar
1 cup flour
1/2 cup chopped pecans
Syrup & butter

Break egg into a large mixing bowl. Beat with a whisk. Add milk and beat until combined. Melt butter in a small bowl in the microwave for about 20 seconds on high. Add to egg mixture. Peel and mash banana on a plate with a fork. Add to mixing bowl. Mix in baking powder, salt, sugar, flour and pecans. Stir until combined to form a thick batter.
Grease a large non-stick skillet with cooking spray and place on medium heat. Wait a few minutes for pan to heat. Spoon out about 1/3 cup batter for each pancake into skillet. Make 2 or 3 pancakes at a time. Cook until bubbly on top and browned on the bottom. Turn each pancake over with a spatula, to brown other side. Don't mash down! Stack pancakes in an ovenproof dish when cooked. Keep warm in a low heated oven while cooking remaining pancakes.
Serve pancakes with soft or melted butter and syrup. (Makes about 10)

For a special treat, top pancakes with syrup, banana slices, whipped cream and chopped pecans.

GENERAL CLASS NOTES

1. A recipe will go together very easily if you read the recipe thoroughly, pull out all ingredients and chop & measure ingredients before actually starting the recipe (mise en place).

2. Always use correct measurers for dry ingredients and liquids. For dry measures, always overfill and level off. For liquids, always leave measurer on counter and bend down to look at measuring line. It's very important to obtain a correct measurement, especially in baking.

3. Get in the habit of using cooking spray on all your cookware and bakeware for easy cleanups.

4. Save on dishwashing by covering baking pans with a sheet of foil---after baking, simply throw foil away.

5. Place a piece of foil under springform pans and tart pans with removable bottoms to catch any drippings.

6. Try using fresh ground pepper---its tastes better.

7. When using dried herbs, crumble herbs in your fingers, before adding to a recipe, to release the oils in the herbs and obtain maximum flavor.

8. When using wine in a recipe, use one that you would drink (not "cooking wine").

9. When a recipe calls for only 1 or 2 Tablespoons tomato paste, don't throw away the rest of the can. Simply measure out Tablespoons of tomato paste onto a wax paper lined baking sheet. Place in freezer to harden, remove and store in a Ziploc bag in the freezer. They can easily be removed individually whenever you need 1 or 2 Tablespoons again.

10. Before cooking meats, especially after being thawed, pat dry with paper towels to absorb any excess moisture.

11. When coating foods with flour before browning, always wait until you're ready to add to the the hot oil before flouring. Otherwise, flour tends to soak into the food instead of coating it.

12. When cooking flour in butter for a sauce or soup, cook at least 2 - 3 minutes, to cook the raw flour taste out.

13. When browning meats and fish with bread crumb or flour coatings, add to hot oil and don't move around initially or the coating will not cook to the meat. Let it cook undisturbed until browned, then turn over to brown the other side.

14. To sauté vegetables, make sure oil or butter is hot before adding vegetables. Test the temperature of the oil by adding a small piece of vegetable. When it starts to cook, then add the remaining vegetables.

15. When rolling out pastry dough or yeast dough, lightly flour the surface and roll from the center, out, in all directions. Don't roll back and forth over just one area, as this will cause thin edges.

16. When proofing yeast for a recipe, the yeast should bubble up, after sitting for several minutes, when a warm liquid and sugar has been added, to prove that it's alive. If it doesn't bubble, discard it and try again with fresher yeast.

17. Liquid temperature ($105°$ - $115°$) is very important in making yeast breads. Don't get it too hot or it will kill the yeast and your bread won't rise.

18. A good warm spot to let yeast breads rise is in the oven. Place dough in a rising bowl, cover and put in a cold oven. Turn the oven temperature knob on to the lowest setting. Leave on for 1 minute and immediately turn off. There will be just enough heat to enable a yeast dough to rise. Don't leave the oven on!

19. When cooking egg yolks in a sauce, especially with lemon juice, use a non-aluminum saucepan. Otherwise, the egg yolks react with the aluminum and will pick up a metallic taste as well as become discolored.

20. An easy way to peel an avocado is to cut in half lengthwise. Remove seed by piercing with a knife. Place a tablespoon between the flesh and the skin and run the spoon from one side to the other, releasing the flesh from the skin in one movement.

21. When a recipe calls for "zest", use a zester garnishing tool to remove just the colored peel of a lemon or orange. A grater tends to pull off the white bitter portion under the peel instead of just the flavorful zest.

22. Peel a tomato by dropping into boiling water and submerging for about 20 seconds. Remove from water and skin will peel off very easily. Can also peel peaches using this method.

GENERAL CLASS NOTES

23. Always store fresh tomatoes at room temperature for maximum ripening and flavor.

24. Wipe mushrooms with a damp paper towel instead of washing. Mushrooms have a high water content and will only soak up more water if washed, adding excess water to a dish when cooked.

25. When cooking pasta, add to boiling, salted water and immediately stir for 1 minute to prevent pasta from sticking together. The addition of oil will not be necessary.

26. Store fresh lemons in refrigerator by double-bagging, so the gases produced by the lemons won't contact other fruits and vegetables, and over-ripen them.

27. Always dissolve cornstarch in cold liquids before adding to hot mixtures.

28. Place plastic wrap directly on the surface of custards and other fillings that might form a skin when refrigerated.

29. When breaking eggs, use a small bowl to break each egg in, then add to mixing bowl. It's easier to remove a shell from a small bowl and, just in case you get a bad egg, you won't ruin the other eggs that were already broken. It's especially important to use an individual bowl when separating eggs. If you get a broken yolk, you haven't ruined the other egg whites.

30. Chocolate holds its shape when melted in the microwave. Be sure to stir frequently to prevent burning.

31. Place small pieces of wax paper just under the edges of a cake when frosting to catch any excess. Remove when finished and the cake plate will be clean.

32. Contrasting colors, textures and ingredients are what make a successful combination in menu planning. Try to compliment your entrées by choosing vegetables that add different colors to your plate. When an entrée is very flavorful, choose a simple, steamed vegetable, so as not to clash with the taste of the entrée.

33. When preparing a special meal for company, pick a menu that can be made in advance. Most desserts can be made ahead of time, as well as many other courses. This way, you can enjoy the meal more if you aren't rushed with last minute cooking and cleanups.

INDEX

A

adobe chocolate cake, 245
Alfredo, fettuccine, 200
almond:
  amaretti, 161
  amaretto bread pudding, 194
    quick bread, 164
  berries & almond cream, 155
  cakes, sweetheart, 94
  candied amaretto cranberries, 164
  chicken, 86
  chocolate amaretto dolci, 208
  cioccolata crema, 213
  floating islands amandine, 149
  orange almond salad, 231
  rice pilaf, 145
  strawberry almond tart, 140
  tartlets, 102
  zabaglione, 211
amandine, floating islands, 149
  roasted Cornish hens, 136
amaretti, 161
amaretto:
  bread pudding, 194
  cranberries, candied, 164
  dolci, chocolate, 208
  quick bread, 164
andouille gumbo, chicken, 122
angel cake, strawberry, 283
anglaise, apples crème, 146
antipasta, 205
appetizers & hors d'oeuvres:
  (cold):
    antipasta, 205
    avocado salsa, 239
    blue cheese dip, 6
    café au lait dip, 163
    cheese pineapple, 183
      stuffed shrimp, 3
    Creole shrimp on pita rounds, 5
    herbed vegetable dip, 180
    hummus dip, 259
    lime vegetable dip, 167
    Louisiana pepper jelly, 167
      spicy shrimp rémoulade, 37
    marinated shrimp kabobs, 5
    party pinwheels, 113
    peppered cheese, 172
    pickled pineapple, 184
    ribbon sandwiches, 114
    salmon cheese spread, 162
    shrimp gazpacho salad, 243
    sugar & spice dip, 176
    sun dried tomato herbed cheese, 160
    tomato egg rounds, 114
    tortilla bites, 3
    vegie Christmas tree, 179
    white shrimp rémoulade, 129
  (hot):
    avocado crab mornay, 4
    bacon cheese toasts, 249
    baked artichoke dip, 124
      potato skins, 252
    Buffalo chicken wings, 6
    caponata, 199
    cheese puffs with mushroom duxelles, 137
    crab stuffed French bread, 4
      stuffed mushrooms, 8
      tartlets, 67
    crostini, 202
    fried mozzarella marinara, 209
      won tons, 73
    frijoles tostaditas, 267
    ham & cheese palmiers, 7
    jumbo shrimp phyllo, 217
    olive cheese balls, 8
    oysters Bienville, 52
    pepper jelly tarts, 7
    phyllo hors d'oeuvres, 220
    sausage stuffed mushrooms, 275
    shrimp & pork egg rolls, 80
      in champagne sauce, 153
      toast, 84
    steamed shrimp dumplings, 88
    stuffed artichoke leaves, 212
    sun dried tomato croustades, 192
    suppli di riso, 195
apple(s):
  bread, cinnamon, 290
  crème anglaise, 146
  crisp, 230
  kuchen, 132
  loaves, sugar & spice, 160
  stir-fried spiced, 79
  tart, pecan, 152
  torte, French, 126
apricot:
  coffeecake, 166
  glazed chicken, 277
  jam, orange, 173
  nectar bread, 173
artichoke:
  dip, baked, 124
  leaves, stuffed, 212
  sauce, fettucine with, 232
  veal with, 193
  soup, cream of, 46
asparagus soup, cream of, 231
avocado:
  crab mornay, 4
  salsa, 239
  soup, chilled, 255

B

bacon cheese toasts, 249
  soup, bean &, 124
baked artichoke dip, 124
  gnocchi, 206
baked potato skins, 252
banana(s) Foster, 233
  nut pancakes, 295

INDEX

sauce, warm, 98
basic cooking methods, 18
    terminology, 19
    equipment, 15
    foods, 18
    measurements, 17
bean(s):
  fresh green bean Caesar salad, 62
  lentil soup, 125
  soup, & bacon, 124
Bea's hot fudge sauce, 235
beef:
  & cheese enchiladas, 271
  brisket, peppered, 244
  Louisiana meat pies, 57
  Mexican spaghetti, 284
  tomato pepper, 78
  spaghetti pie, 234
  Wellington, 154
berries & almond cream, 155
beverages:
  brewed tea, 113
  champagne punch, 106
  coffee mocha punch, 25
  cranberry cheer, 179
  holiday punch, 172
  hot:
    chocolate eggnog, 31
      heavenly, 161
      mocha, 103
    cocoa mix, 292
    spiced cider, 123
  piña colada punch, 249
  spicy tomato juice, 28
  tropical fruit cooler, 258
Bienville, oysters, 52
biscotti, cranberry, 168
bisque, crab corn, 55
  provincial, shrimp, 144
Black Forest torte, 278
blue cheese dip, 6
boiled:
  corn on the cob, 282
  rice, easy, 14
  shrimp, easy, 37
Boston ice cream pie, 262
brabant potatoes, 44
braised rice & vegetables, 135
bread(s):
  amaretto quick, 164
  apricot nectar, 173
  bacon cheese toasts, 249
  brioche twists, 27
  cheese toasts, 46
  cinnamon apple, 290
    candy cane twists, 159
    pinwheels, 32
  coconutty, 169
  cornbread, 240, 277
  crab stuffed French, 4
  crostini, 202

  festive cranberry braid, 178
  Mardi Gras king cake, 30
  oatmeal, 125
  orange carrot, 177
  onion herb, 122
  pita crisps, 259
  pizza, 130
  sesame cornmeal biscuits, 33, 284
  sugar & spice apple loaves, 160
  sugar lump, 182
  sun dried tomato croustades, 192
  sweet scones, 114
  sweet roll Christmas tree, 171
breaded parsley potatoes, 44
bread pudding, amaretto, 194
brewed tea, 113
Brie & walnut salad, 153
brioche twists, 27
brisket, peppered beef, 244
brittlebread, 170
brittle, micro nut, 185
broccoli:
  salad, creamy, 121
  soup, Swiss, 135
  steamed, 286
brownie(s), fudgy, 15
  waffles, 98
bûche de Noël, 99
Buffalo chicken wings, 6

C

café au lait dip, 163
Cajun egg bake, 29
  peppered shrimp & grits, 50
cake(s):
  adobe chocolate, 245
  Boston ice cream pie, 262
  bûche de Noël, 99
  cassata ala Siciliano, 191
  chocolate amaretto dolci, 208
    mousse cake, 95
    pecan gâteau, 143
  hot fudge sundae, 287
  lemon cake roll, 251
    celebration, 51
    meringue cake, 69
  orange tea cakes, 116
  pecan ice cream roll, 39
  petit four hearts, 107
  red velvet, 108
  strawberry angel, 283
  sweetheart almond cakes, 94
  tiramisu, 198
  torte:
    Black Forest, 278
    German chocolate, 96
    lemon torta, 204
    peaches & cream, 63
    pecan, 58

INDEX

candied amaretto cranberries, 164
candies:
  caramel pecan clusters, 162
  chocolate haystacks, 288
    peppermint fudge, 168
  crispy peanut butter, 291
  micro nut brittle, 185
  microwave pralines, 109
  peanut butter fudge, 292
  snowflakes, 163
candy apple cookies, 177
  cane cookies, 174
    twists, cinnamon, 159
cannelloni, seafood, 203
Cantonese, shrimp, 76
caponata, 199
caramel custard, 123
  fruit, 28
  pecan clusters, 162
  popcorn crunch, 181
carbonara, pasta, 192
Caribe, pineapple shrimp, 68
carrot bread, orange, 177
cashew chicken, 89
cassata ala Siciliano, 191
catfish sautéed with
    Creole mustard sauce, 44
    seafood dressing, 60
  sesame, 38
champagne punch, 106
  sauce, shrimp in, 153
chantilly cream, 97
cheese:
  balls, olive, 8
  beef & cheese enchiladas, 271
  Brie & walnut salad, 153
  fried mozzarella, 209
  grits, 25, 50
  jalapeño grits, 33
  mornay sauce, 222
  peppered, 172
  pie, pineapple, 223
  pineapple, 183
  pizza, five, 130
  puffs with mushroom duxelles, 137
  soup, Creole, 59
  spread, salmon, 162
  stuffed shrimp, 3
  sun dried tomato herbed cheese, 160
  toasts, 46
    bacon, 249
cheesecake tartlets, phyllo, 219
cheesy chilie eggs, 32
  potato chunks, 282
cherry tartlets, 117
chicken:
  almond, 86
  andouille gumbo, 122
  apricot glazed, 277
  cashew, 89
  Coca-Cola, 281
  corn tortillas, 270
  Dijon pasta, 228
  enchiladas rancheros, 268
  lemon with pea pods, 81
  melanzana, 210
  moo goo gai pan, 75
  phyllo pies, 218
  pollo d'olive, 197
    limonese, 207
  poulet au vin, 145
  saltimbocca, 190
  Santa Fe, 240
  & sausage jambalaya, 14
  Southern pecan, 41
  tenders, crunchy baked, 285
  walnut, 77
  wings, Buffalo, 6
chilled avocado soup, 255
chocolate:
  amaretto dolci, 208
  Black Forest torte, 278
  Boston ice cream pie, 262
  bûche de Noël, 99
  cake, adobe, 245
  cassata ala Siciliano, 191
  chip chocolate cream puffs, 97
    coffeecake, 180
    extravaganza, 295
  cioccolato crema, 213
  cups, 104
  éclairs, 101
  fudge sauce, 39, 105, 285
  fudgy brownies, 15
    ice cream balls, 285
  glaze, 42, 101, 143, 254, 262
  haystacks, 288
  heavenly hot, 161
  hot:
    chocolate eggnog, 31
      mocha, 103
    cocoa mix, 292
    fudge sundae cake, 287
      sauce, Bea's, 235
  lace cups, 93
  milk chocolate dipped fruit, 33
  mint demitasee cream, 103
  Mississippi mud ice cream pie, 254
  mocha ice cream sauce, 269
  mousse cake, 95
  peanut butter fudge, 292
    fudged ice cream, 228
  pecan gâteau, 143
    tart, 42
  peppermint fudge, 168
  sauce, 48
  snow balls, 291
  snowflakes, 163
  sweetheart brownie waffles, 98
  tiramisu, 198
  torte, German, 96
  white chocolate mousse cups, 104

INDEX

Christmas:
  cookie ornaments, 165
  cookies, 293
    Jell-o, 289
  pinwheels, 185
  tree, sweet roll, 171
  tree, vegie, 179
cider, hot spiced, 123
cinnamon:
  apple bread, 290
  candy cane twists, 159
  ornaments, 169
  pinwheels, 32
cioccolata crema, 213
Coca-Cola chicken, 281
cocktail sauce, 47
cocoa, hot mix, 292
coconutty bread, 169
coffeecake:
  apricot, 166
  chocolate chip, 180
  cranberry, 184
coffee mocha punch, 25
cookies:
  amaretti, 161
  brittlebread, 170
  candy apple, 177
    cane, 174
  chocolate snow balls, 291
  Christmas, 293
    ornaments, 165
    pinwheels, 185
  cranberry biscotti, 168
  homemade fortune, 83
  Jell-O Christmas, 289
  peanut butter crunchers, 288
  shortbread hearts, 115
  tulip cups, 136
cooler, tropical fruit, 258
corn:
  biscuits, sesame, 284
  bisque, crab, 55
  boiled, 282
  relish, fiesta, 243
  soup, velvet corn, 77
  tortilla soup, 239
  tortillas, chicken, 270
cornbread, 240, 277
  dressing, 277
Cornish hens amandine, roasted, 136
cornmeal biscuits, sesame, 33
couscous salad, 260
crab:
  cakes, Louisiana, 47
  corn bisque, 55
  mornay, avocado, 4
  pasta salad, 256
  stuffed French bread, 4
    mushrooms, 8
  tartlets, 67

cranberry(ies):
  biscotti, 168
  braid, festive, 178
  candied amaretto, 164
  cheer, 179
  coffeecake, 184
  dried, 142
  pecan tart, 175
  saucy, 170
crawfish salad, warm, 250
cream:
  almond, 155
  chocolate mint demitasse, 103
  frozen orange, 137
  frozen strawberry, 93
  of artichoke soup, 46
  of asparagus soup, 231
  pastry, 101
  puffs, chocolate, 97
creamy broccoli salad, 121
  garlic salad, 229
  onion soup, 61
  Italian salad, 199
crema, cioccolata, 213
  spumoni, 201
crème anglaise, apples, 146
Creole:
  cheese soup, 59
  mustard sauce, 44
  sauce, 26
  shrimp on pita rounds, 5
  squash soup, 40
crisp, apple, 230
crispy peanut butter candies, 291
crostini, 202
croustades, sun dried tomato, 192
croûte, seafood en, 148
croutons, garlic, 59
crunch, caramel popcorn, 181
crunchers, peanut butter, 288
crunchy baked chicken tenders, 285
curd, lemon, 115
custard:
  caramel, 123
  Monterey flan, 242
  sauce, 149
  zabaglione, 211

D

desserts: (see specific categories: cakes, cookies, frozen, fruit, ice cream, pies, tarts, tortes)
Dijon pasta, chicken, 228
dips:
  avocado salsa, 239
  baked artichoke, 124
  blue cheese, 6
  café au lait, 163
  herbed vegetable, 180
  hummus, 259

INDEX

lime vegetable, 167
salsa fresca, 241
roja, 271
sugar & spice, 176
dolci, chocolate amaretto, 208
dressing, cornbread, 277
seafood, 60
dried cranberries, 142
dumplings, steamed shrimp, 88
duxelles, mushroom, 138, 154

E

easy boiled rice, 14
shrimp, 37
spinach soup, 227
éclairs, chocolate, 101
egg(s):
bake, Cajun, 29
cheesy chilie, 32
frittata, zucchini, 256
shirred, 26
eggnog, hot chocolate, 31
eggplant:
caponata, 199
chicken melanzana, 210
egg rolls, shrimp & pork, 80
enchiladas:
chicken corn, 270
rancheros, 268
beef & cheese, 271
extravaganza, chocolate chip, 295

F

festive cranberry braid, 178
fettuccine, Alfredo, 200
with artichoke sauce, 232
fiesta corn relish, 243
Mexican rice, 267
fish:
catfish, sautéed, 44, 60
sesame, 38
trout au beurre lemon, 139
with seafood sauce, 53
five cheese pizza, 130
flan, Monterey, 242
floating islands amandine, 149
Florentina, veal, 200
fondant glaze, 107
fortune cookies, homemade, 83
Foster, bananas, 233
French:
apple torte, 126
bread, crab stuffed, 4
dressing, spicy, 234
onion soup, 147
fresca, salsa, 241
fresh green bean Caesar salad, 62

fried:
mozzarella marinara, 209
rice, shrimp, 85
spiced apples, stir-, 79
won tons, 73
frijoles tostaditas, 267
frittata, zucchini, 256
fromage, salade de, 150
frosting:
Black forest, 278
chocolate, 191
decorative, 107
orange, 116
powdered sugar, 108
frozen desserts: (see ice creams)
fruit mold, 106
orange cream, 137
strawberry cream, 93
fruit: (see specific types)
caramel, 28
cooler, tropical, 258
milk chocolate dipped, 33
mold, frozen, 106
sauced, 26
fudge:
chocolate peppermint, 168
sauce, 39
sundae cake, hot, 287
peanut butter, 292
sauce, 105
Bea's hot, 235
fudged ice cream, peanut butter, 228
fudgy brownies, 15

G

garlic:
croutons, 59
salad, creamy, 229
soup, roasted, 141
vinaigrette, roasted, 260
garnishes, 9
gazpacho salad, shrimp, 243
German chocolate torte, 96
glaze:
chocolate, 42, 101, 143, 254, 262
fondant, 107
lemon, 51
powdered sugar, 159, 169, 171
gnocchi, baked, 206
gratinée, potatoes, 142
Greek shrimp & pasta, 253
green bean Caesar salad, 62
green chilie potatoes, 244
grits, cheese, 25
jalapeño cheese, 33
with Cajun peppered shrimp, 50
gumbo, chicken andouille, 122
shrimp corn, 43

INDEX

H
ham & cheese palmiers, 7
haystacks, chocolate, 288
hearts, petit four, 107
   salad of, 56
   shortbread, 115
heavenly hot chocolate, 161
herb bread, onion, 122
herbed cheese, sun dried tomato, 160
   fresh tomatoes, 255
   vegetable dip, 180
holiday punch, 172
Holstein, Schnitzel, 229
homemade egg pasta, 196
   fortune cookies, 83
honey mustard shrimp, 260
   nut salad, 49
hors d'oeuvres, phyllo, 220
hot:
   chocolate eggnog, 31
      heavenly, 161
      mocha, 103
   cocoa mix, 292
   fudge sauce, 235
      sundae cake, 287
   jelly, red, 176
   mustard sauce, 74
   spiced cider, 123
hummus dip, 259

I
ice cream:
   balls, fudgy, 285
   frozen orange cream, 137
      strawberry cream, 93
   meringues, praline, 45
   mile high pie, 48
   Mississippi mud pie, 254
   mocha tostadas, 269
   peanut butter fudged, 228
   pie, Boston, 262
   pralines & cream dream, 61
   roll, pecan, 39
   spumoni crema, 201
icing:
   chocolate, 100
   powdered sugar, 94
imperial, pineapple, 76
Italian salad, creamy, 199
   vegetable, 210

J
jalapeño cheese grits, 33
jam, orange apricot, 173
jambalaya, chicken & sausage, 14
Jell-O Christmas cookies, 289
jelly, Louisiana pepper, 167
   red hot, 176

Jezebel sauce, 218
juice, spicy tomato, 28
jumbo shrimp phyllo, 217

K
kabobs, marinated shrimp, 5
Kahlúa mousse, 272
king cake, Mardi Gras, 30
kuchen, apple, 132

L
lace cups, chocolate, 93
layered summer salad, 253
lemon:
   cake roll, 251
   celebration cake, 51
   chicken with pea pods, 81
   curd, 115
   glaze, 51
   meringue cake, 69
   torta, 204
   trout au beurre, 139
lentil soup, 125
lima, sopa de, 270
lime vegetable dip, 167
limone, veal, 232
limonese, pollo, 207
lobster sauce, shrimp with, 82
Louisiana crab cakes, 47
   meat pies, 57
   pepper jelly, 167
   spicy shrimp rémoulade, 37

M
Madeira sauce, 155
Mandarin pancakes, 89
Mardi Gras king cake, 30
marinara sauce, 209
marinated shrimp kabobs, 5
mayonnaise, 129
meat pies, Louisiana, 57
Mediterranean pizza, 131
melanzana, chicken, 210
meringue(s):
   cake, lemon, 69
   crust, 95
   floating islands amandine, 149
   mile high pie, 48
   mushrooms, 100
   praline ice cream, 45
Mexi rice, 272
Mexican rice, fiesta, 267
   spaghetti, 284
micro nut brittle, 185
microwave pralines, 109
mile high pie, 48
milk chocolate dipped fruit, 33

INDEX

mini pizzas, 294
mint demitasse cream, chocolate, 103
Mississippi mud ice cream pie, 254
mocha hot chocolate, 103
  ice cream tostadas, 269
  punch, coffee, 25
  sauce, 269
Monterey flan, 242
moo goo gai pan, 75
mornay, avocado crab, 4
  sauce, 222
mousse cake, chocolate, 95
  cups, white chocolate, 104
  Kahlúa, 272
mozzarella marinara, fried, 209
  veal, 213
mushroom(s):
  crab stuffed, 8
  duxelles, 138, 154
  meringue, 100
  sausage stuffed, 275
  soup, spinach, 85
mu shu pork, 89
mustard sauce, Creole, 44
  hot, 74

N

nectar bread, apricot, 173
New Orleans tartar sauce, 38
Normandy, pork, 151
nut(s) (see specific types)
  brittle, micro, 185
  salad, honey, 49

O

oatmeal bread, 125
olive cheese balls, 8
onion:
  herb bread, 122
  soup, creamy, 61
    French, 147
orange:
  almond salad, 231
  apricot jam, 173
  carrot bread, 177
  cream, frozen, 136
  tea cakes, 116
ornaments, Christmas cookie, 165
  cinnamon, 169
oysters Bienville, 52

P

palmiers, ham & cheese, 7
pancakes, banana nut, 295
  Mandarin, 89
paradise salad, 68
Parmesan vinaigrette salad, 202
party pinwheels, 113
pasta:
  angel hair, 210
  carbonara, 192
  chicken Dijon, 228
  couscous salad, 260
  fettucine Alfredo, 200
    with artichoke sauce, 232
  Greek shrimp &, 253
  homemade egg, 196
  Mexican spaghetti, 284
  salad, crab, 256
  seafood cannelloni, 203
  spaghetti pie, 234
  with peppers & oil, 197
  with squash & shrimp, 62
pastry(ies):
  almond tartlets, 102
  apple kuchen, 132
  beef Wellington, 154
  cheese puffs, 137
  cherry tartlets, 117
  chocolate cream puffs, 97
  cranberry pecan tart, 175
  cream, 257
  cream filling, 101
  cream puff, 101
  Louisiana meat pies, 57
  lemon torta, 204
  mile high pie, 58
  pecan apple tart, 152
  phyllo, 217
  seafood en croûte, 148
  strawberry almond tart, 140
    cream tart, 257
peaches & cream torte, 63
peanut:
  brittle, micro nut, 185
  butter candies, crispy, 291
    crunchers, 288
    fudge, 292
    fudged ice cream, 228
pea pods, lemon chicken with, 81
pears, poached, 105
pecan(s):
  apple tart, 152
  chicken, Southern, 41
  clusters, caramel, 162
  gâteau, chocolate, 143
  glazed, 68
  ice cream roll, 39
  meringue crust, 95
  rice, 53
  salad, honey nut, 49
  tart, chocolate, 42
    cranberry, 175
  torte, 58
pepper:
  beef, tomato, 78
  jelly, Louisiana, 167
    tarts, 7

INDEX

peppered:
  beef brisket, 244
  cheese, 172
  shrimp, Cajun, 50
peppermint fudge, chocolate, 168
peppers & oil, with pasta, 197
petit four hearts, 107
phyllo:
  cheesecake tartlets, 219
  hors d'oeuvres, 220
  jumbo shrimp, 217
  pastry, handling, 217
  pie(s), chicken, 218
    pineapple cheese, 223
  seafood strudel, 222
pickled pineapple, 184
pie(s):
  Boston ice cream, 262
  chicken phyllo, 218
  mile high, 48
  Mississippi mud ice cream, 254
  pineapple cheese, 223
  spaghetti, 234
pilaf, almond rice, 145
piña colada punch, 249
pineapple:
  cheese, 183
    pie, 223
  imperial, 76
  pickled, 184
  shrimp Caribe, 68
pinwheels, Christmas, 185
  party, 113
piquant, sauce, 57
pita crisps, 259
  rounds, 5
pizza(s), dough, 130
  five cheese, 130
  Mediterranean, 131
  mini, 294
plum sauce, 88
poached pears, 105
pollo d'olive, 197
  limonese, 207
pomodori, salsa di, 212
  suppa di, 189
popcorn crunch, caramel, 181
pork:
  egg rolls, shrimp &, 80
  medallions with dried cranberries, 142
  mu shu, 89
  Normandy, 151
  sweet & sour, 87
potato(es):
  brabant, 44
  breaded parsley, 29
  chunks, cheesy, 282
  gratinée, 142
  green chilie, 244
  sauté, 230
  skins, baked, 252

sugar browned, 286
sweet, sauced, 40
  shoestrings, 276
  soufflé, 54
  soup, 276
  wedges, roasted, 150
poulet au vin, 145
powdered sugar:
  frosting, 108
  glaze, 159, 169, 171
  icing, 94
praline(s):
  & cream dream, 61
  ice cream meringues, 45
  microwave, 109
  sauce, 45
Provincial, shrimp bisque, 144
pudding, amaretto bread, 194
puffs, cheese, 137
punch, champagne, 106
  coffee mocha, 25
  holiday, 172
  piña colada, 249
  tropical fruit cooler, 258

Q

quick bread:
  amaretto, 164
  apricot nectar, 173
  cinnamon apple, 290
  coconutty, 169
  orange carrot, 177
  sugar & spice apple, 160

R

rancheros, chicken enchiladas, 268
red bell pepper soup, 49
  hot jelly, 176
  velvet cake, 108
relish, fiesta corn, 243
rémoulade, Louisiana spicy shrimp, 37
  white shrimp, 129
ribbon sandwiches, 114
rice:
  braised, 135
  easy boiled, 14
  fiesta Mexican, 267
  Mexi, 272
  pecan, 53
  pilaf, almond, 145
  risotto, 189
  shrimp fried, 85
risotto, 189
roasted Cornish hens amandine, 136
  garlic soup, 141
    vinaigrette, 260
  potato wedges, 150
roja, salsa, 271

INDEX

Roquefort salade, 138

S

salad(e):
  Brie & walnut, 153
  couscous, 260
  crab pasta, 256
  creamy broccoli, 121
    garlic, 229
    Italian, 199
  de fromage, 150
  fresh green bean Caesar, 62
  herbed fresh tomatoes, 255
  honey nut, 49
  Italian vegetable, 210
  layered summer, 253
  of hearts, 56
  orange almond, 231
  paradise, 68
  Parmesan vinaigrette, 202
  roasted garlic vinaigrette, 260
  Roquefort, 138
  sensation, 13
  shrimp gazpacho, 243
    rémoulade, Louisiana spicy, 37
    white, 129
  spicy French dressing, 234
  vinaigrette, spinach salad, 147
  warm crawfish, 250
    spinach, 47
  wedges, thousand island, 227
salmon cheese spread, 162
salsa, avocado, 239
  crudo, 196
  di pomodori, 212
  fresca, 241
  roja, 271
saltimbocca, chicken, 190
sandwiches:
  party pinwheels, 113
  ribbon, 114
  tomato egg rounds, 114
Santa Fe chicken & cornbread, 240
sauce(s): (dessert)
  almond cream, 155
  amaretto, 194
  Bea's hot fudge, 235
  chocolate, 48
    fudge, 39, 105, 285
  crème anglaise, 146
  custard, 149
  lemon curd, 115
  mocha, 269
  praline, 45, 61
  strawberry sauce, 104
  warm banana, 98
  zabaglione, 211
sauce(s): (savory)
  artichoke, 193, 232
  champagne, 153

  cocktail, 47
  cranberry, 170
  Creole, 26
    mustard, 44
  hot mustard, 74
  Jezebel, 218
  Madeira sauce, 155
  marinara, 209
  mayonnaise, 129
  mornay, 222
  piquant, 57
  plum, 88
  rémoulade, 37, 129
  salsa crudo, 196
  salsa di pomodori, 212
  seafood, 53
  sweet & sour, 74
  tartar, 38
  uncooked tomato, 131
sauced fruit, 26
  sweet potatoes, 40
saucy cranberries, 170
sausage jambalaya, chicken &, 14
  stuffed mushrooms, 275
sauté, potato, 230
sautéed:
  catfish with Creole mustard sauce, 44
    with seafood dressing, 60
  vegetable strips, 139
Schnitzel Holstein, 229
scones, sweet, 114
seafood:
  cannelloni, 203
  dressing, 60
  en croûte, 148
  sauce, 53
  strudel, 222
sensation salad, 13
sesame catfish, 38
  corn biscuits, 284
  cornmeal biscuits, 33
shirred eggs, 26
shortbread hearts, 115
shrimp:
  & pork egg rolls, 80
  & vegetable stir-fry, 78
  bisque Provincial, 144
  Cajun peppered, 50
  Cantonese, 76
  Caribe, pineapple, 68
  cheese stuffed, 3
  corn gumbo, 43
  Creole, on pita rounds, 5
  dumplings, steamed, 88
  easy boiled, 37
  fried rice, 85
  gazpacho salad, 243
  Greek shrimp & pasta, 253
  honey mustard, 260
  in champagne sauce, 153
  kabobs, marinated, 5

INDEX

phyllo, jumbo, 217
rémoulade, Louisiana spicy, 37
   white, 129
toast, 84
with lobster sauce, 82
with pasta, squash &, 62
Siciliano, cassata ala, 191
skins, baked potato, 252
snow balls, chocolate, 291
snowflakes, 163
sopa de lima, 270
soufflé, sweet potato, 54
soup(s):
  bean & bacon, 124
  chilled avocado, 255
  corn tortilla, 239
  crab corn bisque, 55
  cream of artichoke, 41
    asparagus, 231
  creamy onion, 61
  Creole cheese, 59
    squash, 40
  easy spinach, 227
  French onion, 147
  lentil, 125
  red bell pepper, 49
  roasted garlic, 141
  shrimp corn gumbo, 43
    bisque Provincial, 144
  sopa de lima, 270
  spinach mushroom, 85
  sweet potato, 276
  Swiss broccoli, 135
  velvet corn, 77
  zucchini, 233
  zuppa di pomodori, 189
Southern pecan chicken, 41
spaghetti, Mexican, 284
  pie, 234
spiced apples, stir-fried, 79
  cider, hot, 123
spicy tomato juice, 28
spinach:
  mushroom soup, 85
  salad vinaigrette, 147
    warm, 47
  soup, easy, 227
  stuffed squash, 276
spumoni crema, 201
squash:
  & shrimp with pasta, 62
  soup, Creole, 40
  spinach stuffed, 276
  steamed broccoli, 286
  shrimp dumplings, 88
stir-fried spiced apples, 79
strawberry:
  almond tart, 140
  angel cake, 283
  cream, frozen, 93
    tart, 257

sauce, 104
strudel, seafood, 222
stuffed:
  artichoke leaves, 212
  French bread, crab, 4
  mushrooms, crab, 8
    sausage, 275
  shrimp, cheese, 3
  squash, spinach, 276
sugar & spice apple loaves, 160
  dip, 176
sugar browned potatoes, 286
  lump bread, 182
summer salad, layered, 253
sun dried tomato:
  croustades, 192
  herbed cheese, 160
  with baked gnocchi, 206
suppa di pomodori, 189
suppli di riso, 195
sweet:
  & sour pork, 87
    sauce, 74
  roll Christmas tree, 171
  scones, 114
sweetheart almond cakes, 94
  brownie waffles, 98
sweet potato(es):
  sauced, 40
  shoestrings, 276
  soufflé, 54
  soup, 276
Swiss broccoli soup, 135

T

tartar sauce, New Orleans, 38
tart(s):
  chocolate pecan, 42
  cranberry pecan, 175
  pecan apple, 152
  pepper jelly, 7
  strawberry almond, 140
    cream, 257
tartlets, almond, 102
  cherry, 117
  crab, 67
  phyllo cheesecake, 219
tea, brewed, 113
  cakes, orange, 116
tenders, crunchy baked chicken, 285
thousand island salad wedges, 227
tiramisu, 198
toast(s), bacon cheese, 249
  cheese, 46
  shrimp, 84
tomato(es):
  avocado salsa, 239
  croustades, sun dried, 192
  egg rounds, 114
  gnocchi with sun dried, 206

INDEX

herbed cheese, sun dried, 160
   fresh, 255
juice, spicy, 28
marinara sauce, 209
pepper beef, 78
salsa crudo, 196
   di pomodori, 212
   fresca, 241
   roja, 271
   sauce, uncooked, 131
torta, lemon, 204
torte:
   Black Forest, 278
   French apple, 126
   German chocolate, 96
   peaches & cream, 63
   pecan, 58
tortilla(s):
   bites, 3
   chicken corn, 270
   soup, corn, 239
tostadas, mocha ice cream, 269
tostaditas, frijoles, 267
tree, sweet roll Christmas, 171
   vegie Christmas, 179
tropical fruit cooler, 258
trout au beurre lemon, 139
   with seafood sauce, 53
tulip cookie cups, 136
twists, brioche, 27
   cinnamon candy cane, 159

U

uncooked tomato sauce, 131

V

vanilla icing, 262
veal:
   Florentina, 200
   limone, 232
   mozzarella, 213
   Schnitzel Holstein, 229
   with artichoke sauce, 193
vegetable(s): (see specific types)
   braised rice &, 135
   dip, herbed, 180
      lime, 167
   salad, Italian, 210
   strips, sautéed, 139
vegie Christmas tree, 179
velvet cake, red, 108
   corn soup, 77
vin, poulet au, 145
vinaigrette, roasted garlic, 260
   salad, Parmesan, 202
   spinach salad, 147
   warm crawfish salad, 250

W

waffles, sweetheart brownie, 98
walnut chicken, 77
   salad, Brie &, 153
warm banana sauce, 98
   crawfish salad, 250
   spinach salad, 47
wedges, roasted potato, 150
   thousand island salad, 227
Wellington, beef, 154
white chocolate mousse cups, 104
white shrimp rémoulade, 129
wings, Buffalo chicken, 6
won tons, fried, 73

Z

zabaglione, 211
zucchini frittata, 256
   soup, 233
zuppa di pomodori, 189

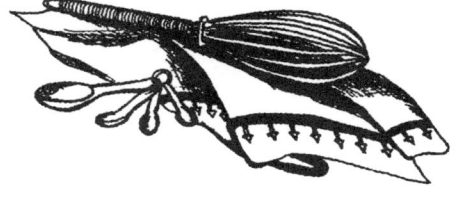

NOTES

NOTES

KAY EWING'S COOKING SCHOOL COOKBOOK

Please send me _____ copies at $14.95 each   _____

+ 8% sales tax LA residents   _____
+ $2.00 Shipping per book   _____

Total enclosed   _____

Check or money order enclosed made payable to:

Kay Ewing's Cooking School Cookbook
17921 Inverness Ave.
Baton Rouge, LA 70810

Charge to:_____Master Card _____Visa

Card Number:_____
Expiration Date:_____
Name as it appears on card:_____

Signature:_____

<u>Ship to</u>:

Name:_____

Street Address:_____

City & State:_____

Zip:_____

Daytime Phone Number:

(_____)_____